ELIOT IN PERSPECTIVE

ELIOT IN PERSPECTIVE

A SYMPOSIUM

edited by

GRAHAM MARTIN

HUMANITIES PRESS: New York

© Macmillan and Co Ltd 1970

First published 1970 *by*
MACMILLAN AND CO LTD
Little Essex Street London W C 2

First published in the United States of America 1970 *by*
HUMANITIES PRESS INC
303 *Park Avenue South New York NY*

SBN 391–00002–0

Printed in Great Britain at the
PITMAN PRESS
Bath

3 3371

Contents

Acknowledgements

Acknowledgements are due to Faber & Faber Ltd for the use of quotations from the works of T. S. Eliot, copyright in which belongs to Mrs Valerie Eliot.

List of Abbreviations

Introduction

GRAHAM MARTIN

I

As a title *Eliot in Perspective* makes a large claim: the poet in the middle distance grouped with peers and inferiors; Literature, or perhaps Tradition, looming vaguely behind him; and a clear, modern, coherent, easily definable 'point of view'. In fact this collection of essays offers something considerably less grand. It developed out of a series of memorial lectures I arranged on behalf of the Extra-Mural Department of London University a few months after Eliot died. The programme was natural for its occasion. There were some general lectures on the poetry, the criticism and the plays, interspersed with one or two on special aspects intended to light up the whole achievement from a particular angle. The question of publication arose only some time after this programme had been agreed, but it made equally natural the inclusion of a group of essays on more specialised topics, and in choosing these topics (the contributors came afterwards) I tried to keep two points firmly in mind. One was to avoid the kind of topic which would lead either to narrowly specialist conclusions or to a discussion of a very limited aspect of Eliot's work. The other was to concentrate on subjects not much attended to so far, and/or likely to matter in future approaches to his reputation. Perhaps the best way to clarify these aims is to refer to Richard Wollheim's essay on the relationship between Eliot and F. H. Bradley. It is an original and distinguished study of Eliot's doctoral thesis *Knowledge and Experience in the Philosophy of F. H. Bradley*, a work only recently available to Eliot's readers, which should enable them to decide about the usefulness of other less rigorous applications of Eliot's philosophical position to his literary work (see, for example, J. Hillis Miller's in *Poets of Reality* (1966) pp. 131–9). But the detailed examination of *Knowledge and Experience* leads

Wollheim to the more general proposal that Eliot had 'a peculiarly empty or hollow way of conceiving the mind' and that 'in the pursuit of a certain kind of security or reassurance . . . [he] was progressively led to substitute, in his mind, on the one hand, ideas of less content for ideas of more content, and, on the other hand, poorer or softer ideas for better and stronger ideas' (see below, pp. 186, 190). Comments like these seem to me to reverberate in every area of Eliot's work, and exactly illustrate the kind of perspective that contributors were invited to work towards. Other essays of this type are F. W. Bateson's discussion of Eliot's erudition, showing it to be partly a product of his inherited American culture, and partly a rhetorical tactic for disconcerting opponents; and Francis Scarfe's survey of Eliot's indebtedness to French poetry, showing it to be substantially confined to his earliest creative years.

This is not to say, though, that more specific assessments were ruled out. On the contrary. Contributors writing on a body of work, as distinct from a particular topic, were invited to reappraise the grounds for its reputation. In this spirit, Katharine Worth proposes a general revaluation of the reasons for continuing to find Eliot's plays interesting, which amounts to defining where Eliot's dramatic, as distinct from his rhetorical, gifts really lie. John Chalker, applying an Arnoldian perspective to the criticism, argues that its permanent value lies less in the separate usefulness of its main ideas (the point links directly with Wollheim's conclusions) than in the interplay between them and the new poetry which they defended. Harold Brooks puts the non-doctrinal, perhaps even the non-religious case for *Four Quartets*, while Ian Hamilton offers a fresh, and refreshingly stringent, approach to *The Waste Land*. The only suggestion of a general reassessment of Eliot's importance occurs in Gabriel Pearson's analysis of 'Gerontion' and the quatrain poems but even here the effect is to question, rather than seriously to disturb the standard account. (Pearson's view of Eliot a little resembles Eliot's of Milton in the 'Chinese Wall' days: an impressive catastrophe from which we may hope eventually to recover.)

Some readers may think the editorial formula critically hesitant, willing to see wounded the reputation of individual works, but afraid to strike at Eliot's general position. But there were two arguments against a more single-mindedly revaluing approach. The first was that for success it presupposed a kind of agreement between the contributors

made impossible by the circumstances leading to the collection, and
without which the end-product would not be Perspective so much as
'perspectives', violently clashing. The second reason is more deep-
seated. Thoroughgoing changes in critical reputation are always
fed by general changes in literary and intellectual culture. They
reflect, sometimes they are part of, the growth of new modes of
literary expression. Collections of essays of this kind may hinder
or assist this process, but not begin it. Eliot, it will be remembered,
thought that while sensibility changed continuously new poetic
languages appeared only at longish intervals,[1] and if it is true, as
several essays indicate, that Eliot's idiom no longer expresses modern
sensibility it is also true that his poems do not yet read as Pope's
must have to the first Wordsworthians. That revolution still awaits
us.

There is nevertheless one general point, made in different ways by
different essayists, which gives the collection a certain coherence, and
points to the consolidation of a definite phase in Eliot criticism. Looking
back over the forty or so years during which his poetry has been under
serious discussion, two fairly clear stages can be seen. There was the
original debate about its importance conducted by Richards, Leavis and
Matthiessen, concluded at the very latest by the middle of the 1930s.[2]
Then followed an assimilative phase, which took over the main judgements of the critical debate, and concentrated on expounding and
explaining whatever seemed to require it. Books in this phase are Helen
Gardner's *The Art of T. S. Eliot* (1949), Hugh Kenner's *The Invisible
Poet* (1959) or, at a more utilitarian level, George Williamson's *A
Reader's Guide to T. S. Eliot* (1955) and J. Grover Smith's *T. S. Eliot's
Poetry and Plays: a study of sources and meaning* (1956). Commentaries
of this type have sometimes been criticised for lacking critical edge, for
pushing the writer's claims instead of assessing them or, worse, for giving
him the academic's kiss-of-death – a purely conventional acclaim. But no
original writer's work can enter into general intellectual culture without
a good deal of direct advocacy, and in Eliot's case a more serious
because a more avoidable weakness in much criticism of this type
derives from another source, a failure to reconsider the close relationship alleged to exist between his poetry and his social and cultural
diagnoses.[3] The chronological coincidence between this phase and
Eliot's activity as a social commentator and ideologue had a good deal
to do with this failure – the imaginative impact of the poetry authorising,

as it were, the opinions of the social thinker. Another factor was the post-1945 political climate, the attendant loss in reputation of the progressive outlook of the thirties, the conviction that this had been responsible for obscuring, or too quickly dismissing, Eliot's profounder insights into the times. Auden, as so often the sensitive barometer of these shifts of opinion, wrote in 1948 that it had been Eliot who, 'not speechless from shock but finding the right/Language for thirst and fear, did much to/ prevent a panic'.[4] Nominally retrospective, the praise made Eliot seem still contemporary, and that he spoke the 'right language' remained the largely unquestioned assumption of his commentators.

But a third phase has now clearly emerged,[5] whose main impulse is to separate the work from the various ideological clouds that have seemed to trail after it, or at least to examine their relationship with a colder eye. Katharine Worth's essay is a case in point. Eliot's plays, she believes, have suffered from the wrong kind of interpretation. A haze of religious allegory, much of it admittedly spun from material which Eliot himself provided, has come to obscure the genuinely dramatic elements, the themes of lost identity and metaphysical despair which combine with Eliot's linguistic and theatrical inventiveness to anticipate the achievements of recent modern drama. It is only putting her case a little bluntly to say that the dramatist of 'Sweeney Agonistes' turned himself into a stage-sermoniser, and that it should now be the critic's business to disinter the drama. Donald Davie's essay offers a more complicated version of the same point. He maintains that the history of Eliot criticism reveals a stubborn and largely successful resistance to Eliot's symbolist methods. *Four Quartets*, he suggests, is a symbolist poem, to be disengaged from its religious and metaphysical framework by the right kind of attention to its language. Where Christian readers will concern themselves with the Logos, others will respond to the operations of the Word, that is, of language itself, the most fundamental of subject-matters. Davie's analysis of some lines from 'Burnt Norton' is – characteristically – persuasive. But (to borrow a good sentence of Wordsworth's) the sense in which words 'are not a mere vehicle, but *powers* either to kill or to animate'[6] is a view felt with particular keenness by poets, and this may explain Davie's having overlooked the fact that the idiom of *Four Quartets* is not homogeneous. Much of the poem's language *is* 'mere vehicle', so that if we are to agree that its main theme depends on a symbolist technique, then, despite the structural parallels and interweaving of motifs which Harold Brooks outlines in his full-length analysis of the poem, it cannot be considered artistically coherent. *Four Quartets*, in other words, may be seen to belong with the plays not just in chronology, but in trying to combine symbolist poetry with rhetorical address. But so much is clear, that Davie's argument (he applies it to other poems as well) joins with Brooks's analysis to disengage *Four Quartets*, wherever possible, from direct entanglement with ideology. For Brooks, this is due to Eliot's having avoided a specifically Christian symbolism or pattern of allusion, adapting instead other religious sources, and using images and symbols open to several interpretations. His concluding paragraphs, moreover, offer an interesting approach to the metaphysical assumptions of the religious theme. Contrasting these with the Time philosophy of ameliorist writers like Shaw, Brooks proposes that Eliot's view of Time amounts to a way of insisting that to conceive human experience only within a category of historical time seriously impoverishes it. Or, as Forster might say, we live in the moment as well as in the future. And the argument suggests the corollary that Eliot's conservatism (like Burke's) ought always to be taken within the context of its opposite, progressivist optimism – as, indeed, a crucially necessary response to its shallower varieties. This seems a valuable perspective on the connection between Eliot's work and the intellectual culture of the earlier twentieth century.

There is, of course, another more straightforward way in which the collection voices a new stage in the discussion of Eliot's work. For several essayists, his opinions have become historical, less to be argued with or cited as authoritative rhetoric than to be examined for their historical connections. Ian Gregor, writing on Eliot and Arnold, is fairly explicit about this. Eliot's social thinking is, he believes, no longer interesting enough to deserve independent attention, but should rather be seen as one motif in the pattern of Eliot's whole identity. This leads him to propose an analogy with Arnold, like Eliot a poet and influential literary critic, who developed into a significant commentator on cultural, social and religious themes, a general similarity in each writer's relation to his own times which helps to clarify the nature of Eliot's greater poetic achievement. The connection with Arnold recurs in John Peter's essay on the *Criterion*. Eliot's editorial policy of providing a European forum for the best available work descends directly from 'The Function of Criticism', and it was his failure to sustain this policy in the thirties that led to the founding of *Scrutiny*. Essentially, Peter views the later *Criterion* as a casualty of history, Communism and the world capitalist crisis of the thirties making impossible the Arnoldian ambition of its first decade. Eliot found himself squeezed between the political commitments of the young poets whose talent he admired and the demands of his own emerging theological position, and in trying to balance the first by drawing in contributors congenial with the second gradually abandoned – perhaps no longer believed in the primacy of – his earlier commitment to disinterested intelligence. Gregor's and Peter's essays have, I think, the further interest of linking up with Chalker's to show not simply how important Arnold was for Eliot, but the extent to which Eliot's tone about Arnold (in, for example, 'Arnold and Pater') can be seen to derive from an unsuccessful effort to shake off a powerful influence.

Two other essays fall in the same category. Terry Eagleton examines in detail Eliot's concept of Culture, with an effect even more powerfully distancing than Gregor's analogy with Arnold. And Adrian Cunningham uncovers a continuity in Eliot's view of Tradition which underlies the ostensible change of views associated with his conversion to Christianity. The arguments of these essays are too detailed to summarise here, but one aspect of Cunningham's essay is worth mentioning. He finds Eliot's debt to Charles Maurras an essential clue to the general continuity he is concerned to trace, and this will throw some light on one aspect of Eliot's later work which must have puzzled many: the fact that his essays on religious themes are so lacking in the devotional content expressed in his religious poems and plays. Cunningham suggests that it was Maurras who encouraged Eliot to think of the Church, as it were, sociologically, as a social and political structure, rather than as the vehicle for individual religious life. One might need further to ask why Eliot was predisposed to be influenced in this way, and to seek the connection in his exasperated revulsion from the whole Puritan tradition in Anglo-Saxon religious history, a topic separately touched upon in Martin Jarrett-Kerr's essay on Eliot's churchmanship. But, as an account of Maurras's relevance, it is to be hoped that this will replace the relatively superficial connection usually made with Eliot's authoritarian political leanings. Cunningham proposes that the Catholic condemnation of the Maurrasian *Action Française* made a peculiar crisis for Eliot, not on political grounds, but because it asserted the anti-Christian character of the writer who had most deeply influenced his concept of the Church, and therefore tended to isolate him from other European Catholic thinkers just when he felt he had been moving towards them. It may be that in this development we ought to seek the reason for the pronounced sectarian character of Eliot's writing on religious and theological matters in the thirties, and perhaps, therefore, one of his difficulties with the *Criterion*.

Finally, one smaller grouping may be mentioned. Wollheim's discussion of the relevance of the Bradley thesis to the literary criticism makes an illuminating counterpart to Chalker's treatment of the connection between the critical ideas and the poetry. And Cunningham makes a different use of the Bradley influence to explain Eliot's critical style and the elusive shifting definitions of key concepts – points also treated by Chalker. Taken together, these three essays seem to me particularly stimulating.

II

'AN adequate Definition of a true *Critick*', observes the supposed author of *A Tale of a Tub*, '[is], that He is *a Discoverer and Collector of Writers Faults*', and it is a definition especially tempting for editors of collections of essays. Nothing is simpler than to slide into the God's-eye view, chiding some contributors for not fitting their work to certain ghostly specifications visible only to the editorial eye, confidently appropriating the findings of others, perhaps even succumbing to the fantasy of Johnson's astronomer of having been responsible for the whole production, except, of course, for some mechanical assistance for which one is anxious to give all due credit. More directly, that is, it is impossible not to have editorial expectations about the way some topics will turn out, and impossible that all of these will be satisfied. The temptation can, admittedly, be resisted. There is the formula of anonymous recommendation. 'Here, dear reader, are these essays. Here, chiefly, is what they say. None is more equal than any other.' On the other hand, since nobody edits collections of essays without having hobby-horses of his own to ride, some direct comment seems the more honest course. I hope also that it may prove the more interesting course. The stimulus which I have taken from the different contributions will speak for itself, and what follows certainly makes no claim either to God's or to 'a true Critick's' voice.

I have already cavilled a little at aspects of Davie's and Brooks's discussions of *Four Quartets*. A more general point to make is the need for a comparative study of Eliot's religious sensibility, and in this

context the obvious figure to think of is George Herbert. Martin
Jarrett-Kerr ends his essay with a comparison between him and Eliot,
but I think he is mistaken in claiming their similarity. It is the differences
which stand out, especially in their respective treatments of a central
religious experience, self-abnegation before God and the need to
worship. Christian commentators appear content with Eliot in this role;
and without sharing the Christian position, it is not easy to comment.
But the literary critic can at least point to some specific contrasts. The
tone of Herbert's poetry, for example, confers no special or separate
value on the worshipping experience – it is a familiar point about the
tradition he writes in – whereas Eliot's is hushed, meditative, withdrawn, never far from the liturgical. Herbert's metaphors, too, are
revealing. Habitually they juxtapose a secular with a supernatural, or
churchly, element. Eliot, on the other hand, uses a generalised symbolism (rose, garden, children, fire) which conflates the natural with the
supernatural. Winifred Nowottny's discussion of Metaphor is helpful
in explaining why Herbert's method is, as I think, so much more
effective.[7] Metaphor is useful to poets, she proposes, because it makes
available a structure of meanings in addition to those which inhere in
the language of common use, a matter of particular relevance to religious
poetry. The structure of Herbert's metaphors obliges the mind to move
between, and therefore to bring into connection, the everyday and the
sacred, the understood and the guessed-at. But the vagueness and
generality of Eliot's symbolism implies that normal experience is not
interesting enough to offer even significant clues about the nature of its
opposite, which therefore – quite understandably – swallows it up. The
sense of being mysteriously related, in all one's ordinariness, to an
awesomely wonderful God is never strong in Eliot's religious poetry.
He never seems able to begin from the firm grounding that Herbert
supplies, a level of experience that is not God, but at the same time is
not worthless. Eliot is too often found to be arguing that though
ordinary experience *looks* empty and dismal enough, it *must* be meaningful because it eventually leads, though in unknowable ways, to God.
And, while the serious feeling can command respect, such an argument
is fatal to the sense of worship.

An equally important comparison needs to be made with other
twentieth-century religious thinkers such as Simone Weil and
Dietrich Boenhoeffer whose Christian belief brought them into such
impressively tragic collision with modern political and social life. In

fact, for the humanist it is all too easy to point the general contrast between the this-worldly character of modern religious thought and the other-worldly character of Eliot's, so that perhaps a special duty devolves upon Eliot's Christian commentators to work out a more critical assessment of his religious writings within the European context. And to return to *Four Quartets* from a different point of view, the 'European' question may be put somewhat sharply. How far does the poem transcend the immediate context which attached to it for Eliot and his Anglo-American readers? Its later stages offer, for example, History as a significant concept, but what recognisably public experience from our history-persecuted times does the concept engage? The London blitz is merely assimilated (though brilliantly) to the private theme; and in 1942 who but Eliot would be likely to have felt drawn away from the contemporary crisis by the 'antique drum' of Charles the Martyr's confrontation with Oliver Cromwell? This aspect of the poem seems unlikely to wear well. It shows the same unawareness as lies behind Eliot's self-questioning after Munich – a late date, one would have thought, to recognise the force of the Marxist view of Western capitalist democracy.[8]

Eliot's attitude to the present naturally brings up his use of the past, a matter which badly needs the historical perspective J. F. Kermode brought to his discussion of 'dissociation of sensibility' in *Romantic Image* (1957) (pp. 138–61). It is fairly astonishing, for example, to find Northrop Frye substantially taking over Eliot's self-identification with Dante,[9] when the question to explore would seem to be what cultural situation made it possible for Eliot to aspire even tentatively to such a remarkable role. Lawrence's remark that Eliot's 'classiosity'[10] was cowardly may be unkindly blunt, but it does put the point that Eliot sometimes uses the past not to extend his own experience (the general function he assigns it in his criticism), but to evade it. The use of Dante in a line like 'I had not thought death had undone so many', a feeling about one's fellow creatures which it would seem proper for the poet to examine, actually sanctions a *withdrawal* from further exploration of the mood. In his essay on *The Waste Land* Ian Hamilton shows this to be a general tendency. Recognition of the allusions to past literature confirms the reader in his sense of possessing a spiritual enlightenment denied to the individuals whose state the poem denounces (or if 'laments' is fairer than 'denounces' then only as a justification for moving off into its own better-instructed condition). The past, that is, acts as a barrier, not an aid, or a stimulus, to a fuller understanding of the present.

The problem touches, of course, on the issue of allusion in the poetry, which F. W. Bateson discusses in his essay on Eliot's learning. He is, I think, too easily content with the heavy degree of allusive dependence in Eliot's poetry, a feature of minor not major art, though one very congenial in the academic environment which we all inhabit. Bateson explains it as, in Eliot's case, a product of his education, and the suggestion can be linked with A. Alvarez's general proposal of several years ago that Eliot's and Pound's cosmopolitan air belongs with a specifically American poetic modernism which English poetry rejected.[11] But, whatever its source, the practice needs more theoretical discussion than it receives. It ought, for example, to be clearer what we mean when we claim that an allusion works or does not work. There are cases of allusion in Eliot's poetry which cannot be reconciled with the immediate structure of feeling, and may even deflect attention from some radical hiatus. How, for example, is it possible to reconcile Tiresias' grave authority, so well embodied in the movement of 'I who have sat by Thebes below the wall/And sat among the lowest of the dead', with the shallowly satirical note of the Popeian couplets which are its context? What has Tiresias to do with marginal snobberies about Bradford millionaires, and bed-divans, with gibes about carbuncles, or with the sniffy distaste on the subject of the young lady's underclothes. To say that Tiresias both generalises and judges the seduction scene – the usual account – is acceptable only if we can square what his name brings to the poem with what is there already. Otherwise, the allusion 'works' only in the sense of claiming profundity for a state of feeling which, on its own, clearly doesn't deserve it. There is also a marked difference between Eliot's earlier and later practice of allusion. Up to *The Waste Land* the allusions are, if not actually ambiguous or confused, certainly open-ended: they leave the work of interpretation to the reader. But in his Christian poetry the allusions both retain a determinate public meaning and directly accommodate themselves to the poems' inner structure. The reader is no longer on his own, or offered merely the vague shifting identity of a cultured person (inclined to wonder whether he is cultured enough), but has to share, or to imagine himself sharing, a communal identity with the poet and other devout persons. A critical study of Eliot's allusions thus directly bears on the problem of the poetry and its audience, a major issue of symbolist aesthetics. The simple-minded explicatory approach to his poems can become a technique for forgetting what sort of poetry Eliot writes; and one way of restoring our sense of this is to sharpen our awareness about what successful allusion actually is.

On *The Waste Land* there are two points to add to Ian Hamilton's discussion, and partly arising from it. The first concerns the standard theme of the commentaries, the poem's special position in the literature of post-war England. I believe this claim needs to be revised. The evidence within the poem for social or cultural relevance appears more and more ambiguous, and Eliot's own remark that some of its original critics had misunderstood the nature of its disillusionment more and more to the point.[12] Its reception, and the commentaries which followed it, are facts about the context; but the text clearly belongs to the record of Eliot's personal search for a religion, and the representative character of *that* can be established only within the broader perspective which I have already suggested we need. The second point is closely related. It is the question whether *The Waste Land* is a whole poem. This is not the place to resume the arguments of the many distinguished critics who have thought it adequately structured and appropriately coherent. But some years ago Eliot made two important comments, which need to be considered. He accepted both that the poem was 'structureless' and that it might be radically obscure, adding weight to both remarks by revealing how central and extensive Pound's editorial role had been.[13] On the point of the poem's obscurity, there is a useful parallel with Coleridge's *Dejection: an ode*. It is now accepted that there are two poems: (1) the published text which Coleridge carved out of (2) the much longer unpublished verse-letter to Sara Hutchinson,[14] and only when the second turned up could an essential hiatus in the first be explained. Now that *The Waste Land* typescript has turned up, maybe there will be a similar clarification of the published text. Donald Gallup's preliminary report[15] certainly confirms Eliot's account of Pound's editorial role, while the extracts reproduced in his article do nothing to contradict the notion of the original being 'just as structureless, only in a more futile way'. In fact they add to the sense of Eliot having worked at very different levels of seriousness, even of success, and strengthen an impression of the published poem's fitful realisation of its themes, sometimes grasping them with great force and economy, elsewhere merely sketching them in with allusive gestures, nervous hints, or handling them in an inappropriate tone, or with indefensible obliquity. We already know how commentary on the poem was affected by the spoof Notes, and soon we will know just what the published poem's structure owes to Pound. It seems reasonable to guess that the poem as we have known it is about to undergo radical change.

III

You've the great American disease, and you've got it 'bad' – the appetite, morbid and monstrous, for colour and form, for the picturesque and the romantic at any price. I don't know whether we come into the world with it – with the germs implanted and antecedent to experience; rather perhaps we catch it early, almost before developed consciousness. . . . We're like travellers in the desert – deprived of water and subject to the terrible mirage, the torment of illusion, of the thirst-fever.[16]

I began by explaining that some topics were chosen on the ground that they were likely to be important in the future. Of these Eliot's nationality is the most outstanding, and for that reason in itself Gabriel Pearson's essay seems to me particularly welcome. It is not too difficult to see, after all, that Eliot's American origins matter.[17] The problem is to discover their bearing on his work, and the failure even to open this issue probably derives from Eliot's successful reconstituting of the English poetic tradition (the most ambitious feat of cultural imperialism the century seems likely to produce). For though the personal element in those revolutionary critical judgements is well known,[18] their specifically American features have still to be clarified. Pearson's essay is valuable at precisely this point because it connects Eliot's departure from America with a phase of American social history when the responsible patrician class to which the Eliots belonged was being politically displaced by the new forces of industrialism and machine-democracy centred in the big cities. Pearson finds that Eliot's work reveals a never wholly successful attempt to leave this American social conflict behind. A disordered emotion persists within, and occasionally surfaces to disrupt the symbolist stasis, the attempted mask of 'impersonality'. There is a withdrawal from social experience coupled with a ghostly hunger for it never entirely appeased. So in the late work we find on the one hand the self-exploration in *Four Quartets* of the most private experiences of the psyche, combined with the well-willing but empty social engagement of the plays. Pearson's essay offers an explanation of a major irony of Eliot's poetry, that his early 'alienated' poems are rich with the presence of people off-stage, of human relationships just outside the poem, while his late work, laying anxious claim to a common humanity, can only assert it through the mechanical interchanges of characters of whom the mildest thing one can say is that they are too slightly realised.

There are other aspects of Eliot's career which his American background clarifies. Some years ago Raymond Williams located the weakness of Eliot's social criticism at the point where he moves from general formulation to a detailed observation of English life.[19] One explanation for this lies in the fact that Eliot observed England as an American expatriate. The source of his valuable detachment, this is also the source of his weakness, since he saw everything English through the spectacles of his own social needs. There is, for instance, the general American hunger for a past generated by, and interacting with, the equally American tendency to abolish it. There is the more specific preoccupation with a responsible aristocracy to guard national culture against erosion by the urban masses ('the red-eyed scavengers'), and the specialised model for the Church of England, derived, as Martin Jarrett-Kerr points out, more from reading and residence in Kensington than from any concrete historical possibility. Eliot's undervaluing of, and active distaste for, the English Puritan tradition can be seen as a symptom of his own flight from the Unitarianism of St Louis, Missouri.[20] And the same cause appears to underlie his extreme mistrust of the Inner Voice – one often feels in the presence of Dryden or Swift battling with the Baptist Boar and Presbyterian Fox – and the more complicated issue discussed by John Chalker and Adrian Cunningham, the opposition between Tradition (constructed by the Individual Talent) and the Individual Talent (impoverished without the aid of Tradition). Eliot's Americanism is obviously not a master-key, and critical discussion is already badly enough littered about with genetic explanations which explain too much, but the Puritan background is so significant in American history, and in Eliot's own family, that his attitude towards it must be considered central. Is it too much to look here for the source of that nervousness about the mind diagnosed in Wollheim's essay? Northrop Frye made the good point recently that Eliot's aesthetic theory lacked the concept of the Imagination,[21] and is not this another aspect of that mental passivity in the face of experience which often appears in his work? Or, rather, it would be truer to say that we find a theory or idea of mental passivity joined to the workings of an intensely active mind, as it were unwilling to conceptualise its own identity. It is this strange juxtaposition, which accounts for the feeling one gets with so much of Eliot's prose that the writer is lurking danger-ously about somewhere out of sight, using his argument to distract or deceive before making an irrational pounce on his victim-reader.

These are general issues, but Pearson's essay raises a more specific matter which certainly needs its American context: Eliot's anti-semitism. I take Pearson's analysis (in the manner of Kenneth Burke) of the language of 'Gerontion' and other poems to provide definitive evidence that anti-semitism is *not* a marginal issue in Eliot's work (revealed only in unfortunate asides, and discernible only to the paranoia of Jewish critics). And, while it is obviously stupid to talk as if Eliot had drafted minutes for Eichmann, I do not myself see how anti-semitism in important poems by a major writer can be lightly forgotten. We know that there *were* consequences to that diffused 'cultured' distaste at work in European attitudes from about 1880 (I choose the date with *Daniel Deronda* in mind for the English context, but perhaps the post-Dreyfus time would be more appropriate), and any contribution by a major writer to that state of affairs has got to be faced. But the immediate roots are worth knowing, and some light may be thrown on them in Eliot's case by a recent autobiography – *Making It* (1968) by the American literary critic, Norman Podhoretz. Its author is a Brooklyn Jew, whose formal education took him to Columbia and Harvard, by a process which imposed, as in the case of an English scholarship boy, a severe cultural strain. But Podhoretz's Jewishness (combined perhaps with the availability of the American democratic tradition?) provided him with a powerful source of resistance. The result was a battle, rather than the elaborate interchange more typical of the English scene, ending in Podhoretz's conscious rejection of crucial elements in the WASP* liberal culture which he had imbibed. The detail of this is not relevant here, but the general issue is. Podhoretz's account suggests that the big immigrations at the turn of the century set up a deep-seated cultural antagonism, not without class overtones, between the inherited Anglo-Saxon traditions and a new thrusting Jewish intellectualism. Socially and economically under-privileged they might be, but the Jewish immigrants were unusual in

* White Anglo-Saxon Protestant.

having access to the cultural weapon of their own history. What I am suggesting is that the ritual degradation of the Jew which Pearson diagnoses in some of Eliot's poems derives from this cultural war, and that Eliot's departure from America may reflect his response to a cultural deadlock with extensive implications. And, when we recall Sartre's analysis of anti-semitism as the ritual creation of outsiders in order to allay (but it can never be allayed) the fear of not belonging within the established social framework,[22] it is possible to see in the shadowy Jew whose rootlessness and vulgarity offends Eliot's inherited culture, a scapegoat for his own expatriation. It is an interesting fact that as Eliot's poetry becomes more social, more at one with its ideal reader, it reveals for its central protagonist a true Romantic Wanderer, a permanent alien, the 'spirit unappeased and peregrine' who haunts *Four Quartets* (descending from such unexpected ancestors as Huck Finn and Isobel Archer). The release of this symbolic figure could come about only within the specially constructed social context of Eliot's England. At an earlier stage, when he was still struggling to attach himself to an acceptable version of English society (in the deepest sense), the uncultured Jew functioned as a fictional whipping-boy for his own suppressed subversive self.

There is at least one other neglected area of Eliot studies where the American background matters: Eliot's relationship with James. We need a historical examination of the different cultural situations each inherited in America and found in England. Unlike Eliot's, James's America was not in process of superannuation when he left for England; and, as *The American Scene* shows, his response to the process which affected the young Eliot was not simply a rejection. Then there is the critical issue, that where James made the complex American fate a major theme of his work Eliot evades or suppresses it. In this connection, Tony Tanner's recent book on American literature, *The Reign of Wonder*, is enlightening. He links the general theme of innocence in the literature with determining aspects of American social experience, and convincingly explains James' International Theme as a version of this inherent pattern, American innocence in both its good and bad points being played off against the European sense either of human limitation, or of corrupting moral cynicism. The thesis can also be applied to Eliot's work (whose absence from the book illustrates how natural it still is *not* to think of him as an American), where innocence is helpless, static, or actually in retreat before the corrupt power of experience, and is embodied only in the paralysis of observers, or the off-stage symbolism of childish laughter in poems like 'Marina' and *Four Quartets*. The oppositions, that is, persist, but as states of being which never meet rather than, as in James, interpenetrating categories of reality.

And to conclude on a domestic note. I doubt if Eliot's place in our own poetic tradition can really be understood without a fuller understanding of his American social and cultural inheritance. It is sometimes said that Eliot and Pound offered English poetry a cultural opening towards Europe which the poets of the last twenty years have been blameworthy for not following up, and for adopting instead a provincial airing of nationality. But this seems to me culture without history. On the one hand, Eliot's European alignment was fed from America, and existed in a form which English culture could not directly use; on the other, towards which Europe could the post-1945 poets responsively turn as Eliot had turned to the French symbolist poets (drawing himself upon a national tradition)? To put it another way: only the End of Empire could make available a genuine Europeanism, and what form this will take is not likely to be clear for some time. Eliot and Pound, then, may point the right way, but they certainly offer no map. And to insist on their American roots may be the best way of refreshing our sense of what they actually contributed to our poetry. What it might have been without them is certainly impossible to imagine.

.   .   .

Finally some acknowledgements for help and advice – to Miss Winifred Bamforth of the Department of Extra-Mural Studies in London University, who suggested the original lecture course, and whose resources of courteous efficiency made my responsibility for the academic side so free from care; for general and specific suggestions for topics and contributors, I have to thank F. W. Bateson and Ian Gregor; for much valuable talk about Eliot and symbolist poetry, Nick Furbank; and, though it will amuse him to hear it, my colleague Donald Hill, for that kind of extended discussion over several years which seems, in the end, the irreplaceable background to all one's more particular projects.

Bedford College,   GRAHAM MARTIN
London.

NOTES

1. 'Johnson's "London" and "The Vanity of Human Wishes" ', in *English Critical Essays: Twentieth Century* (World's Classics: 1933) p. 302.

2. George Watson dates Eliot's 'capture of the young intellectuals of creative energy in England and the United States in the 1920s' ('The Triumph of T. S. Eliot', in *Critical Quarterly*, VII iv (Winter 1965) 328–37). The influential critical interpretation of this event dates, however, from F. R. Leavis's *New Bearings in English Poetry* (1932) and F. O. Matthiessen's *The Achievement of T. S. Eliot* (1935).

3. Leavis called *The Waste Land* 'an effort to focus an inclusive human consciousness. The effort, in ways suggested above, is characteristic of the age' (*New Bearings*, p. 95). See also Matthiessen, *Achievement*, chapters 5–6 passim. The authority of this connection between the poem and the age can be suggested by a casual reference to *The Waste Land* 'as a record of cultural collapse' in the course of a discussion of *Mrs Dalloway* (A. D. Moody, *Virginia Woolf* (1963)).

4. 'To T. S. Eliot on his Sixtieth Birthday', in *Nones* (1952) p. 63.

5. The trend is clear in both C. K. Stead, *The New Poetic* (1964) pp. 148–67, and Northrop Frye, *T. S. Eliot*, Writers and Critics series (1963) pp. 7–24.

6. Cited in Mary Moorman, *William Wordsworth, A Biography: the later years 1803–1850* (1965) p. 442.

7. *The Language Poets Use* (1962) pp. 67–8.

8. 'Was our society, which had always been assured of its superiority and rectitude, so confident of its unexamined premisses, assembled round anything more permanent than a congeries of banks, insurance companies and industries, and had it any beliefs more essential than a belief in compound interest and the maintenance of dividends?' (*ICS* p. 64)

9. Frye, *Eliot*, pp. 50 ff. Dante's general importance to Eliot need not be argued, but it is worth while recalling the character of Eliot's response to writers who influenced him significantly. 'If we stand towards a writer in this other relation of which I speak, we do not imitate him. . . . This relation is a feeling of profound kinship, or rather of peculiar personal intimacy, with another, probably a dead author . . . and when a young writer is seized with his first passion of this sort he may be changed, metamorphosed almost, within a few weeks even, from a bundle of second-hand sentiments into a person. The imperative intimacy arouses for the first time a real, an unshakeable confidence that you possess this secret knowledge, this intimacy, with the dead man, that after few or many years or centuries you should have appeared, with this indubitable claim to distinction; who can penetrate at once the thick and dusty circumlocutions about his reputation, can call yourself alone his friend. . . .' ('Reflections on Contemporary Poetry', in *Egoist*, VI iii (July 1919) 39.)

10. Cited in J. M. Murry, *Reminiscences of D. H. Lawrence* (1933) p. 189.

11. *The Shaping Spirit* (1958) p. 12.

12. 'Thoughts after Lambeth', in *SE* p. 368.

13. '*Interviewer*: Did the excisions change the intellectual structure of the poem? *Eliot*: No. I think it was just as structureless, only in a more futile way, in the longer version. . . . I think that in the early poems it was a question of not being able to – of having more to say than one knew how to say, and having something one wanted to put into words and rhythm which one didn't have the command of words and rhythm to put in a way immediately apprehensible. . . . In *The Waste Land*, I wasn't even bothering whether I understood what I was saying.' (*Writers at Work: the Paris Review interviews*, 2nd Series (1963) pp. 83, 90.)

14. Humphry House, *Coleridge* (1953) pp. 133–8.

15. Donald Gallup, 'The "Lost" Manuscripts of T. S. Eliot', in *Times Literary Supplement*, 7 Nov. 1968, pp. 1238–40.

16. Henry James's story 'Four Meetings'.

17. Matthiessen's well-known comments (*Achievement*, p. 144) throw little light on the social forces at work.

18. 'The Frontiers of Criticism', in *PP* p. 106.

19. *Culture and Society*, 1780–1950 (1958) pp. 233–6. Eliot's banking and commercial experience seems to have been responsible for some of his social knowledge. He wrote to Lytton Strachey in 1919: 'You are very – ingenuous – if you can conceive me conversing with rural deans in the cathedral close. I do not go to cathedral towns but to centres of industry. My thoughts are absorbed in questions more important than ever enters the heads of deans – as *why* it is cheaper to buy steel from America than from Middlesbrough, and the probable effect – the exchange difficulties with Poland – and the appreciation of the rupee. My evenings in Bridge. The effect is to make me regard London with disdain, and divide mankind into supermen, termites and wire worms. I am sojourning among the termites. At any rate that coheres. I feel sufficiently specialised, at present, to inspect or hear any ideas with impunity' (cited in Michael Holroyd, *Lytton Strachey*, II (1968) 364–5). Strachey thought this letter 'grim', and 'hesitated to communicate with Eliot again', perhaps not surprisingly: the tone is very queer indeed, the play with 'the rupee' clearly marks Eliot out as one of the unrecognised masters of gamesmanship.

20. F. R. Leavis has already made this point in his discussion of Lawrence and Eliot in *D. H. Lawrence: Novelist* (1955) pp. 87n – 88, 305–8.

21. *Eliot*, p. 48.

22. *Anti-Semite and Jew* (New York, 1948). Eliot later spoke of 'that stream of mixed immigration, bringing (or rather multiplying) the danger of development into a *caste* system', explaining that 'the essential difference between a caste and a class system is that the former is a difference such that the dominant class comes to consider itself a superior race' (*NDC* p. 45 and note).

I

The Poetry of Learning

F. W. BATESON

I

A LITTLE learning, though no doubt a dangerous thing in the abstract, can act as a creative stimulus on poets of a 'literary' temperament. Pope's own knowledge of Homeric Greek, for example, was scarcely that of one who had drunk deeply of the Pierian spring, but his *Iliad* is one of the most successful translations in English. And the *Essay on Criticism* itself, though not wholly without learning of a sort, is really a very superficial performance, as John Dennis, a man of genuine critical learning, hastened to point out at the time. If Pope's poem continues to be read and quoted, one reason may be the 'danger' he ran of being exposed as a critical charlatan. The liveliness, then, with which Pope enacted the part of critical mentor there is a consequence, at any rate in part, of his own consciousness of a deficiency of critical learning. If he could not perhaps be more learned than Dennis, he could at least put what learning he had to more effective poetic use. And under such circumstances the question of charlatanry does not arise; Pope is a part of English literature and Dennis is not.

The close parallel between Eliot's poetry and Pope's – as in some respects between that of Auden and Dryden – has often struck me. The verbal brilliance that Pope and Eliot share is accompanied in both by a similar uncertainty, occasionally degenerating to sheer clumsiness in the structure of their poems. Eliot bluffs his way out by abrupt transitions, but to the critical reader this defect is a serious and central one. The poems are all too often brilliant fragments only perfunctorily stitched together.[1] It is tempting to connect with this general stylistic characteristic the local stimulus that Pope and Eliot both appear to derive from the moments of learning, or pseudo-learning, whose shallowness constitutes both a challenge and a 'danger'. The thinner the ice the more dazzling the skater's performance becomes. The appearance of sophistication and erudition, not having been honestly earned, has to be maintained in other ways – either by astonishing us momentarily

and then hurrying on to something else, or else by the sheer verbal wit
and delightful impudence of the whole affair, or sometimes by a grammatical obscurity that suggests more than we are certain it can really
mean.

Eliot was not an autodidact like Pope, nervously dependent upon the
approval of his more scholarly friends, but the quality and range of his
learning, in the strict sense of the word, are often exaggerated. As an
undergraduate he was, as Irving Babbitt once told me in a long private
conversation, 'a vurra poor stoodent'. The comment surprised me at
the time. I knew Babbitt had been one of Eliot's early intellectual
heroes, and his general anti-romanticism – superficial though it may
seem today – clearly derives from Babbitt's celebrated Harvard course
on French criticism, which the young Eliot is known to have attended
enthusiastically. I attended it myself, less enthusiastically, some twenty
years later. Whether Babbitt was right in describing the undergraduate
Eliot as a poor student I have no means of knowing. I should add,
however, that when I talked to Babbitt – it was about 1928 or 1929 – he
expressed the highest opinion of Eliot's mature criticism, though this
admiration did not extend to the poetry. (I seem to remember that when
I tried to point out to him that the poetry at its best was the creative
complement of the criticism I got nowhere at all.)

The clever if lazy 'poor stoodent' grew up, largely under Ezra
Pound's influence, into the clever if irresponsible pseudo-scholar of the
early poems and essays. I shall not attempt a catalogue here of the
errors of fact committed by the young Eliot in some of the critical
essays, but it is necessary to illustrate briefly what tends to happen in
them regarded simply as scholarship, so that the air of authority and
expertise can be seen in its true colours. An amusing example will be
found at the beginning of 'Shakespeare and the Stoicism of Seneca'.
This brilliant critical firework – which Eliot inexplicably omitted from
the paperback edition of *Elizabethan Essays* (1963) as unduly 'callow'
– originated as an address to the Shakespeare Association, who had it
published by the Oxford University Press in 1927 as an eighteen-page
booklet. In this decorous format a preliminary apologetic paragraph
opens the proceedings, which may be worth quoting since it is not to
be found in the essay as reprinted in *Selected Essays* (1932) or elsewhere:

> Desiring to make the most of the opportunity which had been given
> me of addressing the inmost circle of Shakespeare experts, I cast
> about, as any other mere journalist would do in the circumstances,

for some subject in treating which I could best display my agility and conceal my ignorance of all the knowledge of which everyone present is master. I abandoned several interesting topics on which I might hope to impress almost any other audience – such as the development of dramatic blank verse or the relation of Shakespeare to Marlowe – in favour of one which, if I am in disagreement with anybody, I shall be in disagreement with persons whose opinions will be regarded as suspiciously by the Shakespeare Association as are my own. I am a timid person, easily overawed by authority; in what I have to say I hope that authority is at least as likely to be of my opinion as not.

The cancelled paragraph shows an Eliot nicely conscious below the irony of what a dangerous thing a little learning may be – though it also shows how intimidating this 'mere journalist' could be in the use of what learning he had. Between the defensive irony of 'I am a timid person, easily overawed by authority' and Pope's 'Tim'rous by Nature, of the Rich in Awe' (*Imitation of Horace*, First Satire of the Second Book, line 7) the parallel is clearly more than accidental. But the consciousness of a necessity to conceal ignorance comes to grief in the very next paragraph – the one with which the essay opens in *Selected Essays* and *Elizabethan Essays*.

Eliot begins there, it may be remembered, by contrasting three modern Shakespeareans (Lytton Strachey, Middleton Murry and Wyndham Lewis) with a nineteenth-century critical trio (Coleridge, Swinburne, Dowden) and an eighteenth-century quartet, who are presented as likely to be 'more sympathetic' to us than their nineteenth-century successors. The quartet is made up of three familiar names – Rymer (of *A Short View of Tragedy*, 1693), Morgann (of *An Essay on the Dramatic Character of Falstaff*, 1777), and Dr Johnson; the fourth eighteenth-century Shakespearean is a certain 'Webster'. ('Whether Mr Strachey, or Mr Murry, or Mr Lewis, is any nearer to the truth of Shakespeare than Rymer, or Morgann, or Webster, or Johnson, is uncertain. . . .') After its appearance as a booklet in 1927 the essay was revised for its incorporation in *Selected Essays* in 1932, but though it has been frequently reprinted since in one collection or another the mysterious 'Webster' has remained in the text. Unfortunately there was no eighteenth-century Shakespearean scholar or writer called Webster; he is what bibliographers call a 'ghost'. Eliot's 'Webster' is clearly a slip for 'Whiter'. In 1927 Walter Whiter, the clever if eccentric

clergyman who wrote *A Specimen of a Commentary on Shakespeare*
(1794), would have been just the man to dangle briefly before an
admiring Shakespeare Association as a guarantee that the speaker was
something more than an agile journalist. But what was dangled should,
of course, have been correct. The fact that 'Webster' persists through
all the various printings of 'Shakespeare and the Stoicism of Seneca'
strongly suggests to me that Eliot had never even skimmed through
Whiter's treatise.

Similar errors can be found in most of Eliot's earlier critical essays.
The 'sense of fact' – which is made the final *sine qua non* of the critic in
'The Function of Criticism' of 1923 – was one that he himself only
acquired, if at all, in middle age. A phrase that he applies in that essay
to Remy de Gourmont, whose influence dominates the early criticism
as that of Laforgue dominates the early poetry, can be applied against
Eliot himself: Gourmont (we are told) was 'sometimes, I am afraid . . .
a master illusionist of fact'. Eliot, too, in the early essays, is often a
masterly illusionist of literary scholarship. I do not wish to suggest that
this mastery of scholarly patter detracts in any serious way from the
value of the early criticism. Eliot is to me the best critic who has written
in English since Matthew Arnold. Taken in the proper spirit – as a
smoke-screen behind which a young critic can display his agility and
conceal his ignorance – the illusionism adds considerably to the liveliness
of the early essays. But the factual fallibility cannot very well be denied.
The Marlowe essay is particularly full of errors, false analogies and
ingenious hypotheses that have no real bases in literary history at all.
In the Middleton essay it is at least unfortunate that Middleton's
occasional poetic brilliance has to be demonstrated by the quotation of
a passage from *The Changeling* which is normally assigned to Rowley.
Somewhat similar is the use in the Massinger essay of a passage from
Henry VIII often – and, I think, correctly – believed to be by Fletcher,
to show that *Shakespeare* writes more vividly than Massinger. In the
Dryden essay some lines from *MacFlecknoe* are said to be 'plagiarized'
from Cowley in what is not a plagiarism at all but Dryden's deliberate
parody of Cowley. The mistakes are not gross ones, but a scholar – as
distinct from a critic who has dressed himself up to look like a scholar
– would not have made them. And there are many more.

The lapses from scholarly precision become noticeably fewer in the
later essays; on the other hand, the critical interest of the literary essays
decreases in an almost exact proportion to the absence of factual error.

It is clear that, so far from a 'sense of fact' being the basic qualification of criticism, in Eliot's own case at any rate a splendid dogmatism and recklessness of assertion, underlying and feeding on his masterly illusionism of fact, were the indispensable prerequisites. Eliot had an important and original critical message to deliver, but he seems to have required the masquerade of scholarship, partly perhaps to get the message heard at all at the time, but principally as a personal stimulus, an aid to his own critical self-confidence. Remy de Gourmont was no doubt the model – a better model than the more scholarly Babbitt for two wholly reputable reasons: his prose style was a much better one, and his wide if superficial learning was used in the cause of contemporary poetry (Gourmont was a minor Symbolist), not in the cause of conventional Protestant ethics (which Babbitt had re-named 'Humanism'). But the special fascination of Gourmont, a minor critic, for Eliot, a major critic, was (I believe) the spectacle he presented of learning used as a polemical device which was also a kind of charade. The impudence of such a comment of Eliot's as that in the Jonson essay – 'It is a world like Lobatchevsky's; the worlds created by artists like Jonson are like systems of non-Euclidean geometry'[2] – is precisely its critical *raison d'être*. We suspect that Eliot knows no more about Lobatchevsky than we do, but we know that the old fogeys he is attacking will *think* he does. It was an effective way in 1920 of silencing the George Saintsburys and Edmund Gosses if they had dared to object to this new interpretation of Jonsonian comedy. Who were they to protest if they did not know who Lobatchevsky was?

II

In the poems the learning is less detachable from the obscurity. I accept at its face value Eliot's statement in 'The Metaphysical Poets' that obscurity is a necessary consequence of the complexity of modern life:

We can say that it appears likely that poets in our civilization, as it exists at present, must be *difficult*. Our civilization comprehends great variety and complexity, and this variety and complexity, playing upon a refined sensibility, must produce various and complex results. The poet must become more and more comprehensive, more allusive, more indirect, in order to force, to dislocate if necessary, language into his meaning.

2

As an example of such linguistic dislocation Eliot quotes ten lines, from the 'Légende' of Laforgue, a passage which represents Laforgue's poetry at its most obscure and most chaotic. Laforgue's formula was to use the learned or unexpected in an ironic context, but the formula is grossly overworked by him and soon becomes monotonous. Eliot's early verse is often reminiscent of Laforgue's, but unlike Laforgue he provided for each poem a solid and self-sufficient dramatic structure. 'Mr Eliot's Sunday Morning Service' is typical of this development. I need only quote the first two stanzas:

> Polyphiloprogenitive
> The sapient sutlers of the Lord
> Drift across the window-panes.
> In the beginning was the Word.
>
> In the beginning was the Word.
> Superfetation of τὸ'ἐν
> And at the mensual turn of time
> Produced enervate Origen.

This is, or might be, Laforgue in English. But there are two immediately obvious differences. One is that whereas Laforgue would have got the learned words right the 'vurra poor stoodent' has made two mistakes; the Greek should be τὸ'ἐν (with a rough breathing), and 'mensual' should presumably be 'menstrual' (the form 'mensual' as recorded in the *OED* has no physiological meaning). The second difference is that Eliot has so obviously *enjoyed* the exercise in theological sarcasm, whereas the prevailing mood in Laforgue is of a self-pitying ennui.

Eliot's enjoyment in this poem communicates itself to the sympathetic reader, whether he is or is not aware of the errors of scholarship. In 'Gerontion', on the other hand, a slightly later poem, the learning or pseudo-learning is likely to be missed or misunderstood by the reader. 'Gerontion' begins with two lines of excellent dramatic blank verse:

> Here I am, an old man in a dry month,
> Being read to by a boy, waiting for rain.

It is disconcerting to learn that the two lines come, almost word for word, from a sentence in A. C. Benson's undistinguished life of Edward FitzGerald (1905): 'Here he sits, in a dry month, old and blind, being read to by a country boy, longing for rain.' Some twenty years later Eliot admitted that the passage had been 'lifted bodily from a Life of

Edward Fitzgerald [*sic*] – I think the one in the "English Men of Letters" series'.[3] By that time he had apparently (and characteristically) forgotten even the name of the author plagiarized, though he is correct in saying the life is in the 'English Men of Letters' series.[4]

An even more bare-faced act of plagiarism occurs in the short third paragraph of 'Gerontion', this time from a nativity sermon by Lancelot Andrewes, the relevant passage being:

> Signs are taken for wonders. 'Master, we would fain see a sign' (Mat. xii. 38), that is a miracle. And in this sense it is a sign to wonder at. Indeed, every word here is a wonder. . . . *Verbum infans*, the Word without a word; the eternal Word not able to speak a word. . . . And . . . swaddled. . . .[5]

Eliot has here only abbreviated the passage in Andrewes without verbal change, though the sarcastic tone is, of course, his own contribution. He continues:

> In the juvescence of the year
> Came Christ the tiger
> In depraved May, dogwood and chestnut, flowering judas. . . .

There is, as it happens, no such word as *juvescence* in English; it is presumably a happy slip for *juvenescence*. The rest of the passage – apart from the Blakean tiger – is a distillation of some sentences in *The Education of Henry Adams* (1918), a book Eliot had reviewed at length in the *Athenaeum* of 23 May 1919. The relevant passage in Adams is part of a description of Washington, as it was in his youth, in the spring: 'Here and there a negro cabin alone disturbed the dogwood and the judas-tree. . . . No European spring had [the] passionate depravity that marked the Maryland May.'[6]

'Gerontion' made its first appearance in print in 1920 in *Ara Vos Prec*. If he had been asked in 1920 to justify the preceding plagiarisms he would no doubt have replied in similar terms to those he used in the Massinger essay of the same year:

> Immature poets imitate; mature poets steal; bad poets deface what they take, and good poets make it into something better, or at least something different. The good poet welds his thefts into a whole of feeling which is unique, utterly different from that from which it was torn; the bad poet throws it into something which has no cohesion.

The argument had itself been stolen from Gourmont's *Le Problème du style* (p. 109), a book praised by Eliot later in the Massinger essay, but Eliot's practice had already justified it several times in the *Prufrock* collection (1917). As an example take the brilliant line from 'La Figlia Che Piange' (a poem apparently written in 1911):

> Simple and faithless as a smile and shake of the hand.

The theft, a clear improvement on its original, was from Laforgue's short story 'Hamlet', which has the incidental phrase, in prose, 'Simple et sans foi comme un bonjour'.

The justification of improvement as an excuse for plagiarism is one with a long history. In English literature the extreme examples are *The White Devil* and *The Duchess of Malfi*, two superb plays that are almost wholly fabricated, according to the latest investigator, from other men's writings.[7] Eliot's special interest in Webster is well known. Perhaps he may have recognized, without realizing why, that he and Webster belonged to the same assimilative poetical tribe. Pope is another English poet who almost always improved what he stole. Unlike Eliot, however, who scarcely ever revised his poems after they had achieved print, Pope was continually improving upon himself either by minor verbal changes or as in the case of *The Rape of the Lock* and *The Dunciad* by completely recasting this poem.

Gourmont's concept of mature poetry as one legitimising verbal theft – even if the stolen passage is improved in the process – raises more questions than it answers. Why is the theft necessary at all? How is the conscientious reader expected to react when such a theft is found out? What is the burglar-poet on the look-out for? An alternative and more useful formula was provided by Eliot himself in the section on Donne in 'Shakespeare and the Stoicism of Seneca'. The crucial sentences must be quoted in full:

> In making some very commonplace investigations of the 'thought' of Donne, I found it quite impossible to come to the conclusion that Donne believed anything. It seemed as if, at that time, the world was filled with broken fragments of systems, and that a man like Donne merely picked up, like a magpie, various shining fragments of ideas as they struck his eye, and stuck them about here and there in his verse.

As a comment on Donne I do not find this particularly persuasive: Donne after all *did* believe in a great many things. But applied to

Webster, and the extraordinary medley of authors represented in his (hypothetical) 'notebook', the formulation is probably correct. And it becomes even more plausible when applied, as so much in the early criticism can be, to Eliot himself. The magpie-instinct – not only for 'fragments of systems', but for all sorts of 'shining fragments' of imagery or phraseology – was unusually highly developed in him. The link between this personal characteristic and the general poetic trend of his generation in Western Europe and America towards 'difficult' poetry is the public use to which Eliot was able to put literary allusion as a mode of symbolism. 'The poet', Eliot had said in the passage already quoted from 'The Metaphysical Poets', 'must become more and more comprehensive, *more allusive*, more indirect, in order to force, to dislocate if necessary, language into his meaning.' The statement dates from 1921, the year of *The Waste Land*'s composition, and the various alternatives listed – comprehensiveness, allusiveness, indirectness, linguistic dislocation – are notoriously all present in that poem. But it is the use of literary allusion that is perhaps the principal synthesizing device in it. The difference between the allusions in 'Gerontion' to A. C. Benson, Lancelot Andrewes and Henry Adams and the more or less learned quotations and references in *The Waste Land* is that the former are essentially private (their function is simply to supply Eliot with poetic material), while the latter are public (their function is to supply a poetic commentary on the modern world and they must therefore be recognizable by the modern reader of poetry).

The role of learning – or what looks like learning – in *The Waste Land* has already received a more than sufficiently detailed treatment elsewhere.[8] An earlier and less familiar example of the same technique is Eliot's 'Burbank with a Baedeker: Bleistein with a Cigar', a poem that has never in my opinion had proper critical justice done to it. Its technical interest is the dual function, private as well as public, to which the not inconsiderable learning packed into it is put. It is also the last and perhaps the best of Eliot's exercises in semi-comic satire. I will confess to greatly preferring its verbal concision and poker-face gaiety to the hysterical sublime of *The Waste Land* and 'The Hollow Men'.

'Burbank' was printed with 'Sweeney Erect' in the same issue of *Art and Letters*. Like its companion-pieces, an epigraph precedes the poem, but instead of the customary extract from some Elizabethan play we are provided with a passage of amusing almost nonsensical prose which proves on inspection to be a cento of phrases from Gautier, St Augustine,

Henry James's *The Aspern Papers, Othello* ('goats and monkeys'), 'A
Toccata of Galuppi's' ('with such hair too') and a masque by John
Marston. The key to a method in the confusion is that most of the
extracts are from English literary classics that are sited in Venice.
Burbank, it is clear, has brought more than a Baedeker with him to
Venice.

On the surface the poem itself is a miniature comic drama describing
Burbank's brief love affair with the Princess Volupine and his displace-
ment in her favours first of all by his compatriot Bleistein ('Chicago
Semite Viennese') and then by Sir Ferdinand Klein, a knight-errant
presumably of Lloyd George's creation. But this simple story of
feminine infidelity is narrated in the poetic diction of high ironic
scholarship. The members of the Shakespeare Association would have
been delighted no doubt to meet in the second verse 'defunctive music'
from 'The Phoenix and the Turtle', which is followed by two passages
from *Antony and Cleopatra*, one diverted to Burbank and the second to
the Princess, a familiar scrap from *The Merchant of Venice* and another
from *Hamlet*. There is also – a more recondite allusion – an echo of a
line in Chapman's *Bussy D'Ambois* which is itself an imitation of an
image in Seneca's *Hercules Furens*. Finally, the poem's fourth line,
('They were together, and he fell') is a comic reversal of the fourth line
in Tennyson's 'The Sisters':

> They were together, and she fell.

Eliot's use of familiar, or reasonably familiar, literary allusions in
'Burbank' gives the poem its special mock-heroic effect. As in such
Augustan mock-heroics as *MacFlecknoe* and *The Rape of the Lock*, the
reproduction of a sordid or trivial modern incident in the magnificent
phraseology of the literature of an earlier age diminishes the modern
participants without in any way degrading the classic models. (Burbank
is equated with Shakespeare's Antony and Bleistein with Shylock for
the light it throws on them, not on their models.) But the total effect of
Eliot's poem is very different from that of the Augustan mock-heroics.
The learning to which it appeals, for one thing, is not public in the
sense in which the conventions of classical epic were public in Pope's
time. In spite of occasional suggestions of Pound's *Mauberley*, 'Burbank'
is very much Eliot's poem and one concerned with Eliot's own personal
predicament.

Negatively, then, Pound was certainly right when he wrote to William

Carlos Williams in 1920, 'Eliot is perfectly conscious of having imitated Laforgue, has worked to get away from it, and there is very little Laforgue in his Sweeney, or his Bleistein Burbank, or his "Gerontion" '.[9] 'Burbank' is *not* Laforgue in English. The self-pitying irony of Laforgue is completely absent from it. But Eliot's positive poetic achievement is not defined in Pound's letter.

A detail that may assist such a definition is a sentence in the *Athenaeum* review of Henry Adams's *Education* already referred to. Eliot wrote in the course of this review that 'Henry Adams in 1858 and Henry James in 1870 . . . land at Liverpool and descend at the same hotel'. 'Burbank', which must have been written within a few weeks of the *Athenaeum* review, begins, it will be recalled:

> Burbank crossed a little bridge
> Descending at a small hotel. . . .

To 'descend', in its special nineteenth-century sense, was to step down from a carriage or cab – a physical impossibility in the Venice of 1919 as the *carrozza* did not ply there. For this brief moment, however, Burbank has ceased to be an American tourist arriving by gondola in Venice and has become the young Henry Adams, or the young Henry James, who is about to spend his first night in Europe. The allusion or error is private to Eliot, but it helps to give the poem a public context. Burbank, who is Adams, James and Eliot, is also a more representative figure – the young American intellectual of Anglo-Saxon stock with the whole of New England culture symbolized in his name and his guidebook.

The poem, therefore, is a sort of Henry James novel in miniature. Its essential subject is the relationship of the American intelligentsia to Western Europe. But its date is 1919; Europe is now in ruins after the First World War; America has passed out of its Burbank phase to a domination by men like Bleistein ('Money in furs'). And so this wry international comedy ends on an almost serious note with the question that is raised by Burbank in the last verse:

> . . . Who clipped the lion's wings
> And flea'd his rump and pared his claws?
> Thought Burbank, meditating on
> Time's ruins, and the seven laws.

If, as seems likely, the seven laws are Ruskin's *Seven Lamps of Architecture*, an element of satire re-enters with them. And the pseudo-scholar is again in evidence here, though for the only time in the poem. The work of Ruskin's that Burbank would have been much more likely to pack with his Baedeker is surely *The Stones of Venice*.

III

The critical conclusion to which I have been leading is that the 'learning' in Eliot's earlier poems must be seen as an aspect of his Americanism. As scholarship it is wide-ranging, but often superficial and inaccurate. At one level, indeed, the enjoyment that he and Pound found – and successfully communicated to their readers – in exploiting their miscellaneous erudition is the same in kind, if not in degree, that every American pilgrim of our cathedrals, galleries and museums experiences. The appearance of literary scholarship parallels the tourist's apparent acquisition of 'culture'. When Eliot in 1920 prefixed to *The Sacred Wood* – facing the title-page – the phrase 'I also like to dine on becaficas', he was merely showing off. Why should the reader recognize this line from Byron's *Beppo*? Why should he be expected to know that 'becaficas' – which both Byron and Eliot misspell – are Italian birds that make good eating? In any case what is the relevance of this particular line of Byron's on the attractions of Italy as a place to live in to a collection of critical essays? This is tourist-erudition.

Such frivolities can be disregarded. Their interest – like that of 'Burbank' (which has other interests too, as I have argued) – lies in the evidence they supply of a certain gaiety of spirit that Eliot never fully recovered after his nervous breakdown in 1921. For the poetry the significance of the 'learning' is that it was an American supplement to the various attempts made by the best European poets of the time to escape from the *impasse* of Pure Poetry. In the end, of course, the expatriate American intellectuals – with the eccentric exception of Pound – had either to adapt themselves to their European surroundings or to return to America. Eliot gradually merged into the Anglo-French literary establishment, though with the poetic consequence that when (in and after 1927) he had formally become an English citizen the 'learning' had lost most of its aesthetic *raison d'être*. He was no longer an American poet with a revolutionary new technique – as Poe and Whitman in their different ways had been before him. After *The Waste Land*, therefore, the learned allusions tend to persist only as a matter of literary habit. In *Four Quartets* (composed 1935–42) in particular it is noticeable how functionless most of the allusions, quotations and plagiarisms now are. The impression one has is of an essayist in the Lamb or Hazlitt manner eking out material that is subjectively and emotionally decidedly 'thin'. The one exception that occurs to me is the half-translation from Mallarmé in the beautiful Dantesque episode in 'Little Gidding'.

The unconscious reminiscences, on the other hand, especially in *Four Quartets*, are not from European literature at all but, as far as I have been able to detect them, from Whitman's *Leaves of Grass*. Pound's curious poem beginning

> I make a pact with you, Walt Whitman–
> I have detested you long enough,

and ending

> We have one sap and one root–
> Let there be commerce between us,

might also have been written, whether Eliot was fully aware of it or not, by the author of *Ash-Wednesday* and *Four Quartets*. The anomalies of attitude and subject-matter should not be allowed to obscure the fact that in a final analysis Eliot was an American poet of enormous talent who happened to live in England – as James was a great American novelist who too happened to prefer living in England.

It is in such a context that the 'learning' of Eliot has ultimately to be explained and justified. In the earlier poems the plagiarism-quotations and the whole façade of erudition are part of the poetry as well as biographically a stimulus to its composition. They make a contribution peculiar to American intellectuals – where a great university still has something of the sanctity of a medieval monastery – to the revival of modern poetry. But, now that it has revived, English poetry has proved not to require flowers of learning as a rhetorical premise or device. Though these things persist sporadically in Eliot's later poems, their place as stimulus and ornament was taken, less successfully, by the English institution caricatured in 'The Hippopotamus' (the earliest of the poems in quatrain form):

> Flesh and blood is weak and frail,
> Susceptible to nervous shock;
> While the True Church can never fail
> For it is based upon a rock.

The scholarship, it is true, was only skin-deep, whereas the Anglo-Catholicism was devoted and sincere, but most of us – English and American – will continue to prefer 'The Hippopotamus' and its progeny to *The Rock* and its successors.

NOTES

1. 'Burnt Norton', the first of the four *Quartets*, grew out of fragments discarded from *Murder in the Cathedral*. See Grover Smith, *T. S. Eliot's Poetry and Plays: a study in sources and meaning* (Chicago, 1956) p. 251.
2. The sentence will be found in *SW* p. 100. It has been omitted in the reprint of the essay included in *Selected Essays* (1932).
3. *Purpose*, x (1938) 93.
4. A second echo from A. C. Benson's *Edward FitzGerald*, p. 29, occurs at the end of the first paragraph of 'Gerontion', which reproduces less exactly part of a letter from FitzGerald to Frederick Tennyson that Benson quotes.
5. *Works of Lancelot Andrewes*, ed. J. P. Wilson, I (1841) 204.
6. When F. O. Matthiessen called Eliot's attention to this echo of Adams years later, Eliot was apparently flabbergasted. Unlike the use of A. C. Benson and Lancelot Andrewes, the reminiscence is an unconscious one.
7. R. W. Dent, *John Webster's Borrowings* (Berkeley, 1960).
8. Smith, *Eliot's Poetry and Plays* pp. 67–98, though heavy handed critically, is the most thorough assembly of the quotations, references and sources. Eliot's own notes are comparatively perfunctory.
9. *The Letters of Ezra Pound 1907–1941*, ed. D. D. Paige (1951) p. 226.

Eliot and Nineteenth-century French Poetry

FRANCIS SCARFE

I

IT would make no difference to T. S. Eliot's achievement if it were said that his knowledge of French literature was in many respects limited and superficial. What matters is the way in which he used that knowledge, which in some domains was profound.

It is true that his approach to French literature was not usually scholarly or systematic. His interests were very personal. He disclaimed any first-hand knowledge of Provençal poetry. We have not his views on medieval French poetry, but he came close to finding *Le Roman de la Rose* a dull poem.[1] He treated Villon always with respect, relating him to Chaucer, Dante and Blake. He had little or nothing to say for the Pléiade poets,[2] and it is surprising that he neither discussed their linguistic aspirations as compared with those of the Elizabethans, nor recognized in their habit of paraphrase and conflation a method similar to his own. He was on good ground, and scholarly, in his remarks on Garnier and Montaigne, and especially Pascal and Racine, the latter being one of his main points of reference. Interesting, also, are his asides about Molière, of which we would have liked more: scholars rarely offer creative statements like the one he made in comparing him with Jonson: 'It is not, at all events, the farce of Molière: the latter is more analytic, more an intellectual redistribution'.[3] In *The Sacred Wood* he made, for his own purposes, similar expert use of writers in whom we would not expect him to show interest, such as Marivaux, Flaubert, Rostand, Maeterlinck (though it is now impossible to take the last two so seriously). Boileau he thought 'a fine poet', and he compared Malherbe with Valéry.[4] For the rest, the 'Baroque' poets, then Corneille, La Fontaine, La Bruyère and the other moralists, then most of the

French eighteenth century, hardly existed for him, while with the exception of Baudelaire he investigated only minor figures in modern French poetry. It might now appear almost perverse to select Corbière and Laforgue, as against Rimbaud, Verlaine and Mallarmé – though Mallarmé was given more respect as Eliot matured. He remarked to me in 1937 that he was 'not particularly interested' in Rimbaud, and added 'we did not read Lautréamont in my young days'. However, he was sufficiently informed to want Dali's illustrations for an edition of Lautréamont. As for the rest, though he knew Apollinaire and André Salmon, his work quickly steered away from that current.[5] Valéry he used mainly as a kind of aesthetic foil, and perhaps with a slight antipathy.[6] Perse he did not manage to bring alive for the English reader.[7] In his early work he referred disparagingly to Claudel,[8] though Claudel later left a mark on some of the *Rock* choruses and perhaps on the versification of *Murder in the Cathedral* and *The Family Reunion*.

The range, then, was not very great, and Eliot's vital relationship with French poetry seemed to wither after his flirtation with the Maurras group. His serious exploration of French poetry had ebbed by the early 1920s. But it is not by a statistical approach that we can appreciate his position, for in the same way he eliminated from his writings vast tracts of Italian and English literature.

Whether limited or not, the essential point about Eliot's French interests (avoiding the term 'sources' for reasons to be given later) is the way in which he exploited them. They appear less as interests, even, than as signposts, tools, even weapons, in Eliot's early efforts to establish and clarify his critical theory and his practice as a poet, his poetic style. The main difficulty in trying to estimate what he was doing is that we are no longer reading the same poets in the same way. Baudelaire was undervalued or wrongly valued for some sixty years after his death in 1867, but now looms so big that it is harder than ever to assess his achievement. Laforgue and Corbière, exciting discoveries for the young Eliot, have shown their limitations and are neglected in France. Verlaine has shrunk to his true modest proportions, while excessive claims are now made for Rimbaud and Mallarmé. These examples are enough to show how original Eliot was in making the choices he did, while it is also significant that he avoided the loose definitions, then and now so popular, 'Symbolist' and 'Symbolism'.[9]

II

Eliot was an undergraduate when he discovered Baudelaire, and later gave him a 'rounder' treatment than to any poet except Dante. In his essay on 'Andrew Marvell' (1921) he associated Gautier, Baudelaire and Laforgue with his definition of Wit as 'this alliance of levity with seriousness (by which the seriousness is intensified)', but particularly with reference to the *dandysme* of the last two (*SE* p. 296) – not a very striking remark for those who believe that Byron's dandyism undermined his seriousness. Then in 'The Metaphysical Poets' (1921) he took a great step forward, writing

> Jules Laforgue, and Tristan Corbière in many of his poems, are nearer to 'the school of Donne' than any modern English poet. But poets more classical than they have the same essential quality of transmitting ideas into sensations, of transforming an observation into a state of mind. . . . In French literature the great master of the seventeenth century – Racine – and the great master of the nineteenth – Baudelaire – are in some ways more like each other than they are like anyone else. The greatest two masters of diction are also the greatest two psychologists, the most curious explorers of the soul. (*SE* p. 290)

Eliot often returned to this comparison of Baudelaire with Racine, which modern criticism approves, but which was first suggested by Remy de Gourmont in his *Promenades littéraires*. In 'Baudelaire in Our Time' (1927, reprinted in *EAM*) the ostensible aim was to discredit those who had misrepresented Baudelaire in the nineties, but it was really a shrewd blow at a whole generation – it is worth remembering that George Moore regarded Laforgue as 'evanescent as French pastry'. Eliot now advanced a more mature view of Baudelaire. Beneath a superficially 'satanist' romantic vocabulary, Eliot was among the first to appreciate the struggle of a remarkably endowed religious sensibility. After a further comparison with Racine, he emphasized Baudelaire's respect for Order, and defined without exaggeration the French poet's situation as a Christian. Eliot's admiration for Baudelaire was by now more than literary: his stress on Baudelaire's humility reveals the growing spiritual affinity between the two poets: 'and Baudelaire came to attain the greatest, the most difficult, of the Christian virtues, the virtue of humility' (*EAM* p. 74). As Eliot's own spiritual quest developed, he departed increasingly from his usual custom, taking the man rather than the poet as his guide.

In his essay on 'Baudelaire' (1930) Eliot referred to his 'theological innocence' and decided that he was 'man enough for damnation', but the study is less satisfactory in other respects. The comparison he makes of Baudelaire with Goethe[10] does not take us far, nor, despite his praise of Baudelaire's 'excellence of form', the decision that he had 'the external but not the internal form of classic art'. It seems odd to us that Gautier and Laforgue should be regarded as having inner coherence, and not Baudelaire: it would now be tempting to reverse Eliot's terms. We now see better the continuity and coherence of all Baudelaire's work, the steadfast principles that unite all he wrote into one indivisible opus, though the 'external' form is generally far from 'classic'. This adjustment would help us to accept Eliot's further remark, that Baudelaire's claim as an artist was 'not that he found a superficial form, but that he was searching for a form of life', after which Eliot praised him for his 'stock of imagery of contemporary life'. This praise is logically related to Eliot's earliest conception of the poet alive to his own time. It is, then, what Baudelaire himself called 'l'héroisme de la vie moderne', an acute awareness of the everyday facts of contemporary life, which made a mark on all Eliot's work, though in his later years he neglected the Baudelairean care for realist detail.

There are certain flaws in Eliot's understanding of Baudelaire. It seems eccentric to set Gautier above Baudelaire for any reason whatever, as in 'He had a greater technical ability than Gautier, and yet the content of the feeling is constantly bursting through the receptacle' (*SE* p. 424) – as if that were a fault. It is not so certain that Baudelaire had 'a greater technical ability' than Gautier. Baudelaire had a grand design, which Gautier was incapable of. He also had a greater creative ability than Gautier. In any case, what is meant here by 'technical'? The expression has no meaning when unrelated to what the two poets were trying to do. Gautier had the acrobatic skill of a Banville (or a Sitwell), but, like them, he did not know what to do with it. Gautier's 'receptacle' – if we must use this odd word, which might apply to artefacts, but hardly to poems – was never threatened. This immunity was not the result of some superior 'classical' restraint or maturity, but the result of a lack of life: the form had become for Gautier an end in itself. Form was never an end in itself for Baudelaire – though he sometimes pretended that it was – for his main intention was always to say something. He was not, as Lionel Johnson said, 'singing sermons': he was, rather, shouting secrets ('c'est un secret de tous connu'). His violent overflow made him an 'Elizabethan' – and this also distinguishes him from Racine, after all. It was no polite restraint that made him 'modern', either; but a constant withdrawal from the conventionally poetic. For instance, in the midst of the rhetoric of 'Crépuscule du matin' he dropped almost into prose with 'Les maisons ça et là commençaient à fumer' before beginning another characteristic spiral of eloquence. Or, at the end of 'Le Cygne', he dropped into a kind of *etcetera*, ending or suspending his poem on 'et bien d'autres encore'. Baudelaire could apply a brake to his own rhetoric, whereas the grand *aria* of the Racinian heroine is checked mechanically, not by the poet but by the *confidante*, who redirects the tone. It is not always wise to compare a dramatist with a non-dramatic poet, as Eliot so often did. Eliot seems to have remained, also, indifferent to many of Baudelaire's faults, forgiving him what he would not forgive others. Rimbaud was better informed when he said of Baudelaire, 'la forme chez lui est plutôt mesquine' (that is, if he meant the external, mechanical form). And, if Eliot saw him as 'a master of diction' comparable with Racine, he must have overlooked many a cliché ('gouffre amer', etc.). Baudelaire's achievement did not lie in any 'invention of form', but in the ironic reversal of romantic values, the creation of an urban poetry set in an impressive though imperfect design, in which the emphasis is not on the outward portrayal but the very meaning of existence.

It is not very profitable to examine Eliot's work for the deposit left there by *Les Fleurs du mal*. The main influence was that of Baudelaire's Paris, 'cité pleine de rêves', where 'tout pour moi devient allégorie', where 'le spectre en plein jour raccroche le passant' – as in both *The Waste Land* and the celebrated meeting in 'Little Gidding' to which Baudelaire's line is a key or an impulse. It is, also, not impossible that *The Waste Land* is to some extent a baudelairean construction, in the sense that the so-called 'architecture' of *Les Fleurs du mal*, with its five parts in the 1857 edition and six in the 1861 edition, might have set Eliot thinking on similar ambitious lines. Also, the *Tableaux parisiens*, which show a night and day of the city's life, might well underly the conception of the 'Rhapsody on a Windy Night' and 'Preludes'.

Apart from such speculations, one can only hope to produce a few footnotes, such as the following. In the 'Rhapsody', in the lines

'Remark the cat which flattens itself in the gutter,
Slips out its tongue
And devours a morsel of rancid butter.'

So the hand of the child, automatic,
Slipped out and pocketed a toy that was running along the quay.
I could see nothing behind that child's eye

there is no clue, for the intelligent reader, as to the connection between the cat and the child. All this is a shorthand précis of Baudelaire's prose-poem 'Le Joujou du pauvre'. Baudelaire compared the poor child receiving a toy, with 'les chats qui vont manger loin de vous le morceau que vous leur avez donné', then went on to show how the rich child might well envy the toys of the poor, which are living things; 'Or, ce joujou, que le petit souillon . . . secouait dans une boîte grillée, c'était un rat vivant!' Thus the 'toy that was running along the quay' was a rat or a mouse. It is noticeable that Eliot introduced overtones of disgust which are far removed from the compassionate insight of Baudelaire, with 'rancid butter', and 'I could see nothing behind that child's eye'. On the contrary, Baudelaire wrote 'un de ces marmots-parias dont un œil impartial découvrirait la beauté', and it certainly took Eliot a long time to learn Baudelaire's essential Christian message, that a critique of society and a powerful sense of evil must not exclude sympathy. The early Eliot played his solemn game of mosaics too coolly: as another instance of his ruthlessness in adapting Baudelaire, the French poet's tenderness in 'Et tes pieds s'endormaient dans mes mains fraternelles' becomes 'Or clasped the soles of yellow feet/ In the palms of both soiled hands' in 'Preludes'. Unlike the Renaissance poets, Eliot paid no heed to context when practising such conflation. Sometimes, also, he seems deliberately to lead the reader astray: for instance, one might imagine he was writing personally at the beginning of The Waste Land, with

Summer surprised us, coming over the Starnbergersee
With a shower of rain;

but the lines were lifted from Valery Larbaud's Poésies d'A.-O. Barnabooth or Poèmes d'un riche amateur (1908):

Et l'odeur du foin frais coupé, comme en Bavière
Un soir, après la pluie, sur le lac de Starnberg.

(Indeed, the whole of lines 8–18 of 'The Burial of the Dead' might be taken as a specimen or parody of Larbaud's manner and typically cosmopolitan subject-matter.)

However, Eliot was not always guilty of arbitrary association. An apparent example of this is in 'The Burial of the Dead':

> 'Oh keep the Dog far hence, that's friend to men,
> 'Or with his nails he'll dig it up again!
> 'You! hypocrite lecteur! – mon semblable, – mon frère!'

Here, Eliot spoils Baudelaire's line (the last) by giving a line of thirteen syllables, and also gives his own punctuation, while, in his note, saying it is from the preface to *Les Fleurs du mal* when it is from 'Au Lecteur', which is not strictly a preface. Further, John Hayward remarked on the allusion to Webster, 'L'Anglais et son chien, son amical "démon familier". La substitution de chien à loup, dans cette allusion, est un exemple frappant de l'usage que fait Eliot des citations pour intégrer le passé au présent.'[11] Much of the point is missed. The basis of the association Webster–Baudelaire lies in the latter's line 'Ne cherchez plus mon cœur – les bêtes l'ont mangé' as well as the Dog in both 'Une Charogne' and 'Un Voyage à Cythère'. The background of association is thus far more massive than it might appear.

Apart from such touches, and the fact that a knowledge of *Les Fleurs du mal* is important for anyone reading *The Waste Land*, as Eliot matured the Baudelairean deposit became less pronounced as it fused with that of Dante. Just enough has been said to show that Baudelaire left some mark on Eliot's practice as a poet, besides helping him in his critical work and even in his private spiritual development.

Reference has been made to Gautier, but the matter cannot rest there. In *Make it New*, Pound praised Gautier's 'hardness' – but the question is, yes, but hard about what? The elegant, brittle shell has no yolk. Gautier showed little sign of being more than one of the cleverer young 'romantic' poets, related to Alfred de Musset, until he changed his style with *Émaux et Camées* in 1852. Before that he had invented much of the morbid imagery and vocabulary which had a negative influence on Baudelaire. With the sudden purging of his romantic style, Gautier identified himself with Art for Art's Sake and dominated the young Parnassiens. A radical change of style in Yeats was accompanied by a maturing of vision, but this was not so with Gautier, who admitted that he wrote *Émaux et Camées* in order to keep real life at a distance. He created artificial forms of great tightness, and showed an occasional Wit (as in 'Le squelette était invisible/Au temps heureux de l'art païen' which is not maintained in the rest of the poem, 'Bûchers et tombeaux') which Eliot overestimated in classing him with 'the school of Donne'. However, it would be ungracious to refuse to enjoy virtuosity for its own sake. Eliot used the above poem, and Gautier's 'Carmen', in 'Whispers of Immortality', and adopted for the 'Sweeney' poems the dry quatrain which Gautier had used for non-subjects. To illustrate this point of view about Gautier's lack of significance, the reader is directed to René Taupin's detailed – but not detailed enough – comparison between Gautier's 'L'Hippopotame' and Eliot's 'The Hippopotamus'.[12] After a few comic quatrains, Gautier ended by comparing himself (i.e. the art-for-art's-sake poet) with the hippo:

> Je suis comme l'hippopotame:
> De ma conviction couvert,
> Forte armure que rien n'entame,
> Je vais sans peur par le désert.

(Similarly, in 'Mélange Adultère de Tout', Eliot describes himself, the outsider, as 'Vêtu d'une peau de girafe'.) Taupin commented only on Eliot's appropriation of Gautier's 'technique' and concluded, dully, that the dissimilarities were more important than the similarities. This was to miss the point completely, which is that Eliot gave significance to the hippopotamus as a symbol through his grotesque identification of it with the Church. The only word in Gautier's poem that might have originated Eliot's creative act is the word *conviction* in the few lines quoted above. This adaptation is characteristic of Eliot's genius for giving meaning to a superficial exercise. The lesson is instructive for students of a comparative literature: it is that Eliot did not 'beg, borrow, or steal', but his habit of reading was such that the original text could be either a 'source' or a *cause* (by which I mean something more than the catalyst theory, which suggests a too passive state). Thus 'L'Hippopotame', like *Les Fleurs du mal*, caused an entirely different mental operation, resulting in a very different work. The same applies to the 'Sweeney' poems and many others in which the quatrain of Gautier is amalgamated with that of Corbière. There is no point in looking for Gautier's hand in them. None the less, Gautier helped Eliot to move away from the Laforguian style.[13]

III

This distinction between *source* and *cause* has sometimes to be remembered when discussing Eliot's relationship to Laforgue, of which Dr

Leavis remarked, 'And to learn as Mr Eliot learnt in general from Laforgue is to be original to the point of genius.'[14]

Jules Laforgue, who died in 1887 at the age of twenty-seven, had in himself the makings of a great poet.[15] With his classical education, his excellent knowledge of the English, Spanish and German languages, music, the fine arts, German philosophy, he was excellently equipped. At the time of his death he had completed several collections of poems, as well as his ironical variations in prose on such themes as *Hamlet* which were collected in his *Moralités légendaires*, while he also promised to be a shrewd critic. Eliot referred to him as 'if not quite the greatest French poet since Baudelaire . . . certainly the most important technical innovator'.[16] Whether this was excessive praise or not, Eliot regarded him as an equal, and as more than a useful source.

Apart from Eliot's debt to him, Laforgue was to have a remarkable fertilizing influence. With his friend Gustave Kahn he was one of the pioneers of French free verse. In his collections *Les Complaintes*, *Les Fleurs de bonne volonté* (a title which is a genial commentary on *Les Fleurs du mal*) and above all the unfinished *Derniers Vers* (a kind of verse-novel), Laforgue invented a new kind of dramatic monologue, usually known as the interior or internal monologue, close to common speech and reflecting his interest in German theories of the Unconscious. (It is not impossible that this form was based on the eighteenth-century 'Héroïdes', epistolary elegies written by Colardeau and others, originating in Ovid's *Heroids*.) From Laforgue, his close friend, Édouard Dujardin, without acknowledgement, developed the technique of his short novel *Les Lauriers sont coupés*. This technique was taken up by Valery Larbaud and James Joyce, and played a major part in the composition of *Ulysses* and *Finnegans Wake*.[17] Round about 1908 Eliot, long before them, had taken the form directly from Laforgue himself, and this community of interests helps to explain Eliot's affinity with Joyce. It is fortunate that Eliot took his monologue form from Laforgue rather than Browning, as it helped him both in his apprenticeship to the drama and his exploration of new verse forms. As he said himself, his free verse 'in 1908 or 1909 was directly drawn from the study of Laforgue together with the later Elizabethan drama'.[18] How this was achieved is something of a mystery, but it is interesting to note that Laforgue had 'cracked' traditional French versification with the help of Elizabethan blank verse.

While Laforgue was employed in Germany as Reader to the Empress

Augusta, he appears to have had a stormy and unsatisfactory love-affair with a lady of the Court. Given his humble circumstances there could be no hope of happiness for them. In *Les Complaintes* and other works he managed to exteriorize and sublimate this situation in the wittiest fashion, by creating a Pierrot or clown as his *persona*, closely identifying both himself and the Pierrot with an adolescent Hamlet, and her with Ophelia. Eliot's character, Prufrock, is in the same way an amalgam of himself and Laforgue's symbolic character, groping at the same time towards an identification with Tiresias. It is not superfluous to note that the psychic split in Prufrock is completed by the complex physical state of Tiresias in *The Waste Land*.

The nucleus of Eliot's two early monologues, 'Prufrock' and 'Portrait of a Lady' is to be found in eleven lines of Laforgue's *Derniers Vers*, III:

> Bref, j'allais me donner un 'Je vous aime'
> Quand je m'avisai non sans peine
> Que d'abord je ne me possédais pas bien moi-même.
>
> (Mon Moi, c'est Galathée aveuglant Pygmalion!
> Impossible de modifier cette situation.)
>
> Ainsi donc, pauvre, pâle et piètre individu
> Qui ne croit à son Moi qu'à ses moments perdus,
> Je vis s'effacer ma fiancée
> Emportée par le cours des choses,
> Telle l'épine voit s'effeuiller
> Sous prétexte de soir sa meilleure rose.

Here we see better the difference between *source* and *cause*, for Eliot neither translated nor adapted any of the above lines, yet they dominate his early work in their import, style and tone. The first line gives the basis of action for 'Prufrock'. The second and third lines set the emotional reaction. The fourth is central to the meaning of both 'Prufrock' and the 'Portrait', for the poet or character is in fact annihilated, not so much by an actual person, as by two things implied in line 4: first, by a split in his own personality, one half destroying the other; second, not so much by an actual woman, but by some unreachable, idealized feminine figure who is largely of his own mental creation, as Galathea was Pygmalion's. Finally (line 9) she is carried away 'par le cours des choses', that is to say, lost to him owing to the social and psychological barriers between them, as well as by the passage of time.

This said, there are fewer transcriptions of Laforgue in 'Prufrock' than might be expected. Where Laforgue writes in *Fleurs de bonne volonté*, XVIII,

> Comment lui dire: je vous aime?
> (Je me connais si peu moi-même)
> Ah! quel sort! Ah, pour sûr, la tâche qui m'incombe
> M'aura sensiblement rapproché de la tombe,

Eliot takes the last line, concretizes and develops it, imagining himself rapidly (*sensiblement*) aged 'with a bald spot in the middle of my hair', then hesitating between the identification Tiresias–Polonius. This rapid ageing is only imaginary, but is also touched off by Laforgue's line which means little more than 'will have put years on me'. Where Eliot writes nostalgically of the eyes and arms, Laforgue has, more mischievously,

> Et suivez-les décolletées
> Des épaules, comme, aussitôt,
> Leurs yeux, les plus durs, les plus faux,
> Se noient, l'air tendre et comme il faut.
> > (*Fleurs de bonne volonté*, XLVII)

To select another detail, the 'eyes that fix you in a formulated phrase' has its obvious source in Laforgue's 'le stylet d'acier de tes yeux inflexibles' (*Derniers Vers*, VIII). The imagery of the sea and drowning, in 'Prufrock' and perhaps in references to Phlebas, is also implicit in Laforgue's 'Préludes autobiographiques':

> Donc, je m'en vais flottant aux orgues sous-marins,
> Par les coraux, les œufs, les bras verts, les écrins. . . .

But it is not these sharp reminiscences, of which there are many more, that really matter. Laforgue had given Eliot the essential subject of 'Prufrock', which he varied on in an original way; offered him numerous models for the internal monologue; suggested the analogy with *Hamlet* which led to the Polonius passage; and given him the basis of his free verse. Here it has to be observed that almost all Laforgue's free verse retained a rhyme-scheme, or the use of rhyme, while there is also a constant use of rhyme in Eliot's early monologues. Laforgue's was not really free verse in the modern sense, or as Eliot was to handle it later: it ought to be called freed verse (*vers libérés*), in which the length and structure of the line is freely varied, the alternation of masculine and feminine rhymes ignored, and the rhymes themselves arbitrarily and irregularly placed, or sometimes reduced to assonance (as in *aime-peine-même*, above).

In the 'Portrait' there is a much greater degree of refinement on the Laforguian theme and technique. Whereas we do not know how many parts the *Derniers Vers* would have had when completed (like the *Fleurs de bonne volonté* the collection does not suggest a very deliberate architecture), Eliot wrote his poem 'symphonically' in three movements, though with strong shifts of tone within each part, which tend to disrupt the structure (just as it is disrupted in *The Waste Land*). He also achieved much subtler rhythmical effects, having by now noticed that Laforgue did not write according to the line, but according to the 'groupe de souffle' and the rhythm of speech. But the 'Portrait' also has a fugal element, with inner meditations alternating with the spoken word. Here (as Laforgue also contrived in some of the *Fleurs*) the central character is silent while the woman's voice is heard. This, of course, is the very opposite of the Browning monologue, in which the protagonist usually speaks.

In this poem Eliot brought to perfection his paraphrasing of Laforgue (already marked in 'Conversation Galante'). The central passage in Laforgue, *Derniers Vers*, IX, with the woman speaking, is as follows:

> Pour moi, tu n'es pas comme les autres hommes,
> Ils sont ces messieurs, toi tu viens des cieux.
> Ta bouche me fait baisser les yeux
> Et ton port me transporte
> Et je m'en découvre des trésors!
> Et je sais parfaitement que ma destinée se borne
> (Oh! j'y suis déjà bien habituée!)
> A te suivre jusqu'à ce que tu te retournes,
> Et alors t'exprimer comme tu es!
>
> Vraiment je ne songe pas au reste: j'attendrai
> Dans l'attendrissement de ma vie faite exprès. . . .

In Laforgue this speech is entirely fictitious, as he clownishly flatters himself that some day the Lady will come and throw herself at his feet, praising him as a kind of demi-god, even lying on the mat which he has put outside his door for that purpose. In Eliot the speech is actual, though heard from a devastating psychological distance ('You are invulnerable, you have no Achilles' heel', etc.). Eliot now gains over

Laforgue in his dignity of phrasing (with nothing like the charming pun, 'attendrai . . . attendrissement'), even though he banalizes Laforgue's fine last two lines into the equally moving 'I shall sit here, serving tea to friends'. In Eliot the exaggerated praise has an ironic, destructive effect, hammering on an already acute distress. Here, the two poets, while writing externally in much the same way, are poles apart. Laforgue never achieved Eliot's formidable counterpoint between speech and silence; but nor was he ever so detached or even cruel: it is surprising that Eliot could complain of D. H. Lawrence's cruelty to his characters.[19]

Laforgue also suggested the concluding lines of the 'Portrait':

> Enfin si, par un soir, elle meurt dans mes livres,
> Douce; feignent de n'en pas croire mes yeux,
> J'aurai un 'Ah, ça, mais, nous avions De Quoi vivre!
>   C'était donc sérieux?'

This is from one of the *Complaintes* that also gave the basis of 'Conversation Galante' (which suggests that the latter might originally have been intended as part of the 'Portrait'). The difference of implication between Laforgue's lines above, and Eliot's, beginning 'Well! and what if she should die some afternoon', is most disturbing. Laforgue was only thinking metaphorically of his lady's death, meaning that she would 'die in his books', cease to be his Laura and Ophelia and to provide him with a theme. Eliot's 'And what if she should die' is meant literally, and the ironical conclusion 'And should I have the right to smile?' then appears in the worst of taste.

'La Figlia Che Piange', despite the brilliant adaptation of 'simple et sans foi comme un bonjour' into 'Simple and faithless as a smile and a shake of the hand', is not a typically Laforguian construction. In its conciseness and gravity it is more like a criticism of Laforgue, and it would suffice, also, as a kind of summary and dismissal of Eliot's own early monologues. (Perhaps Eliot was to some extent condemning his own early work – 'Prufrock' and the 'Portrait' – in 'The Three Voices of Poetry', where he concluded, surprisingly in view of his own and Laforgue's achievement, that 'dramatic monologue cannot create a character'.)[20] Apart from this, it might be wrong to take 'La Figlia' as an intensely personal poem, as some critics have done, for the theme is carefully detached and sublimated by its association with Dido and Aeneas.

Looking back on the Eliot–Laforgue relationship, it is evident that apart from Eliot's willing apprenticeship to him in technical matters there must have been a close affinity depending on more personal factors, such as the attraction of a philosophy of the Absurd, and self-doubt. The psychological situations portrayed by them both, however much the same or different in detail or however personal or impersonal, might be censured in the light of Irving Babbitt's analysis of what he called 'romantic irony' in *Rousseau and Romanticism*.[21] Eliot's temporary identification with Laforgue and Corbière is more significant than any appraisal of 'technique' might suggest, for the three of them portray a self-destructive type of introspection, or auto-irony. Whether Eliot, as a person, felt that way or not, the choice of theme, caustic manner, posture, is not insignificant. If he felt so, that is disturbing: if he did not, but chose to mock at failure, that is worse. Laforgue was engaged in writing a novel called 'Le Raté' (The Failure) which might have been the basis for some of his poems. But even in the most adverse circumstances he managed to write with a stimulating sense of humour (his Polonius is killed behind a tapestry depicting the Massacre of the Innocents), which Eliot lacked. Eliot's early poems show no such catharsis (or any other) and his wry wit suggests some unbalance. Like *Empedocles on Etna*, both 'Prufrock' and the 'Portrait' are 'too painful to be tragic', to use Arnold's words (as well as too painful to be comic). For many readers *The Waste Land* narrowly escapes the same fate, so thickly is the pessimism (and even *Schadenfreude*) laid on. To make the point clear – and it is one which puts all of Eliot's so-called 'debts' to the French poets into proper perspective – when he wrote

> I should have been a pair of ragged claws
> Scuttling across the floors of silent seas

it is immaterial whether he was writing for himself, or for a character. This writing is not, as some have supposed, an example of 'empathy', but of the very opposite: it is a statement of self-disgust and also disgust with the creatures, quite remote from his later grasp of empathy as in 'I have lain in the soil and listened to the worm'. Eliot's two lines, and indeed the two monologues 'Prufrock' and the 'Portrait', betray a lack of faith in normal human relationships, without having (for example) the spiritual nostalgia of Baudelaire's 'Ne suis-je pas un faux accord/ Dans la divine symphonie?' Although Eliot began 'technically' where Laforgue left off, he did not achieve an impersonal distance before

'Gerontion'. The tendency to self-depreciation was fundamental to Eliot's character, and he never shook it off. Though it was his only serious flaw (which yet led him to humility) it emerged at times in a crude form, as in the later poem 'How unpleasant to meet Mr Eliot'. Though written in jest, this poem is meaningful in our context. Why should it be unpleasant to meet Mr Eliot? Why should he constantly see himself from the outside? Why should he or anyone ridicule himself, even for fun? It is the same lack of confidence in themselves or other people that prevented many of Eliot's creations, in his later plays, from becoming characters at all.

Paradoxically, it must therefore be concluded that Eliot's most 'Laforguian' poems were not Laforguian in their essence. Laforgue, though in a tragic predicament and intellectually oppressed by the pessimism of Schopenhauer and Hartmann, shows an inner stability. Eliot, like Baudelaire, had an overwhelmingly tragic, if not pessimistic, view of life, which he transcended only in the *Quartets*. This does not mean that he was inferior to Laforgue, but that he was more vulnerable, perhaps more sensitive.

It is not certain whether Eliot could know before 1925 the letter in which Laforgue attacked the insensitiveness of Corbière, his lack of ear, his scraping, jarring style ('cet éternel crincrin que vous savez') and in which he protested that his own work was aiming at symphonic composition.[22] Eliot not only overestimated Corbière, but made little direct use of him except in his own unsatisfactory poems in French, particularly 'Mélange Adultère de Tout' which is closely based on the two versions of Corbière's 'Épitaphe'.[23] Nor is there much to be said about his relationship to other nineteenth-century poets. A few – Nerval, Verlaine – are honoured by an echo. Mallarmé was adapted on two occasions, the first in 'Burnt Norton' with its reference to 'tonnerre et rubis aux moyeux' and 'bavant boue et rubis', both so much out of context as to need no comment. The second is in 'Little Gidding' where 'To purify the dialect of the tribe' is an unsatisfactory version of 'Donner un sens plus pur aux mots de la tribu' ('Le Tombeau d'Edgar Poe'). Mallarmé did not mean, in some Malherbian sense, that the common language should be purged or purified by the poet; but that the vulgar tongue could or should be made to carry more significant meaning. Mallarmé, like Apollinaire after him, honoured and adapted 'popular' poetry, even using many of its forms (just as Laforgue's form for some of the *Complaintes* was based upon the popular song). Eliot used such things snobbishly and pejoratively, as with 'Mrs Porter'. But Mallarmé's line had enough importance for Eliot, to provide the basis of his social theory of poetic language, advanced in 'The Social Function of Poetry'.

On the whole we must conclude that Eliot's 'debt' to French poetry was mainly to what he had read at an early, impressionable age, and that his subjection to this was by no means total. After that, his contacts with such contemporaries as Romains, Duhamel, Vildrac, Salmon, Larbaud, then Paul Valéry, Perse, Claudel, were less significant, for he no longer needed them.

NOTES

1. 'Dante', in *SE* p. 242.
2. 'Imperfect Critics', in *SW* p. 29.
3. 'Ben Jonson', in *SW* p. 120.
4. Introduction to Valéry's *Le Serpent*, trans. M. Wardle (1924).
5. See R. Taupin, *L'Influence du symbolisme français sur la poésie américaine* (Paris, 1929) 2e partie, ch. VI.
6. Perhaps as a critic, but not as a poet.
7. Preface to *Anabasis*, trans. T. S. Eliot (1930).
8. 'The Possibility of a Poetic Drama', in *SW* pp. 66–7, also contains slighting references to Bergson, viz. 'The philosophy of the latter is a little out of date'.
9. He rightly used the word in its historical sense, viz., in note 4 above, 'What Valéry represents, and for which he is honoured and admired by even the youngest in France, is the reintegration of the symbolist movement into the great tradition.'
10. *SE* pp. 420–1. Such comparisons, based on the notion of 'Representative Men' (Emerson), are unsatisfactory: taken a little further, one would end by comparing Baudelaire with Voltaire, etc. At the same time I am grateful to Mr Graham Martin for drawing my attention to Eliot's review of P. Quennell's *Baudelaire and the Symbolists* in the *Criterion*, IX (Jan 1930) 35, in which he wrote: 'any adequate criticism of Baudelaire must inevitably lead the critic outside of literary criticism. For it will not do to label Baudelaire; he is not merely, or in my own opinion even primarily, the *artist*; and if I compared him with any one in his own century, it would be to Goethe and to Keats – that is to say, I should place him with men who are important first because they are human prototypes of new experience, and only second because they are poets.' However I remain unrepentant: we are interested in Baudelaire, Goethe and Keats, primarily because they were poets, and secondarily for those qualities which other important people manage to possess, but whose works (such as Napoleon's) we have no desire to read. Baudelaire's greatness of mind can be quite well established from a proper consideration of his work, without begging the question in this way. The comparison of Baudelaire with Goethe does no good to either, in the form in which Eliot presented it.
11. See P. Leyris, *T. S. Eliot, Poèmes*, trans. (Paris, 1947) Hayward's note, p. 141.
12. Taupin, *L'Influence du symbolisme* pp. 238–9.

13. Ibid. pp. 236–7.

14. F. R. Leavis, *New Bearings in English Poetry* (1932) p. 79.

15. On Laforgue, see F. Ruchon, *Jules Laforgue* (Geneva, 1924); L. Guichard, *Jules Laforgue et ses poésies* (Paris, 1950).

16. Introduction to *Selected Poems of Ezra Pound* (1928) p. viii.

17. See F. Scarfe. *The Art of Paul Valéry: a study in dramatic monologue* (1954) pp. 107–36.

18. Introduction to *Selected Poems of Ezra Pound*, p. viii.

19. *ASG* p. 36. As for 'conscious cruelty', it would be hard to find a parallel anywhere for Celia's speech, in *The Cocktail Party*, where she compares her lover with 'a beetle the size of a man'.

20. *PP* p. 95. Admittedly, Eliot was referring to Browning, perhaps unaware of the extension now given to the term 'dramatic monologue'. See note 17 above, also B. Fuson's *Browning and his English Predecessors in the Dramatic Monologue* (Ames, Iowa, 1948).

21. Irving Babbitt, *Rousseau and Romanticism* (1919) ch. VII.

22. Laforgue, *Correspondence*, 2 vols (Paris, 1925) t. II, 'Corbière a du chic et j'ai de l'humour. . . . Enfin, Corbière ne s'occupe ni de la strophe ni des rimes (sauf comme un tremplin à concetti) et jamais de rythmes, et je m'en suis occupé au point d'en apporter de nouvelles et de nouveaux; j'ai voulu faire de la symphonie et de la mélodie, et Corbière joue de l'éternal crincrin que vous savez.' Previously, this letter had only been printed in the review *Lutèce*, 1885.

23. The passage in 'Gerontion' beginning 'Spawned in some estaminet in Antwerp' is related by Taupin, *L'Influence du symbolisme*, p. 236, to Corbière, but the connection is tenuous. It is almost impossible to demonstrate to what extent Eliot took a kind of 'cockney' style from Corbière, the early influence being too diffused.

Pound and Eliot: a distinction
DONALD DAVIE

I

REVIEWING Yeats's *Responsibilities* in *Poetry* for May 1914, Pound envisaged a reader who asked, 'Is Mr Yeats an Imagiste?' And Pound replied: 'No, Mr Yeats is a symbolist, but he has written *des Images* as have many good poets before him. . . . .' Later in the review, after quoting the first five lines of 'The Magi', Pound remarked: 'Of course a passage like that, a passage of *imagisme*, may occur in a poem not otherwise *imagiste*, in the same way that a lyrical passage may occur in a narrative, or in some poem not otherwise lyrical.'[1]

It is hard for us to recover the state of literary opinion in which the first, most urgent question to be asked about Yeats is 'Is he an Imagiste?' The literary historian can be called upon to show, by appeal to the historical record, that this state of opinion once existed. It might be thought that to the literary critic, however, these echoes of battles long ago are of no consequence; and, indeed, this is how our critics have proceeded, using for instance 'Imagism' and 'Symbolism' as interchangeable terms. I am sure that this is wrong: for Imagism as Pound promulgated it, or as he later elaborated it into 'Vorticism', is not a variant upon Symbolism but an alternative to it; and this forking of the ways confronts the poet hardly less challengingly in 1970 than it did in 1914.

This is not to say, however, that Pound was in the right of it, that fifty years ago he had laid hold of a distinction which we have since lost sight of, much to our disadvantage. He was right to think that there was a distinction, and a crucial one, but he surely failed to trace the line of cleavage accurately. Except very intermittently, and then in a highly idiosyncratic way, Yeats was surely not a symbolist poet, even though Edmund Wilson in *Axel's Castle* and many another commentator have, like Pound, asserted that he was. Similarly, Pound never to

my knowledge asked whether Eliot was an Imagist or a Symbolist.
And yet, I maintain, it is in relation to Eliot, not Yeats, that the question
is a momentous one. Depending on the answer we give to it, we shall
either succeed or fail in uncovering the structure of the Eliotic poem.
For as I read Eliot he is the one poet writing in English who is centrally
in the *symboliste* tradition. What Eliot puts into his poems is determined
preponderantly by his being an American; how he structures his poems
is determined preponderantly by his sitting at the feet of the French,
in the first place (as is generally acknowledged, and as he testified
himself) at the feet of Jules Laforgue. Four decades of commentary and
explication have been largely wasted, because of the refusal of commentators to explore either the American or the French backgrounds.
Instead, the attempt has been made over and over again to come to
terms with Eliot without going outside the narrowly English tradition.
In this endeavour, Tennyson and Beddoes have lately supplanted
Webster and Donne as the most appropriate and useful points of
reference; and this is a gain, but a necessarily limited one. The urgent
question to ask is: 'Was the late Mr Eliot an imagiste?' And the right
answer is the answer which Pound gave, wrongly, when the question
was asked about Yeats: 'No, the late Mr Eliot was a symbolist, though
he has written *des Images* as have many good poets before him.'

. . .

In this section of my essay I take the relatively obvious and easy case
of the late poems.

It is notable that, as Eliot got older, he could be seen in his critical
writings to give steadily more attention to symbolist poetry, narrowly
considered. The crucial name is that of Valéry. Eliot's long and important introduction to what is called *The Art of Poetry*, a volume out
of the scheduled complete translation of Valéry's prose into English,
was only the last of several considerations, always absorbed and respectful, of what Valéry stands for in the landscape of twentieth-century
poetry. If Laforgue was the presiding genius of Eliot's earlier poems,
no figure presided more insistently over the later ones than Valéry,
deliberately Mallarmé's disciple, and like his master as much high-priest
of symbolist theory as a writer of symbolist poems.

We cannot but suppose, therefore, that it is Valéry, bringing with
him the whole symbolist endeavour to make poetry approximate to
music, who stands behind the title – *Four Quartets* – by which Eliot
explicitly indicates a musical analogy for the work which crowns his

maturity. And we shall not be surprised to find that 'Burnt Norton', the first of the Quartets, is a poem very much à la Valéry – a poem in the first place about itself and about the writing of poetry, even (more narrowly) about poetry and music and the specially close relation between these two arts among the others.

Just as 'The Love Song of J. Alfred Prufrock' and 'A Cooking Egg' are generally considered (wrongly) as stories told in verse with some of the chapters left out, just as 'Mr Eliot's Sunday Morning Service' has been considered (wrongly) as the setting of a scene with certain items of description left out (and impaired by others that bulge out of the frame), just as *The Waste Land* has been misconceived by Cleanth Brooks and numberless others as a cryptic allegory with some of the links in the argument deliberately omitted, so *Four Quartets* is generally misread as a philosophical disquisition or a treatise of Christian apologetics with, again, large and deliberate lacunae. But, if the musical analogy is taken seriously at all, just as the structure of 'A Cooking Egg' cannot be narrative structure (however much disguised and fiddled with), just as the structure of 'Mr Eliot's Sunday Morning Service' cannot be scenic, and just as the structure of *The Waste Land* (at least up to the last two sections, where the poet perhaps loses his way) cannot be allegorical, so the structure of *Four Quartets* cannot be logical, discursive. We should not come to *Four Quartets* with those expectations, we should not give it that sort of attention, we should not try to understand it in that way. And, since it is 'in that way' that we nowadays conceive of what understanding is, it becomes almost true to say that we should not try to 'understand' these poems at all. Consider:

> What might have been is an abstraction
> Remaining a perpetual possibility
> Only in a world of speculation.
> What might have been and what has been
> Point to one end, which is always present.
> Footfalls echo in the memory
> Down the passage which we did not take
> Towards the door we never opened
> Into the rose-garden. My words echo
> Thus, in your mind. . . .

'Thus'! Thus? How? What is the connection, the resemblance, thus confidently asserted? Words spoken one by one are like footsteps – well, yes; the argumentative mind can see that in certain circumstances the comparison might be just. But it turns out that the footsteps never happened, for they are footsteps in a direction which was never taken. So it appears that the poet's words dropping into the silence are like, not any actual footsteps, but only his thoughts of those footsteps. To be sure it isn't the sound of the words that is like the sounds of footsteps, but the words themselves (sounds plus meanings) that are like footsteps, perhaps figurative ones like footsteps in an argument. But then, that argument, it seems, was never embarked upon. It is easy enough – we are too ready perhaps – to see words spoken as identical with stages in an argument: we say the right word and thereby we advance one stage in the argument. But words that are specifically not stages in an argument, but only like such stages – this is harder to conceive of. Yet we can corroborate it readily enough from experience – 'It all sounds very fine,' we say, 'but in fact when you look at what he's saying, it doesn't hang together at all.' This is something that we might want to say in fact about what might have been and what has been pointing to one end, which is always present. 'It sounds very fine but. . . .' And, if that was what we may have wanted to say, suddenly it turns out that we were right: we ought to have said it. For the poet himself is pointing out that that is just the effect he was after and attained. Anyone who sits down and tries to worry out what these lines mean, as a proposition in a treatise, is flying in the face of just what the poet tells him a few lines later: that his labour is wasted, that meaning of that sort isn't there. Yet the warning goes unheeded; the devout exegeses continue.

It would be just as wrong to fly to the other extreme, and to suppose that because we can't understand 'What might have been and what has been/Point to one end, which is always present' these lines are meaningless. They add up to something, they amount to something; as we know from the very fact that the something they amount to can be talked about. We can say, for instance, as the poet says for us, that this something is like remembering how we didn't go down a passage to a rose garden. At the very least we can say that the experience of not understanding them is more like the experience of not understanding a book of mystical theology than it is like the experience of not understanding the drunken confidence of a stranger met in a bar.

'Burnt Norton' opens in precisely the same way as 'The Love Song of J. Alfred Prufrock'. There, 'something' ('Oh, do not ask, "What is it?" ') was, we remember, like going 'through certain half-deserted streets,/The muttering retreats/ Of restless nights in one-night cheap hotels/And sawdust restaurants with oyster shells . . .'. This is different from going or not going down a passage to a rose-garden, if only in this respect – that an encounter with a garrulous drunk is much more of a possibility. In both poems, we have hardly begun reading before we find the poem talking about itself, appealing to the reader with the question: 'So far as you've gone the experience of reading this poem is rather like this, isn't it?'

Put like this, the procedure seems to be no more than a gimmick. And of course that is all it is, in itself. But it can be made to work. In the present case for instance, after six lines of the poem we accept it as self-evidently true that 'What might have been is an abstraction/ Remaining a perpetual possibility/Only in a world of speculation'. But nine lines later we ought to have changed our minds. For 'what might have been' (we might have been reading a treatise of mystical theology instead of a poem) has now been presented to us not as an abstract possibility in a world of speculation, but – extraordinary though this seems – as a manifested actuality in a world of lived experience, the experience of language.

These are vistas to set the clearest head spinning. The same possibilities are opened up, but in a more manageable way, by a passage later in the poem:

> Words move, music moves
> Only in time; but that which is only living
> Can only die. Words, after speech, reach
> Into the silence. Only by the form, the pattern,
> Can words or music reach
> The stillness, as a Chinese jar still
> Moves perpetually in its stillness.
> Not the stillness of the violin, while the note lasts,
> Not that only, but the co-existence,
> Or say that the end precedes the beginning,
> And the end and the beginning were always there
> Before the beginning and after the end.
> And all is always now. Words strain,
> Crack and sometimes break, under the burden,
> Under the tension, slip, slide, perish,
> Decay with imprecision, will not stay in place,
> Will not stay still. Shrieking voices
> Scolding, mocking, or merely chattering,
> Always assail them. The Word in the desert

> Is most attacked by voices of temptation,
> The crying shadow in the funeral dance,
> The loud lament of the disconsolate chimera.

Helen Gardner comments on this, intelligently enough: 'The word itself, like the note in music, has meaning only in relation to other words. It exists in time and in usage; and since contexts and usages change, the life of a word is a continual death.'[2] Certainly the semantic history of word-usages is being alluded to here, though less memorably than in a related passage from 'East Coker'. But the emphasis surely falls much less on the historical time, in which contexts and usages alter, than on the time which a musical composition takes to be performed or a literary composition to be read. And though Miss Gardner acknowledges this she hardly makes it salient enough. For the perceptions at work in these lines are those which lie at the heart of symbolist poetic theory. In Eliot's verse as in Valéry's prose, the first thing to be said about poetry is that it works, it unfolds, only in duration, in lapsing time:

> Words move, music moves
> Only in time. . . .

Unlike 'What might have been and what has been/Point to one end, which is always present', the statement 'Words move, music moves/ Only in time' does not just sound as if it made sense; it makes sense. Yet we must still beware of supposing that (this passage) therefore, unlike that first one, is consecutive argument. For all the primness of punctuation and the earnest dryness of the vocabulary, this passage too is what it talks about: its structure is musical, not logical. Consider, for instance, the force of 'but' in what follows – 'but that which is only living/Can only die'. This means, first, 'Words which live in time as we do, must die as we do'; *but* also 'We on the other hand, because we are living as words aren't, must die as they needn't.' At the point where the semi-colon comes, something has been left out which in normal prose discourse would limit what follows to one or other of these meanings. The poet, wanting to have both meanings at once, constructs around the semi-colon a meaningful silence, a blank place on the paper, where the clause that would have settled the question is felt by us as present, as a 'might-have-been'. And the next sentence makes room for yet another meaning.

3

> but that which is only living
> Can only die. Words, after speech, reach
> Into the silence.

Wondering, as the rhythm carries us over the full-stop, what cluster of mutually incompatible logical links lies concealed in the silent space which that punctuation creates (it could be 'And so', it could be 'And yet'), we realise, as 'Words, after speech, reach' (we reach also, for the next line) another sense in which words can be said to die, the sense in which they may compose a dying fall, a cadence which prolongs itself into the silence after the voice has stopped. This is an effect which poetry shares with music:

> the stillness of the violin, while the note lasts . . .

The fiddle and the bow are motionless, while the note which their movements created still sounds in the air about them.

It's just as well to insist on this because otherwise it will seem as if the poem here (and elsewhere) is discontented with its own medium, language, because that medium, like the musical medium, by locking it into the dimension of time, makes it incapable of rising to the simultaneity, the stillness, of the plastic art which produces the Chinese jar. And indeed many interpretations of *Four Quartets* as a whole, especially those conducted from the standpoint of Christian piety, invite us to see the poems as yearning always for some impossible stasis, 'the timeless moment'. Certainly the poet, by introducing quotations from St John of the Cross and other mystics, invites us to set over against the 'time' which he talks of so constantly the concept of 'eternity'. And so the terminology of mysticism is undoubtedly useful for coming to grips with the poem. Still, in this very poem, it is said, 'Only through time time is conquered.' And for readers of other temperaments and interests it may be useful to see not time as opposed to eternity, but musical time as opposed to pictorial or sculptural space;[3] and to think, when they read, for instance, 'And all is always now', not of the mystic's contemplative trance, but of the perpetual present tense which is the tense of a symbolist poem, where words do not stand for events but *are* those events. Because the very first page of 'Burnt Norton' established it as a poem in the symbolist tradition, a poem which describes and discusses itself, this sort of meaning for 'time' and 'present' and 'now'

ould be, while certainly not the one meaning they will bear, at least
e first meaning to be brought to them.

'Burnt Norton', which stands last in *Collected Poems 1909–1935*,
mploys just the same devices as the poem which stands first, 'The Love
ong of J. Alfred Prufrock'. Like 'The Love Song', 'Burnt Norton'
ontinually feeds upon itself, gnaws its own vitals, postures before its
wn glass. As in 'The Love Song', in 'Burnt Norton' much that is most
rucial and affecting is 'between the lines'; in both poems the syntax
f what is said serves to hint at what is unsaid, to frame the meaningful
lences which may be gaps between blocks of lines but may equally
ell, in both poems, be the pregnant stillnesses around colons or semi-
olons or full-stops.* And there are other resemblances. In 'The Love
ong', there is a point where the syntax ceases to be that of written
rose or studied conversation, and becomes, with a sudden access of
rnestness and anxiety, the dishevelled syntax of speech:

It is impossible to say just what I mean!
But as if a magic lantern threw the nerves in patterns on a screen.

he same thing occurs in *Four Quartets*, as here:

> Only by the form, the pattern,
> Can words or music reach
> The stillness, as a Chinese jar still
> Moves perpetually in its stillness.
> Not the stillness of the violin, while the note lasts,
> Not that only, but the co-existence,
> Or say that the end precedes the beginning,
> And the end and the beginning were always there
> Before the beginning and after the end.
> And all is always now.

ne looks with impatience, among all the exegeses, for a little literary
riticism, which would examine, for instance, the points at which, and
urposes for which, Eliot switches from written to spoken syntax, a
riticism which would note how in the sentence about the Chinese jar
ere is the inversion – 'Only by the form . . . Can . . .' – so as to
oint up its written quality, precisely so that the spoken syntax which
llows can come with all the greater desperation. And again, what of

* cf. Mallarmé: 'L'armature intellectuelle du poème se dissimule et tient – a
eu – dans l'espace qui isole les strophes et parmi le blanc du papier: significatif
lence qu'il n'est pas moins beau de composer que les vers.'

'J. Alfred Prufrock' himself, those syllables which have no reference a
all except the phantasmal one which they conjure up for themselves
This, too, occurs in *Four Quartets*. When we read in 'East Coker', 'O
the edge of a grimpen, where is no secure foothold', we all know wha
a grimpen is, yet we shall look in vain for any dictionary to confirm u
in our knowledge. For 'Grimpen' occurs elsewhere only once, as
place-name in Arthur Conan Doyle's *Hound of the Baskervilles*. It ma
not be so clear that much the same thing happens here, in 'Burn
Norton'. Yet:

> The Word in the desert
> Is most attacked by voices of temptation,
> The crying shadow in the funeral dance,
> The loud lament of the disconsolate chimera.

And, if we ignore the capital letter on 'Word', then it must seem tha
the temptations to which the word is exposed, the vices of language
are not so much described as exemplified, in that last opalescent couple
where the shell of Augustan antithetical balance, as it might be i
Dryden, holds no kernel of sense but only the vast suggestiveness of
most un-Augustan sonority.

Still, 'Word' does get its capital letter; and very important it is. I
permits us, and obliges us, to face up to a restive objection which I dar
say we have had more and more difficulty in suppressing, the furthe
we have penetrated through the looking-glass: the exasperated protes
that poetry which has for subject only itself cannot be other tha
trivial, the narrowness of its scope and focus a damning indictment o
the men who write it. What have we been saying, if not that there ar
no real typists in Eliot's Waste Land, no real flowers and birds in hi
Burnt Norton, but only the names of these things? If it may be objecte
to Yeats that in his poems swans are not really swans but stand-in
('Another emblem there!'), how much more heavily must not the sam
charge be levelled at Eliot? The ancient and arcane doctrine of th
Logos – 'In the beginning was the Word, and the Word was with Goc
and the Word was God' – provides Eliot, as it sometimes provide
Mallarmé himself, with an answer to this comprehensive indictment.

The non-Christian reader, while he may acknowledge that thi
doctrine, so central as it is to twenty centuries of European though
somehow carries more weight than the more eccentric ideas of Yeats
may yet feel that the doctrine of the Logos is no less remote than th

Yeatsian doctrines from his own lived experience. He may object, though respectfully, perhaps regretfully, that however far the poet may have been from seeing in this no more than a pun it is impossible for him, the reader, to take it as other than a pun or a historical curiosity. Yet in fact the doctrine of the Logos – or at least some aspects of it – can be readily translated into secular quite unmystical terms which no one can afford to ignore. Meta-linguistics seems to have established, by thoroughly verifiable methods, that the language we speak determines not only how we communicate to others our sense of the truth, but how we communicate to ourselves; the categories which we find in nature or impose on nature, in order to understand it, are (it now appears) linguistic categories. The speaker of English and the speaker of Chinese will not merely arrange nature differently in order to speak of it, but will arrange it differently in order even to think about it. The syntax of our language determines all our ways of seeing the world and of coming to terms with it. To a personality like Pound's, convinced above all of the plenitude, the variety and multiplicity of experience, this realisation will carry the implication, as it did for Pico della Mirandola, that a poem is in duty bound to deal with experience in terms of as many linguistic moulds as possible. But it is equally possible to believe that all the languages move towards the same point by different methods, that the language anyone speaks provides the method, the form or mould, precisely fitted for him to explore reality. This is to believe that the secret answers are concealed in the very structure of the language one uses. This is one way of understanding that 'the Word was with God, and the Word was God'; and on this showing a poem which examines only the structure of its own language by that very token examines everything else, everything there is to examine. And so when Eliot goes on in 'Burnt Norton', from talking about the poem as a form like a Chinese jar and yet as a process, a sequence of events in time, to talking of Love as 'itself unmoving' yet issuing in Desire which moves continually, he is not 'changing the subject'; he is not even making a witty or fanciful analogy (Poem as achieved form = Love; poem as process = Desire), but simply changing the one discussion into other terms and a new key.

Metaphysicians appear to have pursued the same logic. After retiring in confusion before critics who pointed out that the questions they discussed could not be asked in languages with a different structure from their own, who accused them therefore of being tricked by language

into dilemmas which were merely verbal, they now take heart and as
why 'verbal' must be '*merely* verbal' and whether, if language trick
them, it does not trick them for their own good and to some purpose
Once the structure of language is taken to be the structure of reality
then merely verbal dilemmas are seen to be the most real of all dilemmas
and the hoary topics of metaphysics, having suffered a sea-change
present themselves as no less worthy of attention than they ever were
Let God be called 'Reality'; and then meta-linguists and metaphysician
alike appear to agree that 'the Word was with God, and the Word wa
God'.

Some French theorists have divided all men, in their dealings with
language, into 'terrorists' and 'rhetoricians'. The terms when translated
into English are misleading. The French mean by 'terrorist' the man
who is suspicious of language, who takes it for granted that language i
always trying to trap us into saying what we don't mean, that every
word we use must therefore be scrutinised with a sort of baleful resent
ment. England in the present century has been full of 'terrorists' of this
sort, and our poetry reflects the pressures they have brought to bear
It is only lately, and even so very grudgingly and fearfully, that English
poets and philosophers and theorists of language have come to see the
strength of the alternative position, that of the 'rhetorician' who trust
language to do his thinking for him, who casts himself trustingly into
the sea of language, confident that its currents will carry him to better
purpose than if he insisted on swimming against them. If we had not
resisted and evaded for so long the challenge of symbolist theory and
practice – particular phases of that resistance are signalised by the
names of I. A. Richards and F. R. Leavis – we might not have needed
to learn the hard way. Eliot to be sure is not to be herded conclusively
into either camp; he seems to believe that in the act of successful
composition the poet's dealings with language somehow comprehend
both attitudes, both suspicious vigilance and trustful surrender. But, a
compared with Pound, Eliot presents himself as pre-eminently a
rhetorician, a man who serves language, who waits for language to
present him with its revelations; Pound by contrast would master
language, instead of serving language he would make it serve – it must
serve the shining and sounding world which continually throws up new
forms which language must strain itself to register. Either all the forms
of reality are hidden in language and will be revealed by language if we
only trust it sufficiently; or else nature is inexhaustibly prodigal of new

forms, for ever outrunning language, which must be repeatedly constrained to keep in the chase.

II

In what remains of this essay, I shall attempt to show how the principles
which operate in *Four Quartets* operate also in earlier poems by Eliot.
In particular I shall try to justify my coat-trailing about two of those
earlier poems: 'A Cooking Egg' and 'Mr Eliot's Sunday Morning
Service'.

Reading some famous lines in which Prufrock compares the activities
of a fog to the activities of a cat, sturdy common-sense, whose voice,
alas, is so seldom heard in Eliot-land, would protest: 'It isn't so. I am
not convinced. He can talk for as long as he likes, but he doesn't
persuade me that a fog behaves as a cat behaves.' Similarly, even earlier
in the poem, reading, 'When the evening is spread out against the sky/
Like a patient etherised upon a table', common-sense will retort, once
again and quite simply, 'I don't believe it.' Instead of the voice of
common-sense, the voice of the critic (in this case F. O. Matthiessen)
protests that the comparison of the evening with the etherised patient
is 'too intellectually manipulated, not sufficiently felt'.[4] And this is the
very reverse of the truth. For common-sense is right: the comparison
has no substance at all for intellection to worry out of it, no justification
at all in terms of logic and/or sense-perception. To a normal mind, fogs
and cats, evening skies and operating-tables have nothing in common
whatever. And this is just the point of these comparisons; it is precisely
because to a normal mind they are absurd, that we are led or forced
to conceive of the abnormal mind, or the abnormal state of mind, to
which these comparisons are not absurd but exact. The truth is the
opposite of what Matthiessen says: if the comparison has any validity
at all, it is in terms of feeling – of the feeling of the observer, projected
so intensely upon these disparate objects as to deceive him into
thinking them similar; the comparison has no 'intellectual' substance
whatever.

The moral is so obvious that I blush to draw it. On all sides we have
been told, and are still told, that in Eliot's early poetry the influences of
French Symbolists and of English 'metaphysicals' intersect. The case
of F. O. Matthiessen shows that if the two traditions *do* intersect, if
they *can* intersect (and Rosemond Tuve will tell us that they can't), the
point of intersection is easy to mistake. A reader who comes to Prufrock

from Webster and Donne, will, like Matthiessen, read these comparisons as if they were conceits, and the poem will fall to pieces in his hands before he has got through the first three lines of it.

When Donne compares lovers with compasses he presents two images (that is to say, two human experiences – of love and of mathematics) which are normally regarded as belonging to widely different kinds or orders of human experience as a whole. We may say, then, that to begin with there is a wide gap between them. But when Eliot compares a fog with a cat, or an evening sky with an etherised patient, the object of the exercise, for him, is to leave the gap wide open. Only in this way can he incite the reader to close the gap for himself, by deducing from the two terms given the third term which is missing, the state of mind of the observer, Prufrock, who sees a similarity where none exists.* The poetry isn't a riddle: why are fogs like cats? It is a puzzle: puzzle – find Prufrock. There is left between the images a gap which the reader has to fill for himself; sometimes the gap, the meaningful silence of Mallarmé, exists as a space of blank white paper on the printed page, whereas in the cases we are considering the gap is papered over by what looks like normal syntax. But of course it isn't normal syntax, but the symbolist syntax which is working upon us in ways which have nothing to do with the perception of logical patterns.

This is the view of symbolist procedure which was expressed by one critic when he said that in poems in the symbolist tradition 'images or symbols are ranged about, and the meaning flowers out of the space between them'. But as it turns out this formulation does not get us very far, for it seems to leave the reader free to fill in the gaps with whatever materials he pleases, according to whatever may be the idiosyncratic bent of his own interests. This emerged very clearly from a discussion a few years ago of Eliot's poem, 'A Cooking Egg', from his second collection, *Poems 1920*. This rather trivial poem does not deserve all the attention that has been lavished on it; and indeed in most ways Eliot's second collection as a whole cannot measure up to his first. (This is true, I think, even of the most ambitious poem, which stands first in the collection, the famous 'Gerontion'; for Eliot seems to identify himself with this *persona*, unwittingly, far more than he did with

---

* It is true, of course, that if the reading of Eliot has been distorted by a gravitational pull in the reader's mind towards Donne, the reading of Donne has been distorted by the presence of Eliot. We are asked to read Donne's poems as if the interest in them were the mind we deduce from them.

Prufrock.) But this only means that 'A Cooking Egg' perhaps deserves nothing much better than the fate which has come upon it – to be the occasion of a sustained critical wrangle. The discussion will be found in the quarterly *Essays in Criticism* for July 1953 and January 1954. The spectacle it affords, of several distinguished critics falling out about what the poem means, is instructive and rather shocking, and unfortunately, at the time, it gave a handle to the philistines to pluck up heart and exult, 'I told you so; it's nothing but gibberish.' However the discussion was not so pointless as has been made out. Real progress had been made when at the end of it I. A. Richards could ask, 'perhaps it is a current conception of interpretation which is out of focus, at least for such a poem?'[5]

However, the most instructive contribution was F. W. Bateson's. For he began by quoting the formulation already offered – 'Images or symbols are ranged about, and the meaning flowers out of the space between them.'[6] But the problem then became, for Mr Bateson, how the reader was to supply the links which the poet left out; and he supplied them by making up a story about a love-affair between Pipit, the central figure in the poem, and the narrator. That is to say, he treated the poem, not after all as a symbolist poem or a poem in the symbolist tradition, but as if it were a narrative with every other chapter left out. The critics found themselves solemnly debating whether Pipit was a little girl or a grown up or (agreeable lunacy!) perhaps the poet's nannie. And they posed each other such unanswerable conundrums as: did the narrator when he was an undergraduate buy for his old nannie, *Views of the Oxford Colleges*? This, of course, is a question on a par with 'How many children had Lady Macbeth?' – and even less relevant to Eliot's poem than the question of the children is to Shakespeare's. The whole procedure is ludicrous. For what spaces are left in the poem, for meanings to flower in, when Mr Bateson has busily paved the whole area with fictions of his own devising? The poet leaves spaces, and he wants them left. If the riddles could be solved, why didn't the poet solve them, for himself and for us? A range of possible answers can be found, and a vast range of other answers can be ruled out as impossible. But if there were one clear and conclusive answer, one key which, when found, broke the poet's code, the whole poetic procedure would lose its justification and its point. It's just here, in fact, that we make room for what at first may look like the most disreputable feature of symbolist poetic theory – the value it places upon a deliberate vagueness, and upon the suggestive hint rather than the plain statement. What it amounts to, on this showing, is the never treating any issue as entirely closed.

We narrow the range of possible answers, and close the gap so far as is proper, not by constructing impressive fictions of our own, but by attending to the developing shape of the whole poem, and above all by noticing in particular the tone of voice where it leaves off before the gap and where it picks up again afterwards. In 'A Cooking Egg' tone is determined above all by rhyme and by verse-movement:

> Pipit sate upright in her chair
> Some distance from where I was sitting;
> *Views of the Oxford Colleges*
> Lay on the table, with the knitting.

The silly archaism 'sate', and the rhyme on 'sitting'/'knitting' (worthy of Mr Cyril Fletcher) define the tone as detached and a trifle sourly amused, and rule out at once the shame and disgust that some of the contributors to *Essays in Criticism* wanted to impart to the lines. Similarly,

> I shall not want Honour in Heaven
> For I shall meet Sir Philip Sidney
> And have talk with Coriolanus
> And other heroes of that kidney.
>
> I shall not want Capital in Heaven
> For I shall meet Sir Alfred Mond.
> We two shall lie together, lapt
> In a five per cent Exchequer Bond.

It is the fatuous rhyme of 'Sidney' with 'kidney', and of 'Mond' with 'Bond', together with the very heterogeneity of the proper names, which makes it certain that the unspoken refrain in the space between these stanzas is something of the nature of ('I shall meet Sir Philip Sidney'), 'Like Hell I shall', or else (the poet's voice placing perhaps the anonymous speaker), 'Like Hell you will'.

The poem is in three sections marked off by rows of dots, and I. A. Richards, who alone among the contributors to the discussion was sensitive to tone, rightly perceived that verse-movement dictates a wholly new tone in the last section:

> But where is the penny world I bought
> To eat with Pipit behind the screen?
> The red-eyed scavengers are creeping
> From Kentish Town and Golder's Green;

> Where are the eagles and the trumpets?
>
> > Buried beneath some snow-deep Alps.
> > Over buttered scones and crumpets
> > > Weeping, weeping multitudes
> > Droop in a hundred A.B.C.'s.

In the first quatrain, as the verse-movement changes, the tone becomes, for the first and last time, serious and engaged. A real loss is being really lamented. And this holds over to the line printed by itself. The trumpet echoes through the blank space which follows like the horn of Roland carrying from Roncesvaux the last signal of a noble order doomed. But a trumpet after all is not a horn (the horn sounding through the forest – stock image of European romance) and if we have forgotten – as up to a point we are meant to do, meant to make fools of ourselves – that a trumpet is brassy at best and may be a child's toy, we are made unavoidably aware of it, and of our own stoop to self-indulgent folly, with the conclusively deflating rhyme, 'crumpets'. This changes the tone again, so that when we look back at the space after 'the eagles and the trumpets', a space so lately brimming with our own romantic melancholia, we now hear a voice saying mockingly into that silence, 'It's a shame, so it is.' In fact, that whole line about the eagles and the trumpets forces home the recognition that every word and every poetic line has two contexts, what leads up to it and what leads away from it, and that the second context may spring (here by a cruelly delayed-action mechanism) a trap laid for us by the first. This is language as music, exploiting to the full, as music does, the lapse of time in which it has its being and its operation.

Yet it's essential to realise, even as we begin to recognise how nicely in these ways the range of possible readings can be narrowed, that the range is never narrowed so far as to provide only one right reading. One of the possible readings of 'A Cooking Egg' would begin by dwelling on the title. An egg once fresh now stale; hence (perhaps) a hope once entertained now abandoned. It would read out of the first two stanzas, noting their tone as defined by rhyme and archaism, English upper-class security, continuity and assurance. Oxford (if we remember the date) and Pipit (the excruciating coyness of the name) define class; 'Oxford' means English; 'grandfather and great great aunts' means continuity; sitting upright ('Pipit sate upright') means assurance, even dignity; *Invitation to the Dance* means sentimental

philistinism in the arts. And so much for the first section. The middle
section shows (through a speaker who either mocks himself or is
mocked from the wings by the poet) a ruling class no longer assured of
its right to various good things, no longer assured that its own monu-
mental figures (Sir Alfred Mond, Madame Blavatsky) are equal to the
great figures of other cultures, like Sidney, the Borgias or Coriolanus;
or else, in so far as the class does retain this assurance, its claims are
laughed out of court. We may permit ourselves the self-righteous
reflection that, in so far as this assurance was insufferable complacency,
it is good to see it go. But, says the last section in effect, the loss of
security is another matter from loss of assurance, a real loss and one
which may be mourned – which may be mourned, but only a little;
for, try to inflate it to a tragedy, and the rhyme on 'crumpets' brings
out all the brassiness of the trumpet and the inadequacy of the occasion
for the tears being spilled about it. This reading of the poem may seem
all the more plausible if we remember that the author was at this time
in close alliance with Ezra Pound, another American poet who at just
this time was writing a similar mocking threnody on the British imperial
twilight, in his *Homage to Sextus Propertius*.

At the bottom of the symbolist method, it has been said, is the
discovery that words may have meanings though they have no referents.
And most of the misreadings of Eliot derive from a failure, less frequently from a refusal, to recognise this fact about the way language
works:

> But where is the penny world I bought
> To eat with Pipit behind the screen?

The mind that thinks that looking for a word's meaning is looking for
its referent will ask: What is a 'penny world'? And gravely observing
that worlds cannot be eaten, it decides that 'penny world' cannot mean
what it says, and that 'world' must be a fanciful way of referring to
something else, something that is edible, perhaps a bun. 'Penny world'
thus revised to become 'penny bun', it asks what sort of a person penny
buns may be eaten with, and so comes up with the answer that Pipit
must be a nursery playmate, or else a nannie. Its next question is: In
what conditions are penny buns eaten, with or without dear little girls
or dear old nannies, *behind a screen*? And with that little poser before
him, this dogged reader may be abandoned. For enough has been said
to show that in symbolist poetry a word always means what it says –

always, because what it says is always only itself. 'Art is as realistic as activity and as symbolic as fact,' declared Pasternak. In the world of symbolist poetry worlds can be bought for a penny, and they can be eaten. 'Penny' and 'world' are verbal events occurring rapidly one after the other, the cheapness and littleness of 'penny' crammed up against the vastness of 'world'. The penny, the world, the eating, and the screen are here brought into an arrangement which need not correspond to any possible or likely arrangement of these items in the life which we observe about us. This arrangement of them is possible in language and therefore in the mind of the speaker and thereafter, if the poem is successful, in the mind of the reader. The penny and the world and the screen are in just the same case as the fog and the cat, or the evening sky and the etherised patient, in 'Prufrock'. In every case what seems to be asserted is a relationship between items which is impossible or highly unlikely in the world we observe; and in every case, as a result, we have to realise that the items are arranged thus, not in the world observed but in the mind of the observer. For of course there are dreams and other mental phenomena to tell us that the laws of space and time, which operate outside the mind, do not obtain inside it.

In a brilliant and momentous essay, H. M. McLuhan has traced, over the past two centuries of poetic effort, the logic which led the poets to this startling discovery, that they had been observing, in the stories and pictures they created, laws of temporal and spatial arrangement which in fact did not bear upon their activities at all. In this article, called 'Tennyson and Picturesque Poetry' (*Essays in Criticism*, vol. I, no. 3), McLuhan credits James Thomson, author of *The Seasons*, with the original discovery: that there could be maintained in poetry a constant relationship between external events or appearances described, and the state of the mind which first observed and then described them. Thomson is described in the Literary Histories as the poet who first made description of 'nature' (i.e. for the most part, of landscape and weather) self-sufficient matter for poems. It seems an unexciting, a dubiously useful innovation. Thomson is a much more startling innovator if, as McLuhan suggests, what he discovered was not verse-description as such, but verse-description of such a kind that, in offering and seeming to describe the landscape and weather of the observable world, it described equally the landscape of the observer's mind, the weather in the observer's soul. Whether this claim for Thomson can be allowed, is not here the question; in any case it must be allowed that

the discovery was repeatedly made, if not originally by Thomson,
certainly by his successors in this mode, Cowper, Wordsworth occasionally, Keats and Tennyson certainly. Who can doubt – who has ever
doubted – that Keats's 'Ode to Autumn', offering to describe a season
of the year, describes at least equally a season in the spiritual life of the
poet, a landscape or climate of the human mind? By Keats's time, the
psychological fact of this possible correspondence between inner and
outer was already almost a commonplace, and built into the poetic
theories of, for instance, William Hazlitt and Arthur Hallam. Are we
saying, then, that the 'Ode to Autumn' is already a symbolist poem?
Not at all. For Keats and Tennyson are still, like Wordsworth, Cowper,
and Thomson before them, dependent upon nature to present them
with the landscape and the weather that will, because they correspond
to a state of mind, permit them to express that state. The symbolist
poet, on the other hand, has realised that he can do better than wait
patiently upon nature until she provides what he wants. Knowing the
state of mind he wants to express, he can construct the landscape he
wants, so as to make it correspond. And with that recognition comes
another: being thus free of nature's caprice, the poet when he creates
a landscape is under no obligation to make it observe all the laws which
govern nature's landscapes. In Mr McLuhan's words:

> The romantic and picturesque artists had to take advantage of accidents.
> After Baudelaire there is no need for such accidents. The picturesque
> artists saw the wider range of experience that could be managed by
> discontinuity and planned irregularity, but they kept to the picture-
> like single perspective. The interior landscape, however, moves
> naturally towards the principle of multiple perspectives as in the
> first two lines of *The Waste Land* where the Christian Chaucer, Sir
> James Frazer and Jessie Weston are simultaneously present. This is
> 'cubist perspective' which renders, at once, a diversity of views with
> the spectator always in the centre of the picture, whereas in
> picturesque art the spectator is always outside. The cubist perspective
> of interior landscape typically permits an immediacy, a variety and
> solidity of experience denied to the picturesque and to Tennyson.[7]

The change, I suspect, was hardly such sheer gain all round as Mr
McLuhan suggests; the intent and patient waiting upon nature which
is the constant discipline of a Coleridge, a Ruskin, a Turner or a
Hopkins (and I would add, a Pound) – this may induce a religious
apprehension of the spiritual in nature, which it is not worth losing

just for the sake of a more streamlined poetic method. Nevertheless, McLuhan sufficiently explains the fatuity of asking, about those lines in 'A Cooking Egg': When, in what sort of room, under what circumstances, does one eat behind a screen? To attempt to visualise the scene like this is as woefully wide of the mark as to object to Picasso that he disregards the laws of perspective as conceived by Raphael. Yet this is a not uncommon way of misreading Eliot: having taken from *Essays in Criticism* one example of how-not-to-do-it, I will go there for another, Ernest Schanzer's reading (in the issue for April 1955) of the poem called 'Mr Eliot's Sunday Morning Service'.

Another exegesis would be tedious. 'The poem's setting', Mr Schanzer begins, 'is indicated by its title', and in this setting the narrative (which, like Mr Bateson, Mr Schanzer assumes to exist, waiting for him to reconstruct it) 'is supplied by the wandering eye and mind of Mr Eliot'.[8] If, because of the title, we are led to imagine the speaker at a church-service such as we know from observation, we shall start wondering, as early as stanza three, what sort of church Mr Eliot can attend that has an Umbrian easel-painting inside it. Mr Schanzer becomes indignant when the last stanza presents Sweeney in his bath. For even his imagination cannot accommodate in his mental image of Eliot's church an Umbrian easel-painting and an inhabited bathtub. It is hard not to sympathise: Mr Schanzer wants to know if he is in a church or in a bathroom, and all we can tell him is that he is in a poem. The structure of the poem is neither pictorial nor narrative, though Mr Schanzer assumes it is both; it is sustained on the two axes of reference presented in the epigraph ('Look, look, master, here comes two religious caterpillars') by the last phrase, 'religious caterpillars'. The caterpillars announce the flies of the first stanza, and the bees of the sixth, while 'religious' looks forward to the church fathers of stanza two, to the Umbrian painting, and the presbyters. Throughout, these two sets of images interact, particularly in terms of sexual fertility, sometimes very plainly as in 'epicene' (stanza seven), sometimes subtly as in the half-echo, 'pustular'/'pistillate'; but the interaction is not at all so reducible to the one right and clear reading as would be 'the satiric focus' which Mr Schanzer asks for and thinks he half finds. One begins to misread the poem in Mr Schanzer's way, as soon as one assumes, for instance, that the window-panes of the third line are window panes which Mr Eliot can see from his pew. In these poems the images are ranged about not according to the laws of space nor (in the case of narrative images, actions and events) according to the laws of time, but simply as they are ranged about in the poet's head.

The plain directive to the reader was given once and for all in the poem which stands first in the *Collected Poems*:

It is impossible to say just what I mean!
But as if a magic lantern threw the nerves in patterns on a screen.

The magic lantern is somewhere at the back of the poet's skull. Throwing its beam forward through the meshes of the poet's sensibility, it illumines at last the world which faces him; but he is interested, and his readers should be interested, not in that world itself at all, but only in that world as a screen, on to which are projected 'the nerves in patterns', that is to say, the shape and character of the observer's sensibility.

NOTES

1. See 'The Later Yeats', in *Literary Essays of Ezra Pound*, ed. T. S. Eliot (1954) pp. 378–81.
2. Helen Gardner, *The Art of T. S. Eliot* (1949) p. 7.
3. Pound, in the review which I have quoted from, distinguishes between 'the sort of poetry which seems to be music just forcing itself into articulate speech, and secondly, that sort of poetry which seems as if sculpture or painting were just forced or forcing itself into words'. In *Gaudier-Brzeska. A Memoir* (1917), Pound made the same distinction in almost identical words (see Marvell Press reprint (1960) p. 82). In the Memoir, Pound is fairly plainly vowing himself to poetry of the second sort: imagist or vorticist poetry which works by analogy with sculpture. Symbolist poetry on the other hand works by analogy with the art of music. And according to Valéry this analogy is more important to Symbolism than whatever may be gathered from worrying over what is meant by 'symbol'.
4. F. O. Matthiessen, *The Achievement of T. S. Eliot* (3rd ed., 1958) p. 30.
5. *Essays in Criticism*, IV 104.
6. Ibid, IV 106.
7. Ibid. I 281–2.
8. Ibid. V 153.

Eliot: an American use of symbolism

GABRIEL PEARSON

HUGH KENNER says of 'Gerontion': 'It need not be done twice and Eliot does not do it again.' True, he never exploited to the same degree what Kenner, quoting Empson, calls 'the echoes and recesses of words'.[1] Yet 'Gerontion' must be seen as central to Eliot's poetic practice; here he initiates and exhaustively explores permanent features of his basic idiom. Here also he enacts the logic – the social as well as verbal logic – of the conversion of words into the Word. Thereafter, the Word within the word is immanent as doctrinal justification for each poetic act. 'Gerontion' may well end in Eliot, as Kenner claims, one whole phase of Anglo-American linguistic practice; but emphatically it inaugurates that marriage of doctrine and poetic which determines our final sense of Eliot's career.

Words are not only 'echoes and recesses' of their own literary past. They are equally social deposits and repositories of social acts. Moreover, the disposition of words that makes them 'echoes and recesses' is itself social fact. The words of the solitary poet implicate a society in which they once had meaning and being as communications. They imply a past in which audience was once community; while, of the present audience, some were once of that community and conscious of being so, some are unconscious that they were, while some have never been so. All these states of audience are present in the totality of the poetic act.

Amongst so many auditors and vicarious utterers, words, echoed backwards and forwards in time, become weapons and defences, ideals and iconoclasms, compensations and restorations. The poem is an artificial person, articulated out of the parts of social experience localised and internalised by language. One aim of criticism is to reconstruct the lineaments of this artificial person and in so doing take the measure of those forces which required the artifice.

'Gerontion' by common agreement is a dramatic monologue in which the drama has collapsed into incoherence and the monologuist has disintegrated into fragments of his own memory. So much is indicated by the epigraph, a quotation from the Duke's speech to Claudio in *Measure for Measure*:

> Thou hast nor youth nor age
> But as it were an after dinner sleep
> Dreaming of both.

This describes well enough the situation of Gerontion as a representative human figure, caught in time and shorn of grace. The epigraph serves to insist that Gerontion is not merely an emblem of modern man; his futility is the futility of all men at all times sundered from supernatural power by their refusal of faith. The Duke in the play is offering consolation to Claudio for his premature death. He insists on the insubstantiality of individual existence. But *Measure for Measure* is itself a radically disintegrated work. Claudio, in the same scene, is soon crying out against the horrible substantiality of death ('a kneaded clod'). The Duke continues to play out his obscure game of metaphysical chess with all the protagonists. Angelo, the human angel, turns devil, to be redeemed, against all human grain, by Isabella; and so a moral pattern is forcibly educed, but at the expense of a radical distortion of dramatic credibility and coherence. Eliot's instinct in his choice of epigraph is unerring. If *Measure for Measure* is dramatically disintegrated in favour of its 'truth', then Eliot has pushed beyond every remaining coherence to recover his truth in the heart of the vortex of lost meaning, barely contained by the residual framework of dramatic monologue, a half-fractured shell merely:

> Here I am, an old man in a dry month,
> Being read to by a boy, waiting for rain. . . .
>   Tenants of the house,
> Thoughts of a dry brain in a dry season.

Man and boy have collapsed into 'thoughts of a dry brain'. 'Brain' answers 'rain' in a futile rhyming. The house becomes the scenario of these 'thoughts' or simply that which contains them ('tenants' reverting to the verbal noun of *tenir*; one senses a thread of connection to 'Ash-Wednesday': 'that which had been contained/In the hollow round of

ny skull . . .'). The usefulness of calling 'Gerontion' a dramatic
monologue practically disappears, since the major premiss of the form
– stable personality within an admittedly unstable order – has itself
become one of the ghosts which Gerontion claims not to have: 'I have
no ghosts' (he has just evoked four; but each statement of the poem
disintegrates the proceeding statements, so that each syntactical unity
operates ungeneratively, in a void). One major ghost is the form that
Gerontion' fails to be.

If 'Gerontion' is not a dramatic monologue, then how do we read it?
My sense is that 'Gerontion' is literally unreadable. What we 'read' are
words, syntax, grammar, associations. Consider the line: 'Rocks, moss,
stonecrop, iron, merds'. In an approximate way this could be an inven-
tory of 'the field overhead', and, more generally, of the rubbish dump
of memory. But for the reader the declarative import of the line is its
least important. What he attends to is words as words, isolated in their
strange completeness, as substantives, bonded, adjacent and yet
discrete. We linger on 'rocks' whose plural ending is disturbed by being
echoed by the singular 'moss' to be pluralled in its own turn by the
initial *s* of 'stonecrop'. We can, of course, read the first three substantives as telegraphed process: rocks produce moss which is the crop of
stone. But this happy reconstitution of syntax is aborted at 'iron' which
intrudes into this residual nature as, it seems, a dulled echo of 'stone'.
We may be forced back from 'iron' to the 'cutlass' seven lines above
which after 'the warm rain' and 'the salt-marsh' might naturally repose
a rust upon the rubbish heap of memory. But this is too fugitive an
association. Or we could see 'iron' as there to force a kind of pun out
of 'stonecrop'; one talks of an outcrop of iron ore. One thing is sure:
though one gets images, a landscape of sorts, one hardly reads past and
through the words to a world without.

Finally, we pause upon the word 'merds', sensing a complication – a
social murmur almost – in the term's self-insistence. It is a stunned
term for an explosive category: the silence of the word is noisy with
what it names but does not say. One can attempt only the crudest
translation. We find ourselves silently applauding the century or so's
puritan urbanity that allows Eliot, by a dexterous deviation though his
French culture, to render faeces as innocuous as tea-leaves. 'Merds'
rhymes, as it were (my view being that we need to extend our notion
of what constitutes rhyme in modern poetry), with 'makes tea' at the
end of the next line.

The controlled good form that selects the term enacts an aristocratic repugnance and arrogance bred out of a loss of effective power in the face of bourgeois philistinism and democratic vulgarity. It becomes an exquisite mode of retaliation. As audience, we share, momentarily, in the values that permit the disdainful tact of its handling. Yet we are excluded, too: and before its audacious decorum we crouch as apenecked as Sweeney. The poet's skill and deftness are counters for a lightly carried superiority. There is insult, too, in the term: Eliot murmurs 'merds', and we are insulted and exult in the dexterity of insult.

Northrop Frye gives a name to a quality we all recognise in Eliot when he calls it 'mnemonic adhesiveness'.[2] Scraps of lines, movements of paragraphs, images really do stick. Frye suggests as one cause of this the 'echoic' nature of the verse: the body of English and European literature vibrates behind the lines. We might add that so many lines stick because so much of the poetry enacts the operations of memory itself. Eliot's words and cadences are memories, largely memories of literature. Eliot's world is itself constructed as a huge, sounding memory in search of a contemporary identity to attach itself to. Such a condition arises when the present has lost its meaning. It represents an acute crisis of disinheritedness. Memory, and with it necessarily personal identity, ricochet back, as it were, off the blankness of the present. With no present to order and compose them, they have to form their own order, which often consists of construction and orchestration along associational filaments and zigzags. Often, Eliot imitates the actual production of memory. 'Footfalls echo in the memory' ('Burnt Norton') is, for example, a statement about the process and is the process itself. We pick up the 'echo' of the pre-lapsarian garden in the fall of 'footfalls' while the two syllables of 'footfall' are echo-memories of each other.

This world of arbitrarily echoing and associating memories is typical Eliot hell. There is a much quoted passage in 'Burnt Norton' whose oddity I have not seen remarked:

> Words strain,
> Crack and sometimes break, under the burden,
> Under the tension, slip, slide, perish,
> Decay with imprecision, will not stay in place,
> Will not stay still. Shrieking voices
> Scolding, mocking, or merely chattering,
> Always assail them.

The notion of words being assailed by voices seems very queer. In addition, words take on an active, disintegrative existence of their own. Eliot, in *Four Quartets*, tries to cure this disease of autonomously active words with theology, but his real cure is more words, above all the beautiful cadence that suddenly harmonises the disorder, 'The loud lament of the disconsolate chimera', but which remains, after all, but words. One feels that throughout his career Eliot is shaking his bars, trying to get out, but his means of escape are through the very words that imprison him. The quest for 'the still point of the turning world' clearly goes deeper than theology.

One form of attempted escape is an implicating assault upon the reader. A crude large-scale version of this is the Knights' address to the audience at the end of *Murder in the Cathedral* or Becket's stab at the audience at the end of the first Act when he tells us

> . . . you, and you,
> And you, must all be punished. So must you.

Here, as with 'merds', the words seem calculated to detonate a series of small-scale explosions in the reader: the aim is to trap, arrest and implicate us.

Such verbal violence abounds. Consider the lines:

> My house is a decayed house,
> And the jew squats on the window sill, the owner,
> Spawned in some estaminet of Antwerp,
> Blistered in Brussels, patched and peeled in London.

One notices that 'my house' quickly becomes someone else's, 'the owner's'. We are alerted to submerged paradox by 'And'. What is a Jew doing owning *my* house? is the implied question. The Jew 'squats' (an undoubted filament to 'merds' here), is 'spawned', 'blistered', 'patched' and 'peeled' in a swift aggressive flurry of strong verbs. One can scarcely avoid an impression of inflicted retaliations. Here is the 'jew' placarded, as owner, on an appositional sill, being spattered, degraded and mutilated. Like a veritable Elder of Zion he is made to exemplify the squalor he is accused of causing. Yet the attack is at the same time deftly distanced. The indefiniteness of 'some' is furthered by the allusive knowingness of 'estaminet'. The reader finds himself divided between levels of aggression and disdain which may turn out to be an attack on him.

The uncapitalised 'jew' becomes particularly active in this context. Eliot may have picked up the habit from Pound or from the passage in Joyce's *Ulysses* which Grover Smith proposes as a source.[3] It may have been a feature of anti-semitic literature of the period. The context here makes the difference. As a linguistic act, it reads like paranoic retaliation, a cutting down to size by castration.

The suggestion will be resisted. Yet citation of 'Burbank with a Baedeker: Bleistein with a Cigar' should render it plausible. My argument is that in Eliot's case there is an unusual isolation of, and concentration on, language as direct enactment of social attitudes. Poetry has traditionally mediated social existence through conventions, genres, myths, symbols. For Eliot, this mediation has largely collapsed. Eliot is reputed a peculiarly learned and literary poet, and this is true. It is true also that a good deal of raw personal and social emotion is fed back into the action of the language; this need not involve contradiction. Traditional forms no longer compose an inherited order. Rather, they become themselves manifestations of despair and anxiety, because no longer credited and sanctioned. Hence the ultimate unfruitfulness of reading these poems as reworkings of traditional modes. These have become themselves objects of historical attention within a universe of relative values. They lie exposed on the surface of history like withered roots. When the poet self-consciously uses them and discriminates among them, he can no longer derive nutriment from them. Instead, he has to feed them out of the substance of his own life. From this derives the highly personal impersonality of much modern art, and the inevitably ironic uses of tradition.

In 'Burbank', we have the rigid framework of quatrain, borrowed from Gautier, who is himself using quasi-classical structures and devices as sources of irony. Breaking the framework, there are two violent enjambements, over lines and across stanzas. The second of these works thus:

> She entertains Sir Ferdinand
>
> Klein. Who clipped the lion's wings. . . .

That neatly clips Klein of borrowed robes, borrowed knighthood, the borrowed romance of his 'christian' name. 'Klein' itself represents a sudden shrinkage from the full-blown 'Sir Ferdinand'. The first enjambement works in a rather different way:

> A lustreless protrusive eye
> Stares from the protozoic slime
> At a perspective of Canaletto.
>   The smoky candle end of time
>
> Declines. On the Rialto once.

Reading backwards, we already have Sir Ferdinand's declension pre-figured in 'Declines' ('Ferdinand-Klein'). Bleistein's cigar does not show in the poem. But it seems to lurk in 'the smoky candle end of time', which in turn takes up the 'nil nisi divinum stabile est; caeterus fumus' of the epigraph, a motto on an emblematic candlestick in a painting of St Sebastian by Mantegna.[4] This connects Bleistein's cigar with the decay of Venice and posits both as vanities against the divine permanence which is enacted by the rigid framework of the quatrain and the aerial view of Eliot's satiric perspective. The allusion to the riddled St Sebastian may also be significant as prefiguring Eliot's own concern with martyrdom which culminates in *Murder in the Cathedral*. Eliot's persecution of the Bleisteins and the Kleins in this poem would issue naturally out of a sense of persecution. The Shylock reference ('On the Rialto once.') inevitably brings to mind Shylock's knife and the pound of flesh. I read the act of the poem as, in a sense, the symbolic clipping, lopping and extinguishing of Bleistein's protrusive cigar – a ghostly compensation for the defection of Princess Volupine.

In 'Sweeney Agonistes', this clipping becomes almost absurdly literal in the person of Klipstein whose reduction to Klip precedes and so perhaps suggested Krumpacker's unpacking into Krum. (Klipstein, by some obscure logic is characterised almost wholly by the fact that he cannot remember Dusty's name.) In the second enjambement in 'Burbank', the sense rides over the period to make 'Who' into a relative. Sir Ferdinand has been clipping on his own account: the period that clips him becomes a retributive pun by punctuation; clip for clip, as it were.

Burbank, too, is a figure associated with decline. As such, he is in a state of unwitting complicity with Bleistein. He crosses a 'little' bridge, 'descending at a small hotel'; he 'falls' with Princess Volupine. Bleistein's protrusive gaze at Canaletto is repeated in Burbank's medita-tions on 'Time's ruins'. Yet Burbank, deserted and no doubt deservedly so (how vulgar after all to descend to using a Baedeker!), is clearly close to Eliot himself. The poet, by encompassing Burbank and identifying

and attacking the forces that make him a cultural eunuch, escapes
becoming Burbank himself.

Genesius Jones, an orthodox exegesist, celebrates 'Burbank' for
exhibiting what he calls 'the principle of concrescence' by virtue of
which the poet is in simultaneous possession of past and present.[5]
Grover Smith contents himself with noting, parenthetically, that the
poem 'is in execrable taste'.[6] Both reactions seem true and very partial.
'Concrescence' is indeed the principle of composition, but it is an act
of will, a forcing of perspectives, through violent juxtaposition. Simultaneous possession of past and present turns out, I believe, to be
possession of neither. The pieties of exegesis divert consideration from
the poem's verbal behaviour which amounts to precisely 'execrable
taste'. But that term is a little too bland. It is an odd procedure to
devote minute attention to elucidating the most recondite allusions, and
then sink the poem in a phrase. It is pointless merely to execrate because
execration is precisely what the poem seeks to provoke. It is a hate
poem, and when this is grasped its allusiveness – not to mention that
of the epigraph whose six lines are made up of as many quotations – is
understood as part of its central emotion, the wadding and buffering
of raw places, disguises worn by the violence and despair enacted by
stanza and syntax. This wadding becomes in turn an element of over-
control or repression, which in turn generates further verbal violence.

Yet we must allow that the stanzaic poems of the 1920 volume
represent an attempt to reconstitute what Eliot sees as a fragmented
ruin. Meditation alone will not allow Burbank to put his fractured
world together again. Eliot recognises that his poetry will never take
form from a spontaneous unity of culture and consciousness. Unity
has to be imposed by an act of willed juxtaposition of fragments. One
cannot but feel that the epigraph to 'Burbank' is the doctrinal heart of
the poem; the poem itself depending from it as an emotional *exemplum*.
The epigraph's dashes both sunder and hyphenate their discrete materials.
The order of language survives, at least partially, 'Time's ruins'.

'Burbank' and the other stanzaic poems of *Poems 1920*, are consciously
clever, contrived and wilful. Their rage and social disgust have to be
gathered by a kind of inductive leap behind their paraded façades. The
poems of *Prufrock and Other Observations* are, by contrast, debile,
fluctuating, helpless and self-ironic. Here Eliot with, and to some extent
through, Laforgue's Pierrot finds himself 'Au seuil des siècles charla-
tans' with no answer to Pierrot's question 'Et que Dieu n'est-il à

refaire?'[7] *Poems 1920* represents a deliberate hardening of the will. Fluctuating and self-ironic emotion is forcibly contained until it becomes explosive. The stanzaic poems then constitute a series of cracked and rocking façades. 'Gerontion' represents the cracking open of the façade. Constrained energies are loosed, explode, then die away in

> Gull against the wind, in the windy straits
> Of Belle Isle. . . .
> White feathers in the snow, the Gulf claims,
> And an old man driven by the Trades
> To a sleepy corner.

The basic movement of these lines is from 'Gull against the wind' to 'the Gulf claims', 'Gulf' echoing 'gull'. The tension of 'Gull against the wind' is relaxed – but only after being tightened further through the spondees of 'Belle Isle', 'Gulf claims', 'old man' – into the feeble trochaics of 'To a sleepy corner', whose feminine rhyme finally flickers out in its echo in the last word of the poem, 'season'. Before this, however, is the disintegrating explosion:

> What will the spider do,
> Suspend its operations, will the weevil
> Delay? De Bailhache, Fresca, Mrs Cammel, whirled
> Beyond the circuit of the shuddering Bear
> In fractured atoms.

The question about the spider and the weevil does have the effect of delaying, enforced by the enjambement and the rising interrogative pitch on 'delay'. 'Delay' graphically and auditorily still inheres in 'De Bailhache', who is thus torn away with lingering reluctance out of the texture of the proceeding lines. Analysis of sound values rightly lends itself to the suspicion of being empty and obvious. Where it can be isolated as part of a kinetic enactment of attitude it may, however, have its uses. It really does seem that in this passage the *d* and *s* combinations have the effect of a kind of desperate breaking against gathering speed: 'spider do', 'suspend', 'delay', 'de Bailhache', while the opening diphthongs of 'de*lay*', de B*ai*lh*a*che and the open vowel of Fresc*a*, seem to open up a gulf beneath the words themselves. 'Fresca', with his overtones of 'fresco' – a fresco to be shattered – are caught up in a vortex, which precipitates the whole passage in the ruin of 'fractured'. The explosion is complete. The three personages, implicated in two heavy but now very mobile animals ('Mrs Cammel', 'shuddering Bear')

are brandished, whirled and shattered into bits. Again, we have to see
this as pure verbal act. Gerontion's predicament has culminated in a
cold inferno of endless self-reflection:

> multiply variety
> In a wilderness of mirrors. . . .

The explosion becomes a deliberate attempt to shatter these mirrors
and if they allude, as Hugh Kenner thinks they do, partly to Versailles
and the hall of mirrors,[8] then so much the better: Eliot's predicament
is given a genuine historical dimension. Most critics read what I have
referred to as an explosion as a description of the expulsion and circlings
of the damned. They are right, but failure to read the poem as verbal
enactment, as the distribution towards equilibrium of emotional energy,
means a failure to grasp that the poet himself is engaged positively in
releasing himself from tension. Hell has traditionally been an invigor-
ating climate for poets. The theology of Hell has, one suspects, been
often a convenience as much as a prescription. Self-righteousness is
another matter, which is why, perhaps, Pound's inferno, by general
agreement, is no more than a crude cartoon.

'Gerontion' is haunted by the ghost of Henry Adams ('dogwood and
chestnut, flowering judas' are quotations from *The Education*); Adams's
view that the kinetic theory of gas proved that 'Chaos was the law of
nature; Order was the dream of man'[9] complicates my explanation. One
has to say first that Adams's view of nature was the product of his view
of history which in turn was, fairly avowedly, the product of his own
experience as a disinherited political aristocrat. Eliot, inherits this dis-
inheritance and 'Gerontion' shows its hold on his imagination. The
'flowering judas' of the quotation, however, alerts us to the degree of
Eliot's distrust of Adams: he must have found his instinctive sympathy
insidious. I interpret the presence of Adams in 'Gerontion' much as I
interpret the figure of Burbank. He is there to be encompassed: the
forces which caused his self-ironic despair are to be confronted, attacked
and transcended. None the less, the kinetic theory of gas and Adams's
view of history as a progressive complication and dissipation towards
chaos doubtless excited Eliot's imagery of 'fractured atoms'. Eliot did
believe Adams and only one thing could save him from his conclusion,
the blind leap of faith in a providential divine agency. This explains
why 'Gerontion implicitly demands the Logos, and why, at the same
time, the Logos does not naturally inhere in the ordering of the poem.

Eliot, by creating a self-substantive verbal universe, obviously continues the symbolist tradition into the twentieth century and into
Anglo-American literature. Yet I would suggest that he is not so much
in the tradition as using it and being used by it. Ultimately, his poetics
cannot be made synonymous with his poetry. For Eliot, unlike
Mallarmé, self-substantive verbal structure can never really hope to
create 'un Livre explication de l'homme suffisante à nos plus beaux
rêves . . .'. Such a creed is itself, for Eliot, a manifestation of a social
and historical predicament, and this predicament becomes in turn a
central issue of the poetry. The result is 'the intolerable wrestle with
words' of *Four Quartets*. Verbal art fails to transcend and order social
experience. Instead, social experience gets locked up in words and this
imprisonment, too, becomes an issue of the poetry. The problem for
Eliot was how to get them out again and so master the situation that
necessitated symbolist aesthetic. Eliot's discursive writings, critical,
social and theological, is one attempt to do this. In 'Gerontion' we see
clearly for the first time the escape route that Eliot will use for the rest
of his career.

Eliot took the logic of Symbolism to an extreme and then attempted
to return it to experience by connecting the word with the Word. The
Word, within its creative potency, must contain all experience. It is the
Christ child who contains god and adult man and all creation; but
paradoxically it is all these imprisoned in Eliot's own language, which,
like the child, is dumb:

> The word within a word, unable to speak a word,
> Swaddled with darkness.

The indefinite article of 'a word' seems deliberately to reflect on the
handling of words as discrete objects elsewhere in the poem. '*The* word',
by contrast, is articled but uncapitalised. For light, maturity and the
coronation of the capital, it has to wait until the fifth movement of
Ash-Wednesday. The dance of terms in this and the proceeding lines
seems very problematical: 'Signs are taken for wonders. "We would
see a sign!" ' Read one way, this poem consists of signs that signal
nothing except each other. Yet signs, however non-significant, do of their
nature seem to insist upon significance. The passage from St Matthew's
Gospel alluded to here throws some light:

> And I say unto you, that every idle word that men shall speak, they
> shall give account thereof in the day of judgement.

For by thy words thou shalt be justified, and by thy words thou
shalt be condemned.

Then certain of the scribes and Pharisees answered him, saying,
Master, we would see a sign from thee.

But he answered and said unto them, An evil and adulterous
generation seeketh after a sign; and there shall be no sign
given. . . . (XII 36–9)

Eliot regards himself as living among 'an evil and adulterous generation'. As a poet he lives by the word and is afraid to die by the word.
Moreover, the poet is peculiarly liable to mistake, as Mallarmé mistook,
his signs for wonders. (The figure of the 'familiar compound ghost' in
'Little Gidding' has been partly identified with Mallarmé; the ghost
talks of his lost speech, the word 'wonder' flickers at the beginning of
the sequence; but the connection is too frail to be pressed.)

By converting the word into the Word, even though the Word
remains a silent prisoner of words, Eliot seeks to be justified, even at
the risk of damnation; for, as the later poetry insists, damnation is at
least reality. 'And there shall be no sign given' amid a purely verbal
world is the real despair. This despair is savagely vented by 'The tiger
springs in the new year. Us he devours.' The syntax becomes suddenly
almost over-coherent, particularly in contrast to the syntactical dis-
embodiedness of

> In depraved May, dogwood and chestnut, flowering judas,
> To be eaten, to be divided, to be drunk
> Among whispers. . . .

a ghostly parody of the sacrament. The assertive 'Us' (typographically
assertive, indeed) of 'Us he devours' sounds, amid such whispers and
the sexual, historical and mental involutions that surround it, like a
genuine tiger's roar. This may not be the roar of outer reality, but it
shakes the inner walls of the poem's verbal system.

II

For Eliot, Symbolism is a poetic inheritance but also the manifestation
of a predicament. The inheritance is complicated by the way that
Symbolism is itself a formulated resistance against the debasements of
bourgeois democratic mass society. This alone would explain Eliot's
adoption of this tradition. As an American, he has really only two

traditions to draw on. One – that of Whitman – is prophetic celebration of the very forces that had disinherited him. The other – that of the underground resistance embodied in Poe – is too unauthoritative to offer much in its American version. (Kenner seems to be right, however, when he sees 'Gerontion' as completing certain tendencies in Poe.[10]) The English traditions were too weak and in any case necessarily irrelevant to Eliot's case.

Yet Symbolism offered no way of confronting and mediating the social reality that created it. Inherently, it transforms experience into verbal metaphysic, an autonomous universe as against the autonomisms of society.

We have to say, then, that Eliot remained inside the Symbolist tradition and yet profoundly subverted it by translating it first into doctrine and then out of doctrine back into experience. It is that partial circuit which is the real shape of Eliot's career. I say partial, because the translation back into experience is so tentatively achieved. One senses both the logic and the failure of the logic most clearly within the clumsy schematisms of *The Rock*:

> Out of the sea of sound the life of music,
> Out of the slimy mud of words, out of the sleet
> and hail of verbal imprecisions,
> Approximate thoughts and feelings, words that have
> taken the place of thoughts and feelings,
> There spring the perfect order of speech, and the
> beauty of incantation.
>
> LORD, shall we not bring these gifts to Your service? . . .
> For Man is joined spirit and body,
> And therefore must serve as spirit and body. . . .
> You must not deny the body.
>
> Now you shall see the Temple completed:
> After much striving, after many obstacles. . . .

Obviously Eliot had a great time being the Rock. Of course, he must not be judged by the shabby flatulence of such a passage. But it does represent in its own way a return to the world. So indeed do the three plays written after *The Family Reunion*. They are messages to the world, societal in their concerns if always manipulated by doctrine. It is a matter of critical taste in the end, but my judgment on these plays is that while obviously products of an ingenious and subtle mind, they creak too loudly with the effort of unbending. Their human materials are coerced phantoms, delay is substituted for development and intervention for surprise. No one convinced of their value will be affected by these *ex cathedra* assertions. It is another argument. Yet, if I am right, one has to see their failure of dramatic life as a revenge of life itself. After so much denial of social experience, when Eliot seeks to return to it, all it offers are the shadowy stereotypes of the fictional worlds of Dorothy L. Sayers and Noel Coward. You cannot spend a career firmly informing your fellow men that 'The desert is squeezed in the tube-train next to you' without finding the world, when you want to return to it, a pretty dry terrain.

But there is the marvellous recovery of *Four Quartets*, achieved partly through splitting doctrine down into a core of mystical experience on the one hand, a romantic celebration of the mystery of childhood on the other, and relating these, in a formal pattern, to the experience of history and some guarded personal confession through a structure of musical analogies. *Four Quartets* comes as close as possible to producing a complete coincidence of poetics and poetry. Despite this, the four poems seem to me more flawed than criticism generally allows. One is aware of a good deal of management in the scrambling of the major symbols in the last movement of the poem. 'The Dry Salvages' in particular is full of some very ponderous commentary. The interspersed lyrics have a slightly surprised and ragged air, as though they had been torn out of the prose of the poem rather than naturally condensing it. The assertions of mystical experience remain assertions rather than being proved by the poetry.

These failures are in fact the seams opened up between verbal behaviour, doctrine and experience. This certainly accounts for wonderful moments within the poetry, and the delicate, almost ballet-stepping movement of argument over syntax that we find in, for example, the first section of 'Burnt Norton'. This should not obscure the degree to which the whole poem departs from the movement of experience itself and fails to unify it except as a complex of verbal echoes and associations.

This is the crudest sketch, of course, of what a total view of Eliot's career might look like when viewed independently of the routine critical pieties. It leaves out of account almost everything in omitting discussion of *The Waste Land* and *Ash-Wednesday*. However it will

have to stand and be supplemented with an even more sketchy account
of the forces that gave this particular bent to Eliot's career.

Eliot was an American who was not so much an exile, or even an
expatriate, as one who voluntarily excluded himself from a whole phase
of civilisation. In departing from America, he departed out of the
twentieth century, moving back, through his own family, to the point
at which American experience departed from English Puritanism and
beyond that to the mythically unfissured Catholicism of pre-Reforma-
tion Europe embodied in the work of Dante. Doctrinally, it is true, he
paused at Laudean Anglicanism; one senses that temperamentally,
English Catholicism would have seemed in an English context too
eccentric and 'non-conformist'. Such a movement, once its initial
impulse is in motion, will proceed almost purely through literature and
erudition. England it had to be, because England was familiar enough
to connect on many levels with America while still exhibiting the
hierarchies and sanctioned mystifications of a class system.

But what gave the initial impetus? It is a commonplace to situate
Eliot in a line of disinherited Boston aristocrats whose familiar representatives include Henry Adams and Henry James. In *After Strange
Gods*, Eliot offers himself as a New Englander whose testimony to the
importance of the agrarian movement in the south carries particular
weight. But this inheritance was reinforced and complicated by the
position of the Eliot family in St Louis. Eliot's grandfather, William
Greenleaf Eliot, a Unitarian minister, had left Boston in the early
1830s to establish himself in a role that was to be central in the development of St Louis and the State of Missouri. W. G. Eliot was dead when
the poet was born; but his importance for Eliot can hardly be questioned.
Eliot's mother, herself a pleasant, minor devotional poetess, composed a
biography of her father-in-law whose dedication read: 'Written for my
children "Lest they forget." ' One can hardly suppose that they did.[11]

W. G. Eliot's career encapsulates the rise and fall of Unitarianism
as a moral and social agency. Its energies, channelled through Eliot's
grandfather, helped to make St Louis the once-great city of mid-
America. During the decades that followed the Civil War, St Louis was
at the height of its prosperity and reputation. In the St Louis circle it
boasted an advanced intellectual life – a blending of Unitarianism,
Hegelianism and German social-democracy – a university initiated by
W. G. Eliot himself and the most progressive educational system in the
country. W. G. Eliot's whole being, and with it that of his family, was

invested in the destiny of the city. If the Eliots were aristocrats, then they were the leaders of a practical aristocracy who had evaded the fate of the Adamses and their ilk. Unitarianism, in this instance, still ran in effective harness with that 'virtuous materialism' that de Tocqueville had noted in the eighteen thirties.

It is the case that the formation of Eliot's basic social attitudes coincided with a period of intense disillusionment with St Louis as the ascendent city of mid-America. Eight years before his birth the census of 1880 had brutally revealed that Chicago's population had outstripped St Louis's. (Hence, perhaps, the sneer in 'Chicago, Semite, Viennese'.) Worse still, the Steffans revelations of 1902 and 1904 (incorporated in Steffens's *Shame of Cities*, 1904) revealed St Louis as flagrantly boss-ridden and corrupt. A clean-up followed, in which the Eliots were apparently involved. The Steffans revelations spelt the end of socially committed, progressive Unitarianism; in an era of mass-emigration, it now appeared marginal and was about to turn, with Republicanism itself, finally conservative.

In St Louis, and presumably elsewhere, Boston Unitarianism had prolonged its vitality for over half a century after it had faded in Boston itself. Eliot's youth was passed in the shadow of its final decline. The Eliot clan experienced with greater immediacy and in an exposed manner the death of that practical aristocracy which had been for Henry Adams suddenly eroded decades before. But Adams at least had Boston. St Louis had been the all-American experiment which had failed. For Eliot, I suggest, America had failed with it. In the poet's remove through Harvard and to England he deliberately reversed the direction of the founding fathers.

The significance of Eliot's choosing to become a poet can only be surmised. The Eliots' traditional dedication to public service and the fact that Eliot's father was a businessman indicates that this choice involved radical disjunction. This may explain the hesitancies in Eliot's career, the stint in the bank and even the editorial and publishing work. But to become an American poet involved an even more radical choice between the underground life of Poe and the prophetic role of Whitman. Stevens managed to hollow out for himself a peculiarly plush bunker, but a bunker it was. Hart Crane elected both positions at once and perished between them. Memories of social dominance were presumably too active and recent for Eliot to become a true underground man. Whitman was the prophet of the very forces which had destroyed the pre-eminence of Eliot's class. The career of poetry seems, then, to have necessitated the remove to England and the abandonment of America. William Carlos Williams recognised as much when he recalled in his *Autobiography* the first impact of *The Waste Land*:

> Eliot had turned his back on the possibility of reviving my world. And being an accomplished craftsman, better skilled in some ways than I could ever hope to be, I had to watch him carry my world off with him, the fool, to the enemy. (p. 174)

This comment is brilliantly precise. Eliot did carry off not only Williams's but his own world with him, perhaps more of it than he realised. The defeat of his social values moved him out of America and led him to construct the counter-universe of symbolist aesthetic. Yet within the poetry that societal defeat remains fiercely alive. Apparently impersonal procedures are fuelled by some very raw emotions, the more violent for their being locked up inside a verbal prison.

The grandson is said to recapitulate the grandsire. Eliot himself has referred to his puritan temperament and joked in verse about his clerical features. Eliot, it seems, was able to return to the world of experience only by way of religion: yet, hardly through Protestantism and certainly not through Unitarianism, which was implicated in the virtuous materialism which had finally destroyed its social base. So much seems clear from a suggestive passage in *After Strange Gods*:

> I trust that I shall not be taken as speaking in a spirit of bigotry when I assert that the chief clue to the understanding of most contemporary Anglo-Saxon literature is the decay of Protestantism . . . and that individual writers can be understood and classified according to the type of Protestantism which surrounded their infancy, and the precise state of decay it had reached. (p. 39)

The statistics are tendentious while the classification of 'the precise state of decay' is clearly provocative. Such bad writing suggests the over-control of some very powerful feelings. In fact, the Protestantism that surrounded Eliot's infancy was, by all accounts, remarkable for its practical and intellectual vigour. The emotional charge intensifies when Eliot goes on to cite D. H. Lawrence:

> One might expect the unlovelier forms of this decline to be more deeply marked upon American authors than upon English, but there is no reason to generalise: nothing could be much drearier (so far as

4

one can judge from his own account) than the vague hymn-singing pietism which seems to have consoled the miseries of Lawrence's mother, and which does not seem to have provided her with any firm principles by which to scrutinise the conduct of her sons. (*ASG* p. 39)

This cannot be taken seriously as argument, though it has the force of genuine animus. The terms 'unlovelier' and 'drearier' have class connotations. Puritanism had ended by becoming 'low'; it was something of an accident that in some places and at some phases it was found to be the religion of a social *élite*. Shorn of its *élite* associations, it becomes for Eliot part of the general democratic vulgarity in which he wanted no part.

Eliot saw himself, and came to see his poetry, as essentially priestly. The poetry ends by moving between the confessional and the liturgical, uneasy where to settle. *Murder in the Cathedral* obviously gathers up all these tendencies; but Harry in *The Family Reunion* seems destined for the mission field, Celia in *The Cocktail Party* is actually martyred, while Colby in *The Confidential Clerk* is rather coyly permitted to remain artist as well as becoming priest:

> You'll be thinking of reading for orders.
> And you'll still have your music.

There is something very sad about the punctuation. This, then, is the final issue of the grandfilial recapitulation. It does not seem, as indeed it was not to prove, very fruitful. The real drama of Eliot's career lies in the initial repudiation of America and in the violence of repudiation that rocks and shatters the symbolist aesthetic that sought to contain it. Naturally, repudiation involves the reality that it excludes. We need now to read Eliot not so much for the truth he proffers as for the truth he cannot conceal. He is a seismograph from which, negatively, we can infer the force of the quake. And finally there remains the existential courage with which his absurd choices were assumed and then sustained.

It is, I believe, the violence of the initial motive that has launched Eliot into premature pre-eminence. He is so canonically installed in the landscape that we have lost the ability to imagine what it would look like without him. Practically, we may never have to, but it can be recommended as a wholesome spiritual exercise. Williams in the same passage of his *Autobiography* wrote:

Then out of the blue *The Dial* brought out *The Waste Land* and all our hilarity ended. It wiped out our world as if an atom bomb had been dropped upon it and our brave sallies into the unknown were turned to dust. (p. 174)

Williams's devastations may not have turned out to be as permanent as they then looked. All the American poet's dilemmas and predicaments were his too, despite Pound's view that Williams had 'not in his ancestral endocrines the arid curse of our nation'. But he elected to play it very patient and very cool, to look and to listen, to work and to love among the common noises and sights of his obdurately real city. It is too early to say, but it looks possible that at the end of the game the practising doctor and not the displaced priest may have held the winning card all along.

NOTES

1. *The Invisible Poet: T. S. Eliot* (1959) pp. 120 and 116.
2. *T. S. Eliot*, Writers and Critics series (1963) p. 28.
3. Grover Smith, *T. S. Eliot's Poetry and Plays: a study in sources and meaning* (1956) p. 60.
4. Ibid. p. 51.
5. Genesius Jones, *Approach to the Purpose: a study of the poetry of T. S. Eliot* (1964) p. 296.
6. Smith, *Eliot's Poetry and Plays*, p. 54.
7. *Locutions des Pierrots* XVI.
8. *Invisible Poet*, pp. 114–15.
9. *The Education of Henry Adams* (1918) p. 451. Cited in Smith, *Eliot's Poetry and Plays*, p. 62.
10. *Invisible Poet*, pp. 118–19.
11. Herbert Howarth, *Notes on Some Figures behind T. S. Eliot* (1965) p. 1.

The Waste Land

IAN HAMILTON

THERE can be few poems that have demanded and received as much exegetical piety as *The Waste Land*. It is the supreme puzzle poem and most of it has now been puzzled out. We have the allusions noted in the margins, we have flicked through *The Golden Bough* and *From Ritual to Romance* (comforted here by the information that Eliot's own copy has some uncut pages), we know – or think we know – what *shantih* means. So intimately has our experience of the poem been involved with the business of explication that it has become almost impossible for us to make the right kind of distinction between the words themselves, their actual resonance, and the scholarly murmurings that now encrust them. Lines tend to trigger off labyrinthine, half-remembered footnotes rather than evoke direct emotional responses. Or, to put it differently, and in spite of Eliot's own tag about poems communicating before they are understood, we have been encouraged to suspect that 'emotional responses' are somehow unreliable if they have not first been sieved through the meshes of our mugged-up learning.

Of course, Eliot wanted the poem to be difficult and no doubt conceived of its difficulty as an important aspect of its total meaning. There is the practical difficulty of the poem's wealth of cultural allusion and there is the deeper, but related difficulty of its general structure; a difficulty of detail and of plan. Dozens of attempts have been made to provide plausible solutions, to document the allusions, to guess at Eliot's structural intentions, and the assumption has invariably been that a poem which flourishes so many interesting signposts must know where it's going, that all the critic needs is to be more learned and ingenious in his interpretations than the next man. Eliot's knotty seriousness of aim has hardly been called in question – although when lines here and there have not fitted into the explicator's explication there have been nervous mumblings of discontent.

Explicator-in-chief and now the recognised guide to Eliot's aims is Grover Smith, author of *T. S. Eliot's Poetry and Plays: a study in sources and meaning* (1956) and, if only because thousands of students every year are likely to be poring over his interpretations, it might be worth glancing at a sample of his work. The bracing thing about Grover Smith is that he has so few doubts as to the absolute validity of his analyses. If Eliot hadn't written *The Waste Land*, Smith would surely have been able to invent – or at least paraphrase – it. For instance, he is able to tell us what we might not otherwise have been so sure of, that the opening lines of *The Waste Land* are spoken by Tiresias, and that in them 'Blind and spiritually embittered, Tiresias wrestles with buried emotions unwittingly revived' (p. 72). There is, of course, nothing in the actual lines to tell us who is talking; it is simply that Smith has dutifully taken Eliot's gnomic note to heart and has determined to base a whole edifice of paraphrase upon it. Thus, since 'What Tiresias *sees*, in fact, is the substance of the poem', it is Tiresias who remembers

> another springtime, in his youth, when warm days of the resur-rection season brought rain, the water of life, with sunlight, and he was beside the Starnbergersee near the city of Munich. A voice of a Lithuanian girl who recounted a childhood experience of terror, exhilaration, and freedom comes back to him. Against the double happiness of her memory and his, he must now set the present reality of the loveless, arid desert within him. He thinks of Ezekiel, the 'son of man'. . . . (pp. 72–3)

In his anxiety to forge these neat mimetic links, and to erect a shapely incongruity between past pleasures and present grumbles, Grover Smith blithely ignores what ought, at any rate, to be considered as a *possibility*: that the memories are *not* those of the protagonist himself (whether or not he is Tiresias) but are being recounted to him by someone else, someone he disapproves of. The evidence suggests someone middle-aged, female, of cosmopolitan background, someone neurotically clinging to remembered fragments of childhood experience, someone anxious to assert her aristocratic origins ('the archduke's,/My cousin's': an over-eager parenthesis), someone rather desperate and rather boring. One need look no further than, say, 'Portrait of a Lady' or, indeed, the opening section of 'The Fire Sermon' to find an echo of the exhausted, edgy intimacy of lines like

> In the mountains, there you feel free.
> I read, much of the night, and go south in the winter.

Far from setting a 'double happiness' against his present discontent, it seems likely that the woman's recollections, their fevered, disconnected style, are being invoked by the protagonist in illustration of 'the loveless arid desert' he goes on to contemplate:

> What are the roots that clutch, what branches grow
> Out of this stony rubbish?

Grover Smith glides over these crucial lines, presumably because they are in glaring contradiction of his chosen thesis. But one could wrangle like this for hours. All in all, *The Waste Land* has been a goldmine for explicatory critics and, while valuing many of the nuggets they've dug up, we are still left with the problem of what, as poetry, all the un-ravelled ingenuity adds up to. To what essential poetic purpose are the various quotations, echoes, innuendoes that keep forcing our attention back to other writers, other cultures? At what level of seriousness is the anthropological backcloth deployed? To what extent can the poem be said to justify the claims that have been glibly made for it as an illumin-ating, massively inclusive, revelation of what modern life is really like? Are the ideas really transmuted into poetry or are they just ideas? And are they good ideas? These might seem fairly primitive questions but they are nothing like as simple-minded as four decades of academic tinkering have encouraged us to think. Indeed, these are the only kinds of question now worth asking.

The poem's most obvious peculiarity, that it is packed with lines, or hints of lines, written by other poets, is now contentedly taken for granted. We know where the borrowings came from and can easily persuade ourselves that they are valuably relevant. We know, too, that it was one of Eliot's profoundest feelings that 'The people which ceases to care for its literary inheritance becomes barbaric' Literature has a crucial civilising function to perform and one of the ways in which it can sustain this function in a hostile age is simply to remind the present of the past, to insist that culture is continuous and that if people want a modern literature they can have it only at a price – the price, that is, of caring more about the literature they already have.

But telling people what they should have read is not the same as showing people what they might have felt. It is not simply that Eliot drops more names, more scraps of cultivation, more bits and pieces of odd learning than the poem really manages to make serious use of – though this could well be argued. It is more that at the source of Eliot's confident allusiveness there seems to be a very personal despair which he is more interested in disguising than exploring.

At one level, the poem masquerades as Eliot's *ABC of Reading*, his comfortably pedagogic account of what our literary inheritance most valuably consists of. But his desire to educate doesn't get the sharp edge it needs from his despondent recognition that his audience is not only ignorant about culture but indifferent to it. It is true that Eliot is only prepared to go so far to meet his reader's ignorance and is as concerned to condemn indifference as to cure it, but condemnation is different – colder, duller – than complaint. Alongside the keen anthologising there is a prim, aristocratic aloofness, a determination to keep up the barriers even as he pleads for their removal. Knowledge of some literary source is often a necessary condition of our grasping Eliot's point that such knowledge cannot generally be hoped for. Thus the poem is at once a display and a withholding of that possessed cultural wealth which, it is constantly implied, no one can afford to be without.

What one looks for in *The Waste Land* is something of Prufrock's wry self-knowledge. There is a hint of it in the notes, but not really in the poem itself. Prufrock is fastidious to the point of social paralysis, and it is the sorry interplay between his dreams and his responsibilities that makes his love song moving. In *The Waste Land* there is a similarly sorry interplay implied between poetry itself and its likely audience (between, almost, an overvaluing and an undervaluing of culture's powers) and there is something very Prufrockian in the situation of – shall we say? – a solemn, over-cultivated New Englander whose cultural experience of Europe is far deeper, he discovers, than that of most Europeans, a bookish sensitive adrift among the philistines, cherishing intensities and insights which he's convinced would cure a sickness whose chief symptom is indifference to its most effective remedy. 'I am not Prince Hamlet, nor was meant to be'; there is a similar despondent helplessness in the lines from *Hamlet* which end 'The Game of Chess' but here one is not so sure that Eliot is aware of it. Certainly, one implication of 'goodnight, sweet ladies, goodnight, goodnight' is that if either May or Lil were able to recognise the quotation, place it in context and scrutinise its implications, they would be making a first step towards some kind of spiritual recovery. We who do recognise it are allowed, rather facilely, to feel superior to those who don't. The essential difference between 'Prufrock' and *The Waste Land* is that the earlier poem has a distinct human personality at the centre of it whereas *The Waste Land* merely has a body of ideas and theories. The personality we have to guess at.

There is a sense, certainly, in which May and Lil themselves might be allowed to feel a twinge of lofty compassion for those who habitually observe life through a haze of literature, those who have read more than they are interested in experiencing. The judgements of *The Waste Land* are the judgements of a supremely literary sensibility and one can detect an unacknowledged pathos in the ready stock of futile, apt quotations, the lonely invocation of dead kindred spirits. There is this whole aspect to *The Waste Land*, and the glum pedantry of some of the explanatory notes might seem deliberately to draw our attention to it. But had Eliot been as ready, in the poem itself, to pass judgement on his own peculiar, crippling refinement as he is to condemn other people's peculiar, crippling vulgarity, we would have a different, more complex and affecting work than we are actually left with.

We might not, at any rate, have quite such a facile equation of cultural self-consciousness with spiritual prosperity. In 'Prufrock', Eliot captured a whole species of sophistication in the lines 'In the room the women come and go/Talking of Michelangelo'. The kind of dilletante cultivation, the smart, highbrow chattering that is evoked here expresses lives every bit as desolate and pitiable as those of the 'lonely men in shirt-sleeves, leaning out of windows'. Indeed, the lonely men seem, by contrast, rather worthy, contemplative creatures – had they been, say, quietly meditating on the work of Michelangelo they might even have come close to winning Eliot's approval. One of the troubles with *The Waste Land* is that its whole method tends to play into the hands of the chattering women rather than the lonely men, it tends to flatter those who know the cultural score and to despise those who don't.

It would be sheer simple-mindedness to pretend that being able to spot the allusions in *The Waste Land* guarantees anything about anybody. If one happens, though, to be an ill-read house-agent's clerk one will feel more sharply accused by 'The Fire Sermon' than if one is, say, an assistant professor of English literature. Whatever his sex life is like, the assistant professor will be on to that Goldsmith reference in an instant and will therefore feel himself to be in comfortable conspiracy with the learned poet. Not only that, but when Eliot writes:

> Burning burning burning burning
> O Lord Thou pluckest me out
> O Lord Thou pluckest
>
> burning

and solemnly informs us that 'The collocation of these two representatives of eastern and western asceticism, as the culmination of this part of the poem, is not an accident', the assistant professor might well be able to console himself that he is not the only well-read dabbler.

For Eliot, of course, a superb trinity of culture, sex and religion is humanity's most worthy goal and the sickness of modern civilisation is that the three impulses operate in isolation. In a sense, though, Eliot's treatment of them maintains their separateness; the urged collaboration is mostly in the realm of theory. For example, although his distaste for casual sexuality is emotionally based on a conviction that sexuality is sacred, that it is in some way involved with, or endorsed by, religious feeling, his actual treatment of it in the poem is informed predominantly by revulsion. There is an almost gloating intransigence in his characterisation of the squalidly unfeeling, the cheaply lustful possibilities of human conduct. Indeed, there is scarcely a human gesture in the poem which is accepted, or delighted in, or permitted any mysteries.

We are often told that the key moment occurs with the hyacinth girl episode in 'The Burial of the Dead'; and in a way it does, though the significance of this fragment has little to do with tracking down references to the Grail legend. What matters in these lines is that here is one human contact which *is* fertile of beauty and excitement. In human terms, however, it is clearly an expression of emotional failure; or, more precisely, of a failure to limit feeling to the human object that inspires it. It is not the girl's humanity that matters, so much as her power, being human, to release the speaker from his own humanity:

> I could not
> Speak, and my eyes failed, I was neither
> Living nor dead, and I knew nothing,
> Looking into the heart of light, the silence.

These are very beautiful lines, and they are central for what they tell us of Eliot's distaste not just for casual sex but, in *The Waste Land*, for all behaviour that is inescapably human. (It is significant that in 'The Game of Chess' the hyacinth garden experience is recalled in order to measure the widening distance between the speaker and his ageing Cleopatra; there is no way in which *she* can share in the fruits of the experience.) It is not so much that sex ought to be taken more seriously, nor that – if taken seriously – it can offer a route to certain worthy spiritual objectives. The poem's energy is not directed, as it might have been, towards a deepening exploration of the intuitions experienced with the hyacinth girl but concentrates rather on the less arduous business of symptomatising the condition of those whose lives are undisturbed, or unenriched, by such intuitions. Commentators on *The Waste Land* have talked approvingly of its telling condemnation of 'sex for the sake of sex'. But there is surely as much lacking in Eliot's view of sex as there is in the relationships he presents for our pitying scrutiny. If any one of these were less than extraordinarily dehumanised, we might have a more worrying antithesis to ponder. What really troubles, though, is that the poem aspires to some kind of final, representative wisdom on these matters while at the same time excluding whole areas of experience which are vital to such wisdom. The offered choice is of either a mystical 'transcending' of the body or what amounts to a pornographic debasing of it. This is surely not the choice we are faced with in reality.

No one in *The Waste Land* – though the poem is obsessed with sexual behaviour – 'A Game of Chess' and 'The Fire Sermon' are concerned with little else – actually enjoys sex. It is not even granted to be a pleasurable, exciting evil. It is seen throughout as a kind of enervated reflex, a set of tired, distracting compulsions whose servants would as soon be free. The typist home at tea-time, even though her sole function in the poem is as an erotic object, is scrupulously not permitted even the dimmest erotic appeal. Quite the opposite, in fact; her underwear repellantly comprises 'combinations', 'camisoles' and 'stays'. Her capitulation to the 'young man carbuncular' is 'bored', 'tired', 'indifferent' – this is no passionate folly, no excess of carnal zeal, no fun. The room is in tawdry disorder, the meal is eaten out of tins (why should *that* be so awful? and do we really have to think of it as 'a kind of Grail Repast which the Loathly Damsel has prepared' (Grover Smith, p. 88)), the boy friend has a bad complexion. The simple, nose-crinkling snobbishness that underlies 'One of the low on whom assurance sits/ As a silk hat on a Bradford millionaire' cannot envisage a typist and a clerk having any other kind of relationship. But then the most heroic seduction would stand little chance against the arms-length vocabulary which Eliot employs here: 'endeavours', 'encounters', 'requires', 'assaults', and so on – this is refrigerating language, prissily dignified, fastidiously embarrassed. In a similar way, 'By Richmond I raised my knees/ Supine on the floor of a narrow canoe' seems to take more than legitimate satisfaction in its isolation of crude practicalities; one feels that in whatever spirit those knees were raised it would have made little difference to the way Eliot looked at them. As we have seen, though, no one in *The Waste Land* raises her knees in any other spirit than that of glum complaisance.

The typist episode, of course, is viewed through the blind eyes of Tiresias, 'old man with wrinkled dugs'. Indeed, this is the only point in the poem where the protagonist is explicitly identified. And Eliot's own note, that Tiresias is 'the most important personage in the poem, uniting all the rest', obliges us to regard him with a special interest – though not with quite the interest that Grover Smith takes in him. It has often been assumed that the usefulness of Tiresias is that he can stand for a universal, omniscient view of things – and this is no doubt the way Eliot wanted him to be regarded. In allowing that, of course, we are granting Eliot the same omniscience. But Tiresias is, after all, a freak. Old, blind, bisexual. Why should we take these characteristics to denote unusual wisdom (especially about sex) when they can more easily be taken to confess unusual ignorance? Mainly because the whole impersonal posture of the poem painstakingly discourages us from viewing any of it as vulnerably self-expressive, from attempting to detect any subjective centres. By adopting Tiresias as a key *persona*, Eliot implicitly invites us to modify the poem's judgements, to see them in the perspective of Tiresias's disabilities – add to blindness and bisexuality an excessive literary sophistication and a vaguely transcendental horror of the flesh and we are hardly faced with ideal conditions for impersonal jurisdiction. But Eliot's technique in *The Waste Land* is to proffer personal disabilities as impersonal talents, to allow emotional weaknesses to masquerade as moral strengths. With the character of Tiresias, as with the hyacinth girl, the poem moves just so far towards touching on what looks like a very deep and personal alienation, a simple, experienced inability to settle for the kind of lives that other people settle for, but it quickly stiffens into anonymity and diagnosis. We are shown enough, however, of the poet's personality for us to view with some distrust the sophistry he masks it with.

Most studies of *The Waste Land* have taken it for granted that it is
written to a marvellously intricate plan, that Eliot is godlike in his
remote, clandestine machinations. Typical of much academic criticism
is the assumption that whatever *is* in a poem belongs in it, as by divine
law. Eliot's notes, the information that Pound sub-edited the poem, the
opinion of Eliot's close friend Conrad Aiken that the whole was made
up fairly arbitrarily of bits and pieces which had been around for years,
the tediously demonstrated fact that none of the interpretations is finally
more convincing than the others and that all have been obliged to
embrace suspect ingenuities; none of this has deterred the true disciple
from his conviction that the work is some kind of dense, elaborate
miracle of form which it is the poetry lover's humble, lengthy duty to
attempt to document. But the mysteries remain; just what is Phlebas
the Phoenician doing in the poem; had he not been there, would he have
been missed? Are Madame Sosostris's predictions really necessary?
Just what does go on in Magnus Martyr?

The clue that the Grail Legend is at the back of *The Waste Land* has
been a gift, of course, and its reverential treatment by the critics has
been sadly typical of their elementary reluctance to place any faith in
their own puzzlement. The Legend itself has a simple resonance – it
treats of sickness and health, aridity and fertility, life and death; it is
rich with punishments and rewards, with crucial talismans and cruel
tests. It also has the advantage for scholars of existing in many different
versions, and its symbolism is complicatedly diffused and multi-
significant. None the less, Eliot could hardly be said to have made its
dramas clearer or more lively to a modern reader. He does not select
any single version and he is even ready to express his ignorance of, say,
'the exact constitution of the Tarot pack' (though finding that the
Hanged Man 'fits his purpose' because it ties up in his mind with
Frazer's Hanged God and also with the hooded figure on the road to
Emmaus – the poem is altogether too fond of this kind of tenuous,
loosely evocative kind of coincidence). He makes no effort to redramatise
the legend in terms of its supposed modern significances, but rather
treats it as a repository of primitive lore from which he can arbitrarily
select some useful tokens. The legend itself, as a believed drama,
remains colourfully dead. Eliot takes a kind of antiquarian interest in
its symbolic paraphernalia, but its real attraction for him is less imaginative than theoretical; it represents a particular kind of spiritual
enterprise, one which could assimilate sexuality to sacred ends. The

chief failure is that Eliot employs the legend merely to signal the idea; by using fragments of its symbolism he is able to hold in the reader's mind a general notion of *some* ideal type of religio-sexual feeling. The legend thus supplies a bogus specificity to the criteria by which modern humans have been found guilty.

And this is typical of the poem's overall strategy. To put it crudely, we are given too much judgement and too little evidence. And what evidence we do get seems rigged. But why? Answering that question – or even allowing it to impinge – would surely have produced a richer and more humane text for the Grover Smiths to ponder.

Language and Belief in Eliot's Poetry

GRAHAM MARTIN

The poet has an image-forming power, and his 'philosophy' or body of 'ideas' is arrived at by studying the conceptual implications of the structure of his images . . . a much more valid critical procedure than talking about the poetry and the ideas of a poet as though they were separable things.

Eliot is clearly a major poet in this sense: he cannot be sampled in anthologies, and we understand each poem of his better for having read the others . . . his total work is an imaginative world, and must be approached through his imagery, as Yeats approached Shelley.[1]

NORTHROP FRYE introduces his discussion of Eliot's poetry with these statements of method and aim, and as alternatives to more abstract approaches they seem admirable. But the method is less satisfactory than the aim, and even the aim involves a damaging omission. For, as to method, poets make poems, not images. What the imagery in a completed poem means depends upon whether it is central or marginal, the vehicle for simple or complicated feelings, whether it is reinforced or modified or undercut by syntax, rhythm, tone and genre, all those aspects of the poem which are not imagery. Like so many analysts of imagery, Frye reads Eliot's as a code to be deciphered. But poems are not statements in disguise but 'virtual events';[2] and in Eliot's case the characteristic 'event' is the effort of a mind attempting to discover some order within a chaos of hopes, memories and fears, powerful hardly-to-be-admitted feelings, acute sensuous responses, and speculative abstractions. His imagery belongs within this context, contributes to this total effect. To take it on its own is to end up with a sophisticated abstraction.[3]

Frye's goal of apprehending Eliot's whole imaginative world also seems unexceptionable, but in practice he credits it with an inner homogeneity which the most cursory reading of *Collected Poems* seems certain to upset. In Eliot's poetic career, change has been the rule, and it is so much wasted energy to discuss the work's imaginative unity without accounting for this. Frye's actual project seems particularly pointless because he finds his synthesising clue in an inner spiritual allegory embodied in a pattern of recurring images, yet nowhere takes up the effect of Eliot's adoption of Christian belief. That this must radically have altered the character both of the imagery and the inner allegory – if that is what it is – should not need saying. So, in the first part of what follows, I have taken as central Eliot's conversion to Christianity, and examined what changes took place when certain recurrent images were, as it were, baptised. In the second part, I have pursued one finding of the first, to wit, that the language of Eliot's poems does not simply 'reflect' changes in his 'philosophy', but offers its own evidence about what that change amounted to. The poetry, in other words, does not express general changes whose nature we already understand, and require only to check off in particular poems, but crucial evidence which should guide us in our approach to other more explicit, but less informative material.

I

To begin with a really striking example of the difference between the pre- and post-1927 imagery: of the early poems, Frye remarks that 'the laughter is of the sinister and terrible kind that psychologists say the laughter in dreams is'.[4] Actually, the sinister aspect of Eliot's early humorists is usually mitigated by a grotesque and Quilp-like liveliness: Mr Apollinax laughing 'like an irresponsible fœtus', Sweeney 'letting his arms hang down to laugh', the gothic 'chuckle spread from ear to ear' in *The Waste Land*. Nevertheless, set beside any of them the following:

> Whispers and small laughter between leaves and hurrying feet
> Under sleep, where all the waters meet.
>
> ('Marina')

> Go, said the bird, for the leaves were full of children,
> Hidden excitedly, containing laughter.
>
> ('Burnt Norton')

Most obviously, something unamiable has been changed into something infectiously happy and innocent, and linked with this, partly its cause, is the fact that it is children and not adults who laugh. But there are less obvious differences. The early examples are specific, they name individuals, and deal in physical acts of laughing. The later examples imply or speak of a group, 'children', and of 'laughter', the concept. This introduces a significant vagueness. 'Small laughter' (laughter can't be measured) suggests both giggling or tittering, as well as the laughter of small people (linked with 'hurrying feet' we arrive at, or at least we approach, the notion of giggling children). Then, the phrases 'small laughter *between* leaves' and '*under* sleep' introduce a deeper mystery, arising from the way the prepositions of place promise a kind of concreteness, a location for the laughter, which the nouns at once withdraw. What kind of laughter *is* laughed between leaves? between leaves and feet? or under sleep? Where *is* 'where all the waters meet'? As with Keats's unheard melodies, we can only guess, whereas *The Waste Land*'s 'chuckle spread from ear to ear' can be both seen and heard in a normal way (though there is a certain oddness in a chuckle *spreading*: a grin would do this, but a chuckle is heard, not seen). So in 'Burnt Norton'. Faced with 'the leaves were full of children', we probably begin by thinking of trees or shrubbery with children hiding in them. But the poet says 'leaves', insisting upon a fusion of children and leaves, upon therefore an image which has the effect of disembodying both its constituents. And the syntax reinforces this. 'Containing laughter' attaches both to children and leaves, and the first connection withdraws the laughter from us, while the second makes it myterious. Laughter *contained* by children, that is, is both suppressed laughter, and laughter which will only become actual when we go away ('Go, said the bird, *for* the leaves, etc.' – here maybe is the reason for the causal connective); and laughter contained *in* leaves is certainly not less mysterious than laughter that takes place between them. We may summarise these contrasts as follows: the early poems thrust upon the reader mocking individual guffaws, from vividly presented, unamiable, perhaps ill-willing adults; but the later poems suggest, off-stage, a happy generalised laughter that we can only imagine, perhaps coming from children, but also without physical location. And one further point may be added. If the post-1927 laughter is innocent, the earlier examples combine with their mockery and aggression something not unlike innocence. Certainly a laughing fœtus is nightmarish enough but the keyword is 'irresponsible':

Mr Apollinax doesn't care what anybody thinks of him, because he inhabits a world of superior vitality, threatening perhaps but not evil. Sweeney, too, in the poem in question, is more gross than terrible, chiefly the victim of other people's malice. The point to make, then, is not that this 'proto-innocence' anticipates the later quality, which can therefore be abstracted as the residual meaning of 'laughter', but that the early examples involve much complexity of feeling, a blend of high spirits, harsh mockery, malevolence, indifference, while the later cases are simpler, more homogeneous, easier to identify (though harder to describe). From an initially complex weave of meaning one or two strands have been teased out, and in examining the development of the image, this simplifying process must be added to those already noted: changes of attitude, a kind of disembodying, and withdrawing of the experience, a greater generality, and creation of mystery.

Some of these processes can be seen at work in the development of the images of 'desert' and 'water'. Thus, if we compare *The Waste Land* with *Ash-Wednesday*, we find desert-like scenes in the first, but the term itself only appears in the second: 'the quiet of the desert' where the bones lie scattered (II), and 'the last desert between the last blue rocks/The desert in the garden the garden in the desert/Of drouth' (V). These instances are quite straightforward. Scriptural references identify the deserts as metaphors for the spiritual life, and the poem's protagonist actively seeks the condition they imply. But *The Waste Land* is another story. First of all, the relevant scenes are infertile places in a poem partly lamenting a vanished fertility, so that one meaning for 'deserts' is their undesirability. Then again, each scene is realised in enough detail to convey intricate and distinct states of feeling. The 'red rock' scene in 'The Burial of the Dead' comes closest to *Ash-Wednesday*, but the lesson it teaches ('*fear* in a handful of dust') is very unlike the ascetic calm welcomed by the scattered bones of the later poem. In 'The Fire Sermon' the tone is so elegiac that the 'brown land' (in any case, a winter scene rather than a desert) can fairly be read as emblem of a *regretted* sexual and cultural failure implying the desirability of renewal, rather than its negation in the world of the spirit. And in 'What the Thunder Said', while the journey through barren mountains amounts to a search for spirituality, its culmination in the ruined chapel is only one of several indications that it has taken the wrong direction. *The Waste Land* 'deserts', then – it is no surprise to discover – are elusive, self-contradictory places, linked to shifting ambiguities of feeling which the poem leaves unresolved. And, however we may sense common areas of experience within each example, or subterranean links with later poems, even to speak of a single 'desert' image does a good deal of violence to the richness of individual effect. A more elaborate example of the point is provided by the 'water' imagery. In Frye's analysis, 'water' is mainly connected with innocence through its association with Phlebas, Floret and 'La Figlia Che Piange'.[5] As a cleansing agent, it is opposed to the dirtying effects of experience, and sometimes suggests the spiritual cleansing of Christian baptism. But this is too simple to account for the whole range of examples. Eliot constantly uses water's primary association with life and growth (the opening of *The Waste Land* is the obvious case); and also, in direct contrast, its destructive power. Phlebas in 'Death by Water' may be cleansed, but he is also destroyed ('picked his bones in whispers'), and for a baptism into the nascent spirituality of 'What the Thunder said' his epitaph is remarkably elegiac. Then there are the Mesdames Porter who 'wash their feet in soda water'. In this symbolic baptism, or its sacrilegious parody? simple folly, or a prank to entertain the gallant Sweeney? a cleansing or an abortive cleansing? Or, more explicitly, there is *Ash-Wednesday* IV, where Mary 'made strong the fountains and made fresh the springs', i.e. restored natural water from its post-lapsarian depravity to more cleanly life. Earlier poems offer even more complex cases. For Prufrock, the waves spell romance, successful love, freedom, danger (mermaids drown their lovers), and his aggressive–regressive dream of being a 'pair of ragged claws' links the sea with freedom and self-assertion. In 'Mr Apollinax', the sea again offers a lively, though dehumanising, alternative to social triviality. In fact, with such examples to hand, it is probably muddling to talk about a 'water' image as such. Both 'Gerontion' and *Ash-Wednesday* associate the sea with a dangerous freedom and beauty, while in 'Marina', it is more tenuously linked with the desirable, having to be crossed if Pericles is to reach the pine-scented islands. In 'The Dry Salvages', the sea has come to represent danger without beauty, and a meaningless freedom, and it may even be argued that it takes over the meaning of an earlier and separate image in Eliot's poetic universe: purposeless barren wandering of crowds in 'a ring', or over a 'plain'. It is also worth noticing that *Four Quartets* uses rivers as well as seas, and the distinction is shadowily present in *The Waste Land*. As with 'desert', then, 'water' is too abstract an account of the images actually appearing in the poems. 'Sea' and 'river' are almost distinct complexes, 'sea' itself undergoes radical change, and some of the pure 'water' images yield no simple or consistent meaning.

Further examination of the 'sea' images shows a more revealing change, which can be linked with the general trend towards simpler emotional texture: a 'splitting' effect in which the image keeps some of its early meanings, but sheds others which then re-emerge in a different imagistic form. Thus, 'Prufrock' ends with a complex image (mermaid, sea, song, his wished-for journey) representing an intricate emotional blend, desire for a freer life, for beauty and love, fear of risk, despair and unheroic resignation. 'Marina' also uses the sea as part of a complex image, but shifts its attractive qualities elsewhere: the sea is merely the *condition* of the sea-voyage whose goal is represented in the islands, the birdsong and the pinetrees. Even its latent dangerousness has been diluted since what may wreck the boat is not 'water lapping the bow', but the 'granite islands'. And further, though Prufrock's mermaids have disappeared, some of their qualities remain. The haunting birdsong through the fog embodies their seductive aspect; the relation between Pericles and his daughter fulfils and transforms their promise of love; and, where Prufrock, resigning the heroic role, does not expect the mermaids to sing to him, Pericles hears the birdsong and speaks himself to his daughter. It will be recalled also that 'Marina' provided the first example of innocent 'laughter', and that earlier examples involved something unattractive, even threatening. It is this innocent laughter which conveys the essence of Pericles' experience in discovering his daughter, and in doing so he leaves behind him aspects of existence which resemble the discarded meanings of 'laughter'.

> Those who sharpen the tooth of the dog, meaning
> Death
> Those who glitter with the glory of the hummingbird, meaning
> Death
> Those who sit in the stye of contentment, meaning
> Death
> Those who suffer the ecstasy of the animals, meaning
> Death
>
> Are become unsubstantial, reduced by a wind,
> A breath of pine, and the woodsong fog
> By this grace dissolved in place

The potential malevolence and cruelty of the early 'laughter' images (no longer qualified by 'proto-innocence') are here explicitly named as qualities to be exorcised. The original complex of meanings in 'laughter' has split into mutually antagonistic parts, one as it were responsible for the nullification of the other. This throws some light on the withdrawn, disembodied character of the later 'laughter' image. As readers, we experience this laughter as happening off-stage, drawing us away from the identifiable experiences which the poem directly reports – whispers, footsteps, etc. In fact, of course, this off-stage laughter takes place within the poem. The verbal structure indicates how little its mystery has to do with a vaguely conceived realm of fantasy such as Yeats invokes when his fairies cry, 'Come away, O human child!/To the waters and the wild/With a faery, hand in hand'. Yet it does involve a contrast with the normal, the familiar, both because of the terms that define it ('small laughter', etc.), and because the poem juxtaposes with it kinds of experience, more readily accessible or very much less attractive. In 'Marina', that is, we first meet a polarisation of experience not difficult to relate to Eliot's post-1927 view of life,[6] and the 'splitting' of the image can be viewed as a rhetorical structure which dramatises the actual process of polarisation. The movement of the poem is *from* the world of Death, *towards* the world of innocent mysterious laughter. There is also a related difference in poetic idiom, helping to distinguish positive from negative image complexes. Contrast the delicate intertwining suggestiveness of 'Whispers and small laughter between leaves and hurrying feet', and the first group of lines quoted above. There, the effects are not achieved imagistically. None of the images makes its own point, and the meaning of all four lines beginning 'Those who . . .' is only unified by a weighty liturgical rhythm, crude alliteration and rhetorical typography. And perhaps this is necessary, since the individual images carry little conviction. Thus, of the first, why 'dog' ? why not wolf or hyena, or any fierce, traditionally contemptible carnivore ? And of the second, do hummingbirds really 'glitter' ? apart from its alliterative usefulness, is not 'glitter' to be explained by its link with the moral tone of 'all that glitters is not gold' ? The tone of these lines, too, is noteworthy – moralistic, denunciatory[7] and strangely out of key with the occasion, an intimate colloquy between father and newly recovered daughter. The general point will be returned to. For the moment, it is enough to stress the connection both with the emergence of the post-1927 poetry, and the general change in the imagery already outlined.

One more example of these changes, the last especially, may be mentioned: the eye. In 'Prufrock' we find 'eyes that fix you in a formulated phrase', eyes that impose identity and lack compassion, cruel amused eyes. Prufrock fears them but also they attract him. He is also bored by them. 'Rhapsody on a Windy Night' shows a simpler but related situation. The prostitute's come-hitherish eye 'twists like a crooked pin', the child's eye is empty, the peering eyes in the street are crab-like, mechanically aggressive and acquisitive. Over all this dismal scene, the moon winks its feeble complicity, and the lamp tells the poet to 'regard' it resignedly: it contains all of life, and there is nothing else to see. In *The Waste Land*, the image is more complicated. The speaker's sensory eye fails at the vision of the 'heart of light'; he thinks of Phlebas' eyes, now pearls, and tells us that his own are 'lidless'. Finally, the blind Tiresias 'sees . . . the substance of the poem', the clerk/typist seduction, which leads on to the vision of Magnus Martyr. (Music is linked with this experience, a connection repeated in 'Marina' where the birdsong is heard through fog, which renders the eye useless: hence the likelihood of shipwreck on the 'granite islands'.) In sum, the physical eye is damaged or useless, while a 'spiritual' eye comes to replace it associated with a nascent polarisation of experience into desirable if uncertainly grasped spirituality, and the dismal sensuality of the life rendered in 'A Game of Chess' and 'The Fire Sermon'. 'The Hollow Men' makes this more explicit. Eyes belong only to the spiritual world, 'death's other Kingdom', while the poet in 'death's dream kingdom' fears to meet them, and is 'sightless'. The contrast with 'Prufrock' is instructive. As in that poem, the eyes in 'The Hollow Men' still judge, still confer identity, but they are no longer cruel; and though the poet first shrinks from their glance, he ends by accepting it as the only source of reality. In this development, the 'splitting' effect is clear. In the first examples, the eye image amalgamates feelings of attraction, boredom and fear in the person it observes, and in itself conveys a cold indifference to what it sees, a kind of predatoriness, even deliberate cruelty, but also a kind of truth. But as the sensory eye fails, and the spiritual eye is born, its unattractive qualities fall away, finding other embodiment. What Tiresias sees (though blind) no longer holds for him the half-attraction which complicated the revulsion of the protagonist in 'Rhapsody' and 'Prufrock' (nor does what he sees see him); and, where the latter are drawn into and partly constituted by what they see, Tiresias is detached and draws away from the scene. Even though he foresuffers what occurs, his identity is not compromised:

he can go on to hear the music of the 'fishmen' and wonder at the beauty of St Magnus Martyr. In 'The Hollow Men', the potentially beautiful eyes are so different from what they might see in 'death's dream kingdom' that they can only make symbolical appearances in it. Thus, what the judging eye now sees, an empty value-less existence, is the condition which it once partly symbolised; and what the poet-protagonist now is, empty, valueless, is what he once surveyed with his physical eye. This division culminates in *Coriolan*. The spectators see nothing that matters and end by asking for 'light', while the hero, whose physical eye is indifferent to what it lights on, is spiritually absorbed in a private vision.

> O hidden under the dove's wing, hidden in the turtle's breast,
> Under the palmtree at noon, under the running water
> At the still point of the turning world. O hidden.

It is interesting to see that, as in 'Marina', this inner vision requires an imagistic language quite distinct from the one used to convey the world perceived by the physical eye: the flat, unmusical tone of the spectator, the bald list of things that he sees, whose meaning he cannot understand. The 'splitting' of the image, whereby all value accrues to the spiritualised eye, and the attributes it once represented – indifference and aggression – have been given separate expression, is once more associated with the development of a new poetic idiom.

Images, of course, only tell a certain amount, and often to establish that we have had to move away from the image into the poem that uses it. But there is one persistent element in Eliot's poetry, which takes imagistic form but also exists as an idea in the consciousness of the poem's *persona*, or is actually central to the poem's structure. This element is the journey. Eliot's poems are full of taken and untaken journeys, along streets, down rivers, over mountains, across seas. The lover in the 'Portrait' reports visits to his mistress, one an unwilling climbing of stairs, and ends with thoughts of going abroad. Prufrock invites to a journey through streets, imagines his return from the dead, and ends standing on a beach looking over water which he would like to but will not cross. Gerontion's mind is full of vain journeys, real and metaphorical, and he thinks of death as a journey into nothingness. *The Waste Land* refers for its main structure to a legendary quest, and its protagonist is constantly on the move, both in his various manifestations (Tiresias, Phlebas, Mr Eugenides, the 'young man carbuncular',

Elizabeth and Leicester, the wronged girl), and in his own concluding tramp over the mountains to the ruined chapel. 'Journey of the Magi' concentrates on the journey taken (instead of the traditional moment of arrival), and 'Marina' presupposes a nearly concluded sea-voyage. *Ash-Wednesday* III recounts a journey upstairs, and VI exhorts to a final move away from the sea into the desert. *Four Quartets* adopts the endless journey as the appropriate metaphor for human life, whether on the sea, up a river, or along 'the edge of a grimpen'.

In Christian thought, the journey is of course a venerable image, and Auden has given a cogent explanation for this which throws light on the difference between Eliot's later and earlier use of journeys.

> The Christian concept of time as a divine creation, to be accepted, and not, as in Platonic and Stoic philosophy, to be ignored, made the journey or pilgrimage a natural symbol for the spiritual life.[8]

Up to and including *The Waste Land*, journeys are merely dreamt of, or vainly aspired towards, or, if taken, disappointing, of uncertain value. But in 'Marina' the journey is fruitful, though dangerous, and the speaker has to build his own boat to make it. (Contrast Prufrock's dreams and the hypothetical boating-trip at the end of *The Waste Land*.) Again, in *Ash-Wednesday* III, the speaker struggles purposefully upstairs past a vision of renounced, innocent sexuality (innocent because renounced), instead of – like Prufrock – hesitantly towards a corrupt sexuality which bores and frightens him. 'Journey of the Magi' reveals a significant element in the later 'journey' image. The speaker recognises that his expedition was valuable, indeed revolutionary, but also very puzzling: 'were we led all that way for/ Birth or Death?' This is the character of journeys in *Four Quartets*. Though they provide the crucial definition of reality, their goal is absolutely mysterious, their meaning can never be properly understood: 'I can only say, *there* we have been: but I cannot say where.' The clearest case is the exhortation to the old men in 'East Coker' that they should continue journeying, not as in 'Marina' across seas dotted with islands, but into the desolate emptiness of the deepest ocean. We meet here an important aspect of Eliot's use of the traditional 'journey' image. Unlike Dante's or Langland's or Bunyan's quests, with their definite stages and clearly envisaged goals, Eliot's journeys are open-ended. In the traditional use, the journey is also a progress. The traveller learns something at each stage, which helps to qualify him for his ultimate destination. Eliot's journeys are relatively formless, a mere trudging on. While their goal is certain enough in a general way, the traveller, being human, always misconceives it, and the experience of journeying is not valuable in any terms that he can make use of. Time may be a 'divine creation', but human life in time, the experience which the journey symbolises, is not finally meaningful in human terms. The difference between this and meaning-lessness is perhaps narrower than Eliot understood. Nevertheless, in comparing the early and late instances, it is a crucial difference: instead of being dreamed about, or proving illusory, the journeys are now taken, and are valued. The vague promise imagined by Prufrock becomes the unknowable certainty pursued by the traveller in *Four Quartets*. 'Marina' is the earliest poem to show what this involves: the necessary access of purpose (the boat), and the taking of the risk (the granite that will wreck the boat), which Prufrock both lacks and fears. This is the point at which to mention again the change in the handling of the sea imagery which first occurs in 'Marina'. The 'splitting' effect which makes the sea merely a medium, and which projects its original promise of freedom and romance onto the island images, takes place when the journey across the sea *is* undertaken. The 'laughter' image becomes innocent when purged of certain malevolent possibilities, and this purging actually occurs in the poem. So with the 'eye' image. The transcendence of the 'eye', the complete submission to its definition of identity, takes place in 'The Hollow Men', who have become resigned to their journey into 'death's other Kingdom'. We may interpret, then, that the *valuable* journey, with what it suggests of choice and will-power, of 'resolution and independence', is intimately related to the general development of the imagery, to the processes of simplification, clarifica-tion of emotional texture, growing generality, to the polarisation of experience and the withdrawal from the reader of its most significant level.

This last process, in fact, can be seen indirectly at work in the way the journey image itself develops, if we examine not its structural aspect, but the texture, the actual scenery of the journey. The new decisiveness that takes the traveller onto the sea, towards islands, deep into the ocean, also takes him away from streets, houses, cities and people. The transition begins in *The Waste Land* where the observer-protagonist starts in the city (Madame Sosostris, the crowd on London Bridge, the church clock, the boudoir, the pub), moves to the river bank, then downriver ('O city city') towards the sea that drowns Phlebas, and on whose shore the Fisher King finally sits meditating. (Meanwhile various centres of Western civilisation have been declared unreal, and London Bridge is falling down.) The germ of this movement lies in the early poems' use of the sea as a means of *imagined* escape from the stifling triviality of metropolitan culture, and in *Coriolan* we see its full flowering. This poem's action, part political, part military, takes place *in* a city, and a city crowd watches it, but both are relegated to the sphere of illusion, while reality is imaged as an oasis, a pastoral retreat accessible only to the hero's spiritual insight. Finally, in *Four Quartets*, cityscapes have become phantasmal, mere occasions for something more real to declare itself. The authentic scenery is found in gardens, the country, the villages of the titles of each poem, the journeys on marsh, cliff and sea; and the traveller is always on his own, 'a spirit unappeased and peregrine'.

Finally, one image may be mentioned which appears less extensively: fire. Fire appears for the first time in *The Waste Land*, where, as the opposite of water in its creative aspect, it destroys life altogether, offering the only remedy for the spiritless sexuality recorded in 'The Fire Sermon'. But, unlike the imagery already discussed, 'fire' is hardly an image at all: all we have is the word 'burning', and allusions to St Augustine, Buddha and Dante. We only need to recall the wealth of 'water' imagery to underline how slightly the purgatorial experience (to which these allusions point) has actually been realised in the poem. What is more remarkable, however, is the failure of subsequent poems to make any use of 'fire' imagery. *Ash-Wednesday* and 'Marina' deal in some thoroughness with the spiritual aspirations tentatively essayed in *The Waste Land*, and we have already seen how this is reflected in changes in the 'desert' image. But there is no fuller realisation of the 'fire' image. We have, in fact, to wait for *Four Quartets* for other examples – those in 'East Coker' I and II, and more significantly in 'Little Gidding' II and IV. Yet even here the 'fire' image is not very fully realised. The lyric in IV depends heavily on its allusion to Hercules' poisoned shirt, and while in II the associated scenes of destruction offer a fuller presentation the image itself remains significantly indirect. The closest approach occurs in 'that refining fire/Where you must move in measure, like a dancer', yet even here the 'fire' image, already general and qualified in the direction of allegory by 'refining', merges at once into that of the 'dance'. Almost any passage describing the 'timeless moment' offers from the poem itself a criterion which underlines the

relative imaginative weakness, while for the purgatorial experience
Yeats's well-known lines from 'Byzantium' provide a direct comparison.

> Flames that no faggot feeds, nor steel has lit,
> Nor storm disturbs, flames begotten of flame,
> Where blood-begotten spirits come
> And all complexities of fury leave,
> Dying into a dance,
> An agony of trance,
> An agony of flame that cannot singe a sleeve.

'Fire', that is, is an image which Eliot's development into a religious
poet gives birth to, but one which never achieves more than a shadowy
realisation in actual poems. The purgatorial transformation for which
it stands remains a state which the poem's protagonist aspires to, rather
than an experience which has been conveyed to us as a 'virtual event'.
Drawing conclusions from this is a delicate matter, but crucial to a full
discussion of Eliot's Christian poetry. Something of its significance
may be clearer if we contrast it with the later 'laughter' image. We have
seen that this articulates an *experience* of spiritual aspiration. The image
structure directs the reader's imagination to something 'off-stage', seen
but not seen, heard but not heard. In contrast, the 'fire' image is not
more than a signpost, a gesture towards a received idea, a generalised
notion rather than a specific structure of feeling.

II

I have tried so far to establish two points. One is that a general account
of Eliot's imagery will not yield evidence for the simple concept of
imaginative unity proposed by Frye. On the contrary, the images
change so radically that interpreting their recurrence is a complex
matter, and may even lead one to question whether 'recurrence' is a
particularly fruitful way of discussing them. The second point is that
these changes in imagery intimately connect with the difference between
Eliot's view of life before and after 1927. They therefore provide an
approach to the poetry which respects its integrity and does not involve
a reduction of the poems to 'expressions of the thought'. I want now
to look more closely at the significance of the fact that the onset of
Eliot's post-1927 religious phase generates a new kind of poetic idiom,
as well as changes in the imagery.

'Marina' and *Coriolan* both employ a contrast between two poetic idioms to assert a conviction which dominates Eliot's post-1927 work, namely, that experience divides into two mutually antagonistic kinds, which we can call the secular and the spiritual. 'Marina' makes the point very directly: aspiring towards the 'new life', Eliot-Pericles denounces the old world of 'Death' in markedly didactic tones. *Coriolan* treats the antagonism more subtly: in the distance between the hero and the spectator-reporter of events in 'Triumphal March', and in the juxtaposition in both poems of Coriolanus' inward glimpse of 'the still point of the turning world' with his public role. *Coriolan* also resembles 'Marina' in conveying its glimpses of the spiritual world in an imagistic mode, but in place of the earlier poem's liturgical–moralistic summary of the realm of Death *Coriolan* shows the emergence of a satirical-documentary manner which figures prominently in Eliot's later poetry (dramatic and other).

> (And Easter Day, we didn't get to the country,
> So we took young Cyril to church. And they rang a bell
> And he said right out loud, *crumpets*.)
>   Don't throw away that sausage.
> It'll come in handy. He's artful. Please, will you
> Give us a light?
>
> Arthur Edward Cyril Parker is appointed telephone operator
> At a salary of one pound ten a week rising by annual
>   increments of five shillings
> To two pounds ten a week; with a bonus of thirty shillings
>   at Christmas
> And one week's leave a year. . . .
> A commission is appointed
> For Public Works, chiefly the question of rebuilding the
>   fortifications.
> A commission is appointed
> To confer with a Volscian commission
> About perpetual peace: the fletchers and javelin-makers
>   and smiths
> Have appointed a joint committee to protest against
>   the reduction of orders.

The substance of this idiom – the absurd military procession, the paraphernalia of a modern holiday, Cyril's promotion prospects and Coriolanus' political manœuvrings – are secular activities which lead

only to 'Dust/Dust/Dust of dust', and in that phrase the moralistic
denunciatory manner of 'Marina' still sounds with traditional force
But the accumulation of detail, the dry satirical tone, adds something
else. The secular world is not only death-like, it is worthless, empty
vain. Value and permanence are only to be found in the half-glimpsed
vision of the 'still point' with its associated imagery of dove, turtle
breast, tree and running water, all pastoral detail making its own sharp
contrast with the world of man and the city. It is this contrast that gives
rise to the un-Shakespearean pathos of Eliot's Coriolanus. Living in
both worlds, and sensing their antagonism, he appears incapable of
even a *vain* struggle to reconcile them. He reports his secular trans-
actions with weary indifference to the outcome, and an unchallengeable
certainty that they can never reflect ultimate values. None the less,
this meaningless world is sufficiently powerful to change the Nietzschean
conqueror of 'Triumphal March' into the broken figure who soliloquises
in 'Difficulties of a Statesman'. The secular world thus may be said to
be worthless, yet real enough to enforce its variously trivial demands
And it is this combination of qualities that accounts for the 'secular'
idiom, for its combination of bleak assent and ironical deflation.

Another point about this idiom emerges in the contrast between
'Prufrock' and Coriolan. In both poems, the protagonist vainly struggles
to escape from a meaningless and threatening world, but in Coriolan
this world exists independently of the protagonist's perceptions and
attitudes.[9] It is a mistake even to suggest any clear demarcation between
Prufrock and *his* world. To say that he is 'in conflict with it' is not
more than a rough-and-ready indication of one of the several conflicts
that make up his consciousness. Everything in Prufrock's world is
invested with a blend of attraction-revulsion – the seen and heard, the
desired, the remembered, the dreamt-of. It is impossible to distinguish
'inner' and 'outer' worlds, to separate the valued aspiration from the
valueless actuality that obstructs its fulfilment. Beside Prufrock's,
Coriolanus' experience is certainly more straightforward, and clearer,
but is also duller, more ordinary in its juxtaposition of what is valued
and desired from what is perceived and put up with. Thus, the dual
poetic idiom which renders this separation corresponds not simply to
a new moral decisiveness (as 'Marina' suggests), but also to a new
epistemology. Coriolan assumes for the first time in Eliot's poetic
universe the existence of an external world existing independently of
the perceiving subject, not solely to be defined in terms of his

ympathies and revulsions. (For Coriolanus, that is, mermaids – had he hought of them – would be imaginary, where Arthur Edward Cyril ²arker would be real.) But the idiom which affirms the objective reality ▸f this secular world also robs it of value. It is there, but it has no neaning, and between it and the realm of the meaningful no negotiation eems possible. This is the paradox at the centre of Eliot's Christian ›oetry, of the poetic languages he developed to express his new con- victions.

J. Hillis Miller's recent discussion of Eliot's work in *Poets of Reality* pp. 131–89) throws a good deal of light on this development. Starting rom Eliot's doctoral dissertation on F. H. Bradley, Miller argues for a lirect reflection in the early poetry of the philosophical position outlined n the thesis. His account is too detailed to be usefully summarised here, ›ut it will be enough for my purposes to indicate that the sensibility ιt work in the early poetry is genuinely illuminated by the attention which Miller has given to *Knowledge and Experience*. Thus, for example, ˨liot states that

> consciousness . . . is reducible to relations between objects, and objects we shall find to be reducible to relations between different states of consciousness; and neither point of view is more nearly ultimate than the other.[10]

The dream-like character of the world observed in Eliot's early poetry, ts interpenetration of subjective and objective viewpoints, the sense in which all perceptions are suffused in the emotions of the perceiving ιubject, and have no reality apart from these emotions derives from this nterdependence of 'consciousness' and 'objects'. So also does our lifficulty in deciding whether, in 'Prufrock' and 'Gerontion', we are :onfronted with anything truly resembling a person, or whether the ιames are not simply passive containers for an associational flux of ›erceptions, memories and desires. Eliot shared with Bradley the view :hat the 'self' as well as the 'world' is a construction from Immediate Experience, and that while all 'selves' give valid partial truths, none ξives ultimate truth. To any one 'self', other 'selves' appear as con-ιtructions, opaque as any other 'object'. There are no categories, ›bjective to all 'selves', which would make communication possible. Experience, therefore, is always private, and the 'self' always locked within its valid but limited conceptions. But Miller's summary of the :elationship between *Knowledge and Experience* and the earlier poetry

requires a drastic qualification. 'The pathos of the human condition'
he remarks, 'is man's inescapable exclusion from absolute experienc
. . . [and] this pathos . . . is the chief subject matter of Eliot's earl
poetry.'[11] But the 'pathos' of the poetry is precisely the quality whicl
cannot be derived from the philosophy of the thesis. *Knowledge an*
Experience offers an analysis of reality which makes feelings of exclusior
'from absolute experience' pointless. Eliot specifically categorise
the longing for the Absolute as delusive (*KE* p. 202), so tha
feeling 'pathos' about it is exactly on a level with feeling exalted, o
depressed, or stoical, or hysterical, or defiant, or as having no feeling
on the subject at all. There is only one way in which the pathos of th
poems can be said to derive from the epistemology of *Knowledge an*
Experience, and that is in its entertainment of concepts which directl
conflict with it.[12] Far from 'reflecting' its philosophy, the poetry shoul
be seen as exploring some of its consequences, even as a dim intuitior
that a different account of knowledge must be sought. Contrast, fo
example, the different meanings of 'time' in the philosophy and in th
poems. Philosophically, to both Eliot and Bradley, 'time' is not ar
objective category but a mental construction out of Immediate Experi
ence, and not more ultimate than the unstable 'self' which creates it.[1]
But, to Prufrock at least, 'time' offers a much more traditional problem
Like the 'Bo-um!' in the Marabar Caves, 'time' makes nonsense of th
difference between murder and creation, decision and indecision, tea
parties and love-affairs. 'Time' for Prufrock leads towards death ('
grow old, I grow old'), and in this sense is felt to stand over agains
the subjective flux of his desires and anxieties. Here is one source o
Prufrock's melancholy, and another is his inability to communicate t
someone else the seriousness of feeling which 'time' brings into play
Prufrock's sense of exclusion and resulting 'pathos' derives from thi
situation rather than from epistemological anxiety, and his very fain
struggles to surmount it imply a kind of communication with other
which *Knowledge and Experience* actually rules out. In a quite specifi
sense, that is, the poem invokes concepts which the philosophy excludes

Miller's general thesis is nevertheless very helpful in its account o
the relation between Eliot's early and late poetry. He shows that Elio
moves away from the Bradleyan idealism which dominates his though
up to about 1923 to the position of a Christian for whom a transcenden
God has established the objectivity of time, space and the natura
world. *Ash-Wednesday* registers this in the first poem when it announce

that 'time is always time/And place is always and only place/And what
is actual is actual only for one time/And only for one place'; and in the
last with its nostalgic affirmation of the independent beauty of the
natural world. We may add to this that it is Eliot's first poem organised
around an identifiable personality, an experiencing 'I' who records a
world separate from himself, and from his symbolising habits, a 'self'
with a *moral* reality denied to Eliot's earlier *personae*. Again, Miller
points out that history in *Four Quartets* constitutes a pattern only
understood by God, but in which man lives. Though in 'timeless
moments' he can have direct experience of God, time and history
remain the medium for his flawed and limited existence.[14] Thus, we may
contrast with the 'familiar compound ghost' of 'Little Gidding', whose
time and culture remain distinct from the poet's, the voices echoing
through *The Waste Land*. Here there is no real past to be set over
against a real present but the co-existence in the protagonist's consciousness of notations from different realms of his experience (reading,
observing, feeling) wholly susceptible to any pattern he cares to impose.
It is from this 'wilderness of mirrors' that the Christian poet has
escaped.

The connection between this philosophical progress and the development of the double poetic idiom should now be clear. The post-1927
manner records the discovery of an objective world separated from the
self who experiences it, and by a self equally real, no longer a mere
'consciousness . . . reducible to relations between objects'. The new
reality of the self means that moral experience now becomes possible,
or, to put it in Eliot's imagistic terms, real journeys to worth-while
goals can now be undertaken, and as we have seen this late form of the
journey image emerges at the same time as the genesis of the two poetic
idioms. So, also, the moral polarisation of experience into the spiritual
and the secular occurs in the poems registering the epistemological
change. But these poetic changes are not simply 'reflections' of Eliot's
philosophical development: they also tell us what that was. It has been
shown that the poetic idiom affirming the existence of an objective
world also robs it of value. Miller's argument ends with the claim that
'the idea of the Incarnation' dominates the religious poetry, and leads to
an affirmation both of 'the human body and the world's body'.[15] But
the language of the poems fails to support him. It attributes to experience an ineradicable poverty, explicit when the subject-matter is human,
but spreading even to nature, which withers into allegory or, at most,

a neutral framework for the illusionary life of mankind. The point cannot be developed in detail here, though *Coriolan* offers some evidence for it. The fact remains that *Four Quartets* offers nothing so confident as an affirmation of the 'human body and the world's body', and the language of its most original passages (the handling of the 'timeless moments') reveals a highly qualified assent to the new non-Bradleyan epistemology. That the poem communicates the *effort* towards such an affirmation may be conceded – easily: Eliot would be the first to agree that poetry is not a product of the will (*UPUC* pp. 144–5). This is the qualification which should guide our view of his final phase.

NOTES

1. Northrop Frye, *T. S. Eliot*, Writers and Critics series (1963) pp. 48–9. The phrase 'conceptual implications of the structure of his images' suggests an examination of metaphorical structure on the lines of W. K. Wimsatt's 'The Structure of Romantic Nature Imagery' (*The Verbal Icon* (1954) pp. 103–16, where Romantic assumptions about reason, feeling and the mind's relation to external nature are located within a particular metaphorical type. Such an analysis of Eliot's metaphors would be valuable, but Frye's actual discussion takes a more familiar form. He disengages a pattern of metaphors, and interprets it not by revealing its 'conceptual implications', but by linking it with traditional associations.

2. 'Virtual events are the basic abstraction of literature, by means of which the illusion of life is made and sustained and given specific, articulate forms' (Susanne K. Langer, *Feeling and Form* (1953) p. 217).

3. F. O. Matthiessen's comment on Eliot's imagery is still worth quoting '. . . in considering Eliot's relatively narrow stock of repeated images, it is gradually discovered that what enables them to embrace a wider range of experience than would at first appear is the fact that *they release markedly different shades of feeling according to their contexts*' (*The Achievement of T. S. Eliot* (1935) p. 136. My italics).

4. Frye, *Eliot*, p. 48.

5. Ibid. p. 61.

6. 'What I do wish to affirm is that the whole of modern literature is corrupted by what I call Secularism, that it is simply unaware of, simply cannot understand the meaning of, the primacy of the supernatural over the natural life: of something which I assume to be [a Christian's] primary concern.' ('Religion and Literature', in *SE* p. 398. The essay first appeared in 1935.)

It is not much of a simplification of Eliot's religious poetry and plays to say that their main concern is to assert the 'primacy of the supernatural over the natural life'.

7. It is a tone increasingly evident in Eliot's subsequent work, both in prose and poetry.

8. W. H. Auden, *The Enchafèd Flood* (1950) p. 8 n.

9. It may be argued that 'protagonist' is too energetic a term for the shadow Prufrock, but the symbolist view that there is *no* person in the poem fails to account for Prufrock's sense of having an identity, for the poem's forward movement.

10. *KE* pp. 29–30; cited in J. Hillis Miller, *Poets of Reality* (1966) p. 133.

11. Miller, *Poets of Reality*, p. 136.

12. Susanne Langer is again very much to the point on this whole issue: '. . . all poetry is a creation of illusory events, even when it looks like a statement of opinions, philosophical or political or aesthetic. The occurrence of a thought is an event in a thinker's personal history, and has as distinct a qualitative character as an adventure, a sight, or a human contact; it is not a proposition but the entertainment of one, which necessarily involves vital tensions, feelings, the imminence of other thoughts, and the echoes of past thinking.' (*Feeling and Form*, p. 219.)

13. Miller, *Poets of Reality*, pp. 139–40.

14. Ibid. 183–5.

15. Loc. cit.

Four Quartets: the structure in relation to the themes

HAROLD F. BROOKS

I

Four Quartets, to my mind, stands in little need of revaluation: there
is nothing revolutionary about the perspective in which I shall try to
show it. It remains the crown of Eliot's achievement in religious poetry
a religious poem, moreover, as I shall suggest before we leave it, that
speaks not only to orthodox Christians, but to many who (like myself
do not share their creed.

Even in my immediate concern with the themes and structure of the
work, my aim is not to reinterpret, but to clarify. For greater detail
there are previous expositors to consult. The structural pattern of
changes in form and style, for example, has been closely analysed by
Professor Helen Gardner, in studies no serious reader of the Quartets
would ignore.[1] If I believe that many such readers can still be given
further help, it is because I have met a good many (particularly among
teachers and the taught) who could annotate the poem almost line by
line, but who confess they have no sufficient understanding of the
whole. Their need is for a broad view, in which the major themes, and
the general structure movement by movement and Quartet by Quartet
will be plainly visible, with very little else. So that is the perspective I
am adopting.

Four Quartets is an exploration of spiritual experience: the experience
of God (or, if we prefer it, of timeless reality, timeless value) in time.
Near the end of 'The Dry Salvages' Eliot writes of

> The point of intersection of the timeless
> With time. . . .[2]

It is on a momentary instance of this intersection that the first movement of the first Quartet, 'Burnt Norton', is centred: the light-created
vision of water and the lotos (symbol of godhead) in the dry pool. The
moment of grace, filled with a sense of the divine or of an intense,
profound meaning in life, is in fact the first of several leading concepts
(or better, formulations of experience) which are essential to the poem.
Such moments or brief hours of revelation have had a high place in
literature, not least in modern literature. From influential ancestors of
the moderns, one may cite the best-known lines in 'Bishop Blougram's
Apology', beginning

> Just when we are safest, there's a sunset-touch . . .

and Blake's

> There is a Moment in each Day that Satan cannot find,
> Nor can his Watch Fiends find it; but the Industrious find
> This Moment & it multiply & when it once is found
> It renovates every Moment of the Day if rightly placed.[3]

Among the moderns themselves, Proust takes as the starting-point, in
his recovery of time past and gone, his moments of involuntary memory.
Virginia Woolf, and Joyce in *Portrait of the Artist*, take what Joyce
calls 'epiphanies' as their climaxes. Even more germane to Eliot's
'moment', no doubt, is Dante's *stupor* on seeing Beatrice. For descriptions, as literal as possible, of brief unanticipated occurrences of
illumination in the course of ordinary life, one could turn to William
James's *The Varieties of Religious Experience*;[4] instead, I will quote
Yeats:

> My fiftieth year had come and gone,
> I sat, a solitary man,
> In a crowded London shop,
> An open book and empty cup
> On the marble table-top.
>
> While on the shop and street I gazed
> My body of a sudden blazed;
> And twenty minutes more or less
> It seemed, so great my happiness,
> That I was blessèd and could bless.[5]

As in Dante, Blake and Proust, so in *Four Quartets* the moment is a
starting-point, a datum; for Eliot, an experience granted from time to

time by the divine grace. It belongs, characteristically, to 'our first world', either in childhood, or (as the Beatricean experience) in first love, or whenever that innocent eye for the Creation returns. It belongs, that is, to the Earthly Paradise or the rose garden (the Virgin, as she by whom, through grace, God enters our world, is Rosa Mystica, Hortus Conclusus, Fons Signatus). Finally, in the last movement of the last Quartet, the poet calls it 'the moment of the rose'.

He uses, in *Four Quartets*, and has previously used, various metaphors and symbols for this intermittent experience of reality in time, 'the one veritable transitory power' of *Ash-Wednesday*. In 'Burnt Norton' there is the central symbol noted already, the chance effect of sunlight which fills the dry pool as if with water, prompting the vision of the lotos and of the 'heart of light', the absolute at the opposite pole from Conrad's *Heart of Darkness*. Here, too, is the most recurrent of all Eliot's images for the 'moment': the laughter of unseen children in the leaves, which figures in *The Family Reunion*,[6] 'Marina', and the 'Ode' never reprinted from *Ara Vos Prec* (1920), and reappears in 'East Coker' and 'Little Gidding'. Subsequent to 'Burnt Norton', the moment is recalled in each Quartet: in 'East Coker' (III):

> Whisper of running streams, and winter lightning.
> The wild thyme unseen and the wild strawberry,
> The laughter in the garden;

in 'The Dry Salvages' (v):

> . . . the unattended
> Moment, the moment in and out of time,
> The distraction fit, lost in a shaft of sunlight,
> The wild thyme unseen, or the winter lightning
> Or the waterfall, or music heard so deeply
> That it is not heard at all, but you are the music
> While the music lasts;

and in 'Little Gidding' (v):

> The voice of the hidden waterfall
> And the children in the apple-tree.

But the moment, in which we experience the meaning of existence, gives place to other experience, in which we feel that existence has no meaning. The moment happens to us: it is a manifestation of God's grace in his created universe. Yet it *is* momentary; and it is mysterious:

a manifestation in a universe of time and mortality; a manifestation in itself elusive and baffling. 'Human kind cannot bear very much reality': no long, or plain manifestation of it. And the manifestation is withdrawn (*Ash-Wednesday* begins after such a withdrawal). By contrast, we are left the more aware of our experience of what is not reality; aware of it as devoid of meaning. This denial of meaning is a second among the concepts essential to *Four Quartets*. The phase of negation, of desolation which supervenes upon the moment, is again expressed in various metaphors and symbols; the wind and twittering in 'Burnt Norton' (III):

> Men and bits of paper, whirled by the cold wind. . . .
> Not here the darkness, in this twittering world;

the unsafe, uncanny path in 'East Coker' (II):

> . . . not only in the middle of the way
> But all the way, in a dark wood, in a bramble,
> On the edge of a grimpen, where is no secure foothold,
> And menaced by monsters, fancy lights,
> Risking enchantment;

in the 'Dry Salvages' (II, IV), 'the soundless wailing', the 'withering of autumn flowers', 'the drifting wreckage', 'the bone on the beach', 'the sea's lips', 'the dark throat which will not reject them'; and in 'Little Gidding (II, V) the images which objectify the deaths of air, earth, water and fire, and the mortal destinations of men, in the sea's throat, at the stake or the block, or beneath an illegible stone.

The negation, the denial of meaning, is an ambiguous experience. In the order of nature, for the natural man, it is simply one of the extremes between which he oscillates. His experiences of the meaning and value of existence are merely balanced by his opposite experiences of existence as unmeaning and valueless. There is no question of any process taking place, or progress being made. But for the spiritual man, starting upon the way of the soul, the descent into negation may, paradoxically, be the second step of his ascent. The first step having been accorded him by the moment of revelation, the second depends on acceptance of the opposite experience; on embracing its testimony that in the order of nature existence is indeed meaningless. This is to set out on the Way of Negation known to mystics as one of the two Ways of approach to the reality they seek, and leading, to use the same terms

as St John of the Cross, through the Dark Night of the Senses and later
the Dark Night of the Soul.[7] It is characterised in 'Burnt Norton' (III):

> Internal darkness, deprivation
> And destitution of all property,
> Desiccation of the world of sense,
> Evacuation of the world of fancy,
> Inoperancy of the world of spirit.

Acceptance of it is expressed (for example) in 'East Coker' (III),

> I said to my soul, be still, and let the dark come upon you
> Which shall be the darkness of God.

That acceptance is the necessary condition of the next step: the
transformation, with the reconciliation of opposites, which is a third
essential concept of the poem. The moment, now, proves to be

> Not lost, but requiring, pointing to the agony
> Of death and birth.

so that

> . . . the darkness shall be the light, and the stillness the dancing.

Transformation is imaged in 'East Coker' (III) by the progressive series
of three similes: the stage-blackout, for the scene to be changed: the
Underground train, stopped between stations; and the mind under
ether, 'conscious but conscious of nothing'. In the 'Dry Salvages' (III)
the second simile is recalled by the metaphors of the train between start
and terminus, and the liner in her sea passage. In the corresponding
movement of 'Little Gidding', the poet exemplifies the reconciliation
of opposites by the reconciliation, in historical perspective, and to the
eye of faith and charity (represented by Juliana of Norwich) between
Charles I, Anglican royal martyr, and the apologist of his execution,
John Milton, Puritan and republican hero.

Transformation leads to communion with the divine reality; a sense
of God in the world, not confined to the moment, nor dependent on its
coming and going. This concept is easily recognised in each Quartet
since it is embodied in a lyric devoted to one of the sacred persons: the
Creator, the Redeemer, the Holy Spirit, or the Virgin. Finally, following
upon transformation and communion, comes integration, forming a

new whole, indicated in 'Burnt Norton' (II) as what the moment, while
it lasts, is an experience of:

> . . . both a new world
> And the old made explicit, understood
> In the completion of its partial ecstasy,
> The resolution of its partial horror.

The integration, glimpsed here, is fully realised in the last five lines of
the Quartets.

Having looked at these successive aspects of spiritual experience in
the poem, we are ready to relate its structure to its theme. The structure
springs from the progressive exploration of the experience, from movement to movement in the single Quartet, and from each Quartet to the
next.

The progressive pattern is the same in each Quartet, except for an
occasional modification appropriate to the particular subject of the
Quartet in question.[8] All the first movements are movements of proposition. They indicate the order of time in which the experience is met
with – except in 'Little Gidding', where, since the experience is outside
time, the first movement tells us so. The propositions also introduce
the experience, as it is met with in the course of living. While in 'Burnt
Norton' (I) we have the momentary glimpse of reality, 'East Coker' (I)
presents the pattern of the lifetime and succession of lifetimes. The
pattern is focused in the dance, which reconciles opposites and fosters
transformation, for it unites the opposite sexes, and, as a fertility-rite,
brings life out of death every season and in each generation.

All the second movements are movements of negation, antithetical to
the first. They stress what appears to deny the meaning; they pose the
problem which arises if we try to accept the revelation in the preceding
movement. 'East Coker' (II) shows how the merely natural flowering
of one generation after another, and the merely natural growth to
maturity and age fail to provide an adequate meaning for men's lives.
Appropriately, 'Burnt Norton' (II) differs somewhat from the rest,
confronting us not with a denial of meaning, but with its baffling,
paradoxical nature. The sheer revelation in the rose-garden thus finds
its true antithesis; it is seen to be the revelation of a paradox, still
mysterious.

The third movements are turning-points; movements of acceptance,
reconciliation, and transformation. They begin with a restatement of

the negative experience, which is then accepted as a springboard to something beyond it. In 'Burnt Norton' (III) it is accepted that the meaning cannot be discovered among the time-ridden faces,

> Distracted from distraction by distraction. . . .
> Not here the darkness, in this twittering world.

But this recognition directs the search elsewhere: 'Descend lower', into

> . . . that which is not world,
> Internal darkness.

Reconciliation and transformation are most fully depicted in 'East Coker (III) in the three similes and the other lines quoted from it earlier to describe these processes. In 'Burnt Norton' (III), transformation is hardly yet under way; but the lapse from the worlds of sense, fancy, and spirit is sought as the beginning of it:

> This is the one way, and the other
> Is the same.

The fourth movements are lyrics of communion between the divine and the temporal: their subject is the sense of the divine in its continual presence – as in *Ash-Wednesday* (v) – whether individually one is having a particular revelation of it or not. In 'Burnt Norton' the Creator, immanent in the Creation, is the theme. While we hope uncertainly for a sign of his presence in nature, and when, in the flash of the kingfisher, the sign has come and gone, the divine immanence is 'still'

> At the still point of the turning world.

In 'East Coker', the theme is the Redeemer incarnate as a man, suffering for the sin of men in his healing Passion;[9] in 'Little Gidding', the Holy Spirit descending in Pentecostal flame, challenging men with the fire of justice (Hell), the fire of purification (Purgatory), and the lambent fire of union in Paradise.* 'The Dry Salvages' concerns the most inhuman aspects of man's place in time, and so the sense of God that is reached in it is as it were indirect, reached by the agony of supplication that ascends to the Virgin as Intercessor. Instead of the divine

---

* One might be aware, here, only of the choice between the first two: the third becomes plain at the very end of the Quartet, when 'the tongues of flame are in-folded'. But even here, I believe, it is already present, since the choice is also between the burning preoccupations of the world and the self (so designated in the Buddha's and Eliot's Fire Sermons), and the love of God, which includes the ultimate union in Paradisal fire. (Cf. Gardner, *Art of T. S. Eliot*, p. 182.)

reality immanent in or descending into the temporal world, she represents it as we ascend to it out of our distress.

The fifth movements are movements of integration, in three phases.

First in these movements of integration, the truth attained is applied to the poet and to us, so that he in his vocation, and we in ours, are seen to have a place in the experience depicted. Thus in 'East Coker', of which the subject is the human lifetime as the span in which value can be created, Eliot considers what a poet like himself, in his single lifetime, can do of value: namely, achieve a succession of ends – poems or styles – that prove to demand his starting afresh,

> Because one has only learnt to get the better of words
> For the thing one no longer has to say, or the way in which
> One is no longer disposed to say it.

He cannot surpass the best already achieved; he can only try to re-achieve it for his own time. It is the same for us, in the vocation of our personal lives:

> There is only the fight to recover what has been lost
> And found and lost again and again: and now, under conditions
> That seem unpropitious. But perhaps neither gain nor loss.
> For us, there is only the trying. The rest is not our business.

Next comes recapitulation: earlier themes, particularly from the preceding Quartet when there is one, are recalled and integrated into new wholes, since at the stage now attained they can be seen differently. For example, whereas in 'Burnt Norton' the moment seems by its intensity to leave the rest of time meaningless by comparison, in 'East Coker' (v) we see that this is not so. For that intensity can now be matched by the intensity of the experience explored in 'East Coker' (I–IV):

> Not the intense moment
> Isolated, with no before and after,
> But a lifetime burning in every moment
> And not the lifetime of one man only. . . .

In 'The Dry Salvages' (v), we are reminded that 'the unattended Moment' remains, for most of us, the spiritual datum. But now, when the incarnation of God in life has been recognised in 'East Coker', the moments can be taken as witnessing to that: they are 'Hints followed by guesses', and

The hint half guessed, the gift half understood, is Incarnation.

They are now related, besides, to the process by which they are made to bear fruit in an ordinary lifetime, and in the history of the race, which last is a topic of 'The Dry Salvages' itself; the process of 'prayer, observance, discipline, thought and action'.

In each of the first three Quartets, the problem proper to it is then resolved in a way that is adequate on its own plane. But the resolution raises further problems in the orders of experience treated in subsequent Quartets. Only at the end of 'Little Gidding' is the resolution a full one. These resolutions, however, can best be reviewed when we have looked at the course of the poem from Quartet to Quartet.

II

In each Quartet the theme of one movement is dominant, or at most the themes of two. Revelation in temporal experience, the subject of all the first movements, is dominant in 'Burnt Norton'; in 'East Coker', transformation with regeneration, the subject of the third movements; and in 'The Dry Salvages' negation, with acceptance, the subject of the second movements and the beginnings of the third. In 'Little Gidding', the dominant themes are communion, the subject of the fourth movements, and integration, the subject of the fifth. The correspondence is not mechanical. With five movements and four Quartets it could not be one-to-one, but in addition the order of the themes differs; negation and transformation characterise the second and third movements, but the third and second Quartets.

The Quartets represent four ways of experiencing reality, or God, in three different kinds of time, and in a timeless dimension. The time in 'Burnt Norton' is the moment which comes and goes, revealing reality to everyone, whether or not he recognises it or makes it a point of departure. Because this is a grace in the natural order of things, the regent of 'Burnt Norton' is the Creator. Personal and social time is the subject of 'East Coker'; the lifetime of a man, and the succession of men's lifetimes. The due pattern of life, from birth to death, with newborn generations to succeed the old, carries meaning and value. But in the natural order, death denies as much as birth affirms, and the generations face extinction. The liberating possibility is the opportunity a man has, during his life span, of a transformation that will allow the divine to incarnate itself, as far as may be, in his life. Hence the regent in 'East Coker' is God the Son, who was incarnate, perfectly, in Jesus; who, in his Incarnation and Passion, bridged the gulf between the human and the divine natures; and who, in the span of his single lifetime and in his death, transformed, by becoming a member of it, the whole series of human lifetimes and deaths.

Time in 'The Dry Salvages' is that of universal history and objective nature; not only the history of the race or even the biological history of life on earth, but also the astronomical history of the cosmos, before those histories, and after them. It is inhuman: 'Time not our time'. Here the divine is experienced through its opposite: our experience of time and the temporal universe of nature as alien, even hostile. A man's unconscious and biological life with its heritage of imperfectly tamed instincts, its cargo of original sin ('the bite in the apple'), is part of this impersonal, alien, objective nature: 'The River is within us'.* Taking us with it whether we like it or not, it runs through the course of our life, and empties itself, at death, into 'the Sea' of objective nature and cosmic time, the inhuman environment that was always 'all about us'. Judged as part of this kind of time, the moment and the lifetime appear to lose their value, to be negated. In the personal life, we appear to be caught between the impersonal biological life within us, and the indifferent Hardeian universe outside, both of them slaves of 'Time not our time', one bringing the man to an end, and the other the race of men. And we encounter calamities, other people's even more than our own, which nothing in the time-process can reconcile us to, agonies (one of them most intimate for Eliot himself) that no future, achieved by Creative Evolution, could make up for. In the time-process, therefore, the 'partial horror' of life is just as real as its 'partial ecstasy': the moments of 'sudden illumination' do not mitigate 'the moments of agony', which 'are likewise permanent/With such permanence as time has'. How can such an experience of the time-process be also an experience of divine reality?

First, it reveals the process as something in itself valueless, the destroyer not the creator of value: and that is a vision of reality – a negative vision. Like the Bell on the Trois Sauvages, it warns us to go

---

* Symbolising also the biological, instinctive factors in the life and death of communities and civilisations. Cf. Gardner, *Art of T. S. Eliot*, pp. 170 f.

elsewhere. We are not to cling to the dimension of past and future in our search for value. By the calamitous annunciation of what God's will is for us in the time-process, we are brought where we must look beyond. All that is left, is the 'hardly, barely Prayable prayer of the one Annunciation': 'Be it unto me according to Thy word'; accepting, like the Mater Dolorosa, our role, however calamitous by temporal standards, if only it enables God to incarnate himself, so far as may be, in us, and so to exist in the world's history. For in the second place, although the time-process is meaningless in itself, and certainly cannot lend value *to* human life, from another angle we can see that it is not meaningless but borrows meaning and value *from* human life. Krishna's admonition to Arjuna instructs him in detachment from the time-process, and the creation within it of what has real worth; the means being disinterested, right action now, not dictated by the past, or calculated to bring this or that profit in the future. History, then, has its significance in the opportunity it offers for the lifetime of disinterested, right action. On the temporal plane, it is because we have gone on trying to live such a life that we may hope to have done our part to enrich temporal existence by a contribution 'not too far from the yew-tree', not too remote from the true, central, human tradition; a contribution that will help to maintain the meaning of history, and so to keep it a 'significant soil' for other fertile lives. But (to the orthodox Christian) the great event which gave history meaning and focus was the advent of Christ; and therefore the human person who did most for that meaning was Mary his mother.

Hence the regent of 'The Dry Salvages' is the Virgin. And this is not only because she enabled godhead to enter the time-process, but because it was by her assent to the Annunciation that she did so: a calamitous annunciation by all temporal reckoning, since it brought her the role of Mater Dolorosa, in which her suffering was of the kind singled out by the poet as the most unbluntable: 'the agony of others, nearly experienced,/Involving ourselves'; for her, the agony of her Son. As humble companions in this kind of suffering, she has the wives and daughters of the lost fishermen; fishermen who are ourselves on our ultimately fatal time-voyage. She is patron of such voyages: Stella Maris, through whom intercession is made when *in extremis* on the sea, or when (to translate the metaphor), the inhumanities of cosmic, or historic, or biological time leave no resource but prayer – become, indeed, a call to prayer. For then (resembling the Eumenides in *The Family Reunion*)[10] what were formerly Trois Sauvages may be recognised as Dry Salvages; their 'tolling bell' a 'perpetual angelus'.

The negative revelation of 'The Dry Salvages' shows that in the time-process the divine is experienced, at best, as incarnate in an alien environment. It drives, or warns, or summons us, therefore, if we would conceive a fuller communion or ultimate union, to seek it in another, a timeless dimension. And this is the theme of 'Little Gidding'. At Little Gidding, 'prayer has been valid'; there, 'to apprehend

> The point of intersection of the timeless
> With time . . .

was the vocation of Nicholas Ferrar and his saintly community. That in this Quartet the experience of reality is outside time is made clear at once. The season is 'Midwinter Spring', no season of the four in the temporal sequence: 'This is the spring time', says the poet, 'But not in time's covenant.' And what we are in search of is 'the unimaginable Zero summer'. The seeker learns 'to care and not to care' (for non-attachment is not indifference) and to recognise his vocation in the challenge from the Trinity of regents in the fourth movements of 'Burnt Norton', 'East Coker', and 'Little Gidding' itself: 'the drawing of this Love and the voice of this Calling' (FQ p. 43). The regent of 'Little Gidding' is that person of the Trinity to whom, since Pentecost, is committed divine communication with men, and whose tongues are fire. From this theme of communication and communion, the Quartet mounts finally to contemplate the ultimate eternal union with God of all that is redeemable.

Quartet by Quartet, the resolutions with which they conclude have become more complete, and the unresolved discords have diminished. 'Burnt Norton', having asserted the eternal value of the moment, leaves all other time apparently absurd. By the end of 'East Coker', the poem can affirm the value of a significant human life and of the significant tradition of human lives. But, when those who live them would seek 'a further union, a deeper communion', it can only be by passing through the experience and recognition of the alien universe which surrounds them. 'The Dry Salvages' concludes in the assurance that what would otherwise be the mere flux of existence in cosmic time, is given sense by the moment's hint of a divine incarnation in the temporal universe, and by the lifetime's opportunity for endeavour at disinter-ested, right action. Yet it raises the question whether this bringing of sense into history and the cosmic process is man's sufficient end. For it is shown as a second-best beside the saint's full apprehending of 'the point of intersection of the timeless with time'. That point is the gateway, in time, to the timeless dimension of 'Little Gidding'. It is also the moment of 'Burnt Norton'. But there, and even in the two Quartets that followed, 'We had the experience but missed the meaning' (*FQ* p. 28) – at least the full meaning. Now the nearer

> . . . approach to the meaning restores the experience
> In a different form. . . .

In its timeless order of Charity, the final Quartet recapitulates, completes and unites the values discovered by the others in their three different kinds of time. The end of the poem fulfils the beginning. From the moment in and out of time, it has arrived, beyond time, at the Beatific Vision.

The images for that Vision are conceived after Dante's, but are prefaced by words of a wider charity than he possessed. The words are Dame Juliana's, expressing her faith that ultimately all souls shall be saved and all temporal experience redeemed.[11] The Beatific Vision comprehends the divine nature and the union with it of the Church Triumphant. In the *Paradiso*, the Triune Godhead is imaged as a mathematical figure.* For Dante and his age, mathematical symbolism carried an emotional and spiritual charge it hardly has today. Instead of Dante's fiery circles, Eliot invokes 'the crowned knot of fire': a knot of three strands, so tied that they cannot fray; an endless knot of burning love.[12] His image of the ultimate union reflects two phases of Dante's vision. The first is when the Church Triumphant ('all that of us hath won return up yonder') displays itself in the form of a white rose with the angels like bees descending into it, 'their faces all of living flame'. In the second, Dante sees 'ingathered . . . the scattered leaves of the universe . . . as though together fused after such fashion that what I tell of is one simple flame'.[13] In our temporal world leaves shrivel at once in fire. What mortal beauty or value can hold out,

> Whose action is no stronger than a flower?[14]

---

* The likeness in which man was made is added to the vision a few lines later. (*Paradiso* XXXIII 230 f.)

But in the lambent fire of the empyrean, it will never shrivel. The union
Dante speaks of is symbolised by Eliot in a single and final line, where

> . . . the fire and the rose are one.

'The division', wrote Eliot in 1937,[15] 'between those who accept and
those who deny Christian revelation, I take to be the most profound
difference between human beings'; and no doubt there is an irreducible
difference between the meaning of *Four Quartets* to the author and those
who share his theology, and to those who do not. Yet wisdom, Eliot
himself reminds us, inheres in poems by men of very diverse beliefs.
In 'Goethe as the Sage', he has discussed the attitude that can enable
a reader to profit by the wisdom where he does not endorse the belief
(*PP* pp. 208–11, 220–7). If one does not endorse Eliot's, one may hold
that a poet who penetrates so far into the meanings of his own creed
penetrates beyond it; to the region where 'All Religions are One'.[16]
To him, the four regents of the Quartets are the most august Persons
of his faith: to others, who take the standpoint of comparative religion,
they will be metaphors for certain truths of religious experience. Why
should the Christian formulation, and even what for the non-Christian
are the Christian myths, alone be denied their place among significant
expressions of man's religious sense? That man has a religious sense is
probably common ground among almost all readers of the Quartets,
including those to whom it is a delusion, pointing to no reality other
than the working of human psychology itself. Even for them, the poem
can be a marvellous mirror of psychological processes and human
values whose importance they do not question. In short, *Four Quartets*
does not compel us to choose between conforming our interpretation
to the orthodoxy of the author, or finding it a work, for us, of no deep,
acceptable meaning. One reason is that few if any of its leading concepts
are without analogies outside orthodox Christian tradition. That this is
true not only of the moment, but also of the denial of meaning, reconciliation of opposites, transformation, non-attachment and the rest, I
could illustrate from Blake, Carlyle, E. M. Forster and Virginia Woolf;
from William James and C. G. Jung; from Yeats, and the Platonists
behind him, explored by F. A. C. Wilson; and from Persian, Indian
and Chinese sages quoted by Aldous Huxley in *The Perennial Philosophy*.

Yet whatever liberty of interpretation *Four Quartets* may allow, it is
uncompromising in its rejection of the 'time-philosophies' attacked by
Aldous Huxley[17] and Wyndham Lewis:[18] philosophies which search

the past and future and look to evolutionary or revolutionary time-processes as creators of value,[19] sufficient to justify all past and present growth-pains. Fascist and (with higher ideals) Communist idolatry of the future has sacrificed millions of victims. Brecht in *St Joan of the Stockyards* has advocated, and Sartre in *Les Mains Sales* has dramatised a morality which, since it judges solely by the hastening or hindering of the idolised future, condemns as 'objectively' wrong what by all humane instinct and tradition is 'right action'. Even the humane time-philosophy of Shaw claims too much when it supposes the problem of evil to become tractable once the evil is seen as the price of a creative evolution which makes the pain it causes intelligible and worth while.[20] Here the creative evolutionist is vulnerable to Hardy's 'Pain has been, and pain is'; no future 'can remove pain from the past', and make up for it to 'those who are its infallible estimators, the bearers' of it.[21] If there is to be any answer to Hardy, temporal experience while it is present must carry its own redeeming value. This is what *Four Quartets* affirms: the continual presence and accessibility of timeless values in the very present where the suffering, too, occurs. So far Eliot carries me with him. But his faith in the timeless value of the present goes with a want of any additional faith in the future. For Shaw, time is open-ended, with limitless scope for man or his successors to evolve perhaps beyond the trammels of matter altogether, but certainly to a higher civilisation. For Eliot, in accord with certain scientific hypotheses, the time-span of life is finite: man inhabits a 'valley of dying stars'.[22] The interim is his: an opportunity to incarnate the divine and so find union with God; but, though what 'right action' contributes to history is important, 'all times are corrupt' (*SE* (1932) p. 363) and no doubt will be: Eliot foresees no radical improvement. Idolatry of the future kills men: but (one must protest) the rejection of evolutionary or revolutionary hope can be lethal too, inhibiting temporal effort to save them from suffering and premature death. Should not the rival truths of which Eliot and Shaw are such effective champions be recognised as contraries that are both valid? For myself, I cannot do without either: I must think of the present as capable in itself of timeless value; and as valuable also because there runs through it the creative effort, divinely inspired, towards a far better future.

NOTES

1. 'Four Quartets: a commentary' (in T. S. Eliot: a study of his writings by several hands, ed. B. Rajan (1947)) and The Art of T. S. Eliot (1949) ch. 2. Earlier versions of the 'commentary' are listed in the preface to the 1949 volume. I owe more to Professor Gardner than to my other predecessors, but have learned in various ways from too many to specify here. For detail, especially of the wealth of cross-reference in the poem, see H. Blamires Word Unheard (1969).

2. Four Quartets, first English Edition, 1944 (Donald Gallup, T. S. Eliot: a bibliography (1952) A44b) p. 32. I use this edition throughout. Whether in Eliot or in other authors, I give the references for my citations only where there might otherwise be difficulty in tracing them.

3. Poetry and Prose of William Blake, ed. G. Keynes, 1 vol. Nonesuch ed. (1927) p. 535.

4. 1902 (1910 ed., pp. 393–9). Eliot would know the book well.

5. 'Vacillation' IV in Collected Poems (1950) pp. 283–4.

6. (1939) p. 107; also, more literally, in 'New Hampshire', in CP p. 148.

7. See. e.g., Raymond Preston, Four Quartets Rehearsed (1946) pp. 30 f.

8. Precisely what Professor Gardner demonstrates for the pattern of forms and styles.

9. Of all the movements in the poem, this is the one which most evidently must hold a unique significance for orthodox Christians that for others it cannot. Yet, as Aldous Huxley reminds us (The Perennial Philosophy (1947) p. 265), the ideas of 'vicarious suffering and . . . of the transferability of merit are based upon genuine facts of experience'. For the Buddhist, the Unitarian, or for others of no religious faith, what is here predicated of the Christ can still have its application to the incarnate Buddhas and reincarnate Bodhisattvas, to the human Jesus, or to all who are of inspired and sacrificial life.

10. As remarked in Gardner, 'Four Quartets: a commentary' (see n. 1 above).

11. See Gardner, Art of T. S. Eliot, pp. 180 f. Cf. the Bodhisattvas' vow in Huxley, Perennial Philosophy, p. 266.

12. Cf. The Cloud of Unknowing, quoted by Elizabeth Drew in T. S. Eliot: the design of his poetry (1950) p. 239 n. The crowned knot is, I understand, nautical.

13. Paradiso XXXI 1–21 (cp. XXX 61–6, 109–15), and XXXIII 85–90. Eliot quotes XXXIII 85–96 in his Dante (1929) p. 54, with a translation slightly modified from the Temple Classics edition; on which edition, see his preface, p. 13. The translations I give are taken from it.

14. Shakespeare, Sonnet LXV.

15. In Revelation, ed. John Baillie and Hugh Martin, p. 2; quoted in Eliot, ed. Rajan, p. 89 n. 2.

16. Blake, ed. Keynes, p. 148.

17. Perennial Philosophy, ch. 12.

18. Time and Western Man (1927) pp. 3 f.

19. FQ p. 32; cp. above, pp. 141f.

20. See Back to Methuselah (1921) pp. lv–lvi; Doctors' Delusions &c (1932 ed.) p. 313.

21. F. E. Hardy, The Life of Thomas Hardy (1962) p. 315.

22. CP p. 89; contrast Back to Methuselah, p. lxiii.

Eliot and the Living Theatre

KATHARINE WORTH

1

No playwright of our time has been more difficult to 'see' than Eliot
The poetry and the piety have worked a potent spell, obscuring both
dramatic weaknesses and actual or potential strengths. The argument
of this essay is that to be seen in perspective Eliot's plays must be seen
in the context of the living theatre, not as an extension of the poetry
and the dramatic theory, nor as a special kind of activity called 'religious
drama'.

We know that Eliot desperately wanted to elude the kind of audiences
who attended his early plays expecting 'to be patiently bored and to
satisfy themselves with the feeling that they have done something
meritorious'.[1] His anxiety to make contact with 'real' audiences was an
important factor in the evolution of his post-war style. He put the
poetry on a thin diet and overlaid his symbols with a conventionally
seductive façade.

Yet the plays seem to keep their place in the not very jolly corner
labelled 'verse and religious drama'. Is the reason for this simply their
inadequacy as plays? Must they always be performed in what Ivor
Brown jocularly called 'the crypt of St Eliot's' and have they no relevance to the development of the modern theatre? Are they quite out
of the main stream, as far out as the plays of Masefield, Drinkwater
and Stephen Phillips are now seen to have been?

I do not believe that we have to answer 'yes' to these questions
though much of the existing criticism of the drama, no doubt against
its intention, forces us to do so by emphasising so heavily moral
patterns, Christian solutions and thematic progressions. What in my
view emerges as theatrically interesting, and what gives Eliot a place

however tentative, in the main stream, is his feeling for alienation and violence, his gift for suggesting metaphysical possibilities in the trivial or absurd and his exploration of new dramatic means for working upon the nerves and pulses of an audience.

Of course these potentialities are imperfectly realised. Again and again he seems to be on the verge of striking out an entirely new line, of creating, even, the modern theatre. Then he abandons the promising experiment, conceals the real experience. *Sweeney Agonistes* must be one of the most exciting beginnings ever made by a poet turning towards the theatre, a Yeatsian concept of total theatre, full of primitive power. *The Family Reunion* showed that the impulse of the fragments could be sustained in a full-length piece and opened out still new vistas; even in *The Cocktail Party*, though not acknowledged for what it is, sounds the note of Beckett and Pinter; not irrelevantly, as M. C. Bradbrook has noted,[2] do the title and situation of the play bring into mind *The Birthday Party*.

What these experiments grew from, why they were not followed up and Eliot's dramatic powers fully realised, are the questions we might expect criticism to be asking. But, on the contrary, critics tend to accept the idea of painful self-improvement from *The Rock* to *The Cocktail Party* which Eliot offers in *Poetry and Drama*. Few would be found, of course, to place the last plays, *The Confidential Clerk* and *The Elder Statesman*, at the summit of his achievement. These are fairly generally admitted to show a falling away of power, though even here, to some minds, the edification in the subject-matter is more than compensation for thinness of texture.[3] And there will, no doubt, always be some for whom *Murder in the Cathedral* has no need to abide our questions: 'Of the greatness of *Murder in the Cathedral*, there can be no doubt – it may even be the greatest religious play ever written – and the other plays will survive if only as parts of the unity of which it is the finest element.'[4] But setting aside these acts of homage to the subject-matter, it has still been common form for Eliot's own chart of his progress to be taken as a basis for study, for *The Cocktail Party* to be seen, as he presents it, as a dramatic advance upon *The Family Reunion*, and for *Sweeney Agonistes* to be totally ignored.

Eliot is, then, not without responsibility for a situation in which his real theatrical powers are not recognised. In small ways, too, he has encouraged an untheatrical view, by allowing recordings of the choruses detached from their dramatic context; indeed, by making them himself,

in a voice admirably suited to *Four Quartets* but hardly likely to increase
our belief in the real existence of the Women of Canterbury. The
early publication of *Sweeney Agonistes* in *Collected Poems* (1936) and
its subsequent omission from *Collected Plays* (1962) has also served to
misdirect. Even critics such as Northrop Frye and G. S. Frazer here
referred to this most exciting theatrical piece as a 'poem'.

Criticism of poetic drama in our time has often taken untheatrical
directions for want of a theatrical context, but there is no need for this
in Eliot's case. A wealth of theatrical material exists, from reviews and
actors' accounts of their roles to records of the growth of the texts
under the pressure of stage requirements.

Two kinds of interest attach to this material. It has, in the first place,
the interest which first-hand accounts of plays in preparation and
production must always have for students of drama, offering a perspective which can never be quite the same as that from the study.[5] In the
second place, it raises questions about Eliot's special kind of relationship
with the theatre world. Some of those involved in production of his
plays were deeply committed to the idea of a 'religious drama'; their
commentaries often combine shrewd stage judgements with a tendency,
common in non-theatrical criticism, to look through what is there in
the play to what ought to be there.

How important was the influence from within the theatrical milieu
in turning Eliot towards the morality patterns of the late plays is,
indeed, one of the as yet unanswerable questions with which future
criticism must be concerned. It is already clear from E. Martin Browne's
illuminating accounts of his share in the plays (especially from *The
Making of a Play* (1966)) that his own influence was of the greatest
importance. In giving Eliot much needed advice on stage necessity, he
was also moving him towards a less ambiguous and equivocal expression
of theme; suggesting such changes as the replacement of the word
'daimon', by 'guardian' in Edward's analysis of his own condition and
requiring an exact account of Celia's fate, which Eliot, we are told, had
in the first draft left 'as vague as, at the end of *The Family Reunion*, he
had at first left Harry's' (p. 22). Whether this last change really was an
improvement is a question to which different answers have been and
will be given, according to whether the play is seen as the Christian
morality it purports to be, or as an abortive attempt at a less easily
defined structure, in which the word 'daimon' is in fact the right one.

The many critics, in and out of the theatre, who are in sympathy with

Eliot's doctrinal intentions, will hardly recognise the existence of such alternatives, or will at least have no hesitation in emphasising the orthodox interpretation of any play under discussion. But even the criticism uncommitted to a religious viewpoint sometimes seems slightly out of focus with what is happening in the plays, perhaps because critical argument is so often conducted in a context composed almost exclusively of Eliot's own theory and practice. Much light has been thrown on the plays by studies of the relation of theory and practice and of the plays to the poems, of sources and meaning, ritual and symbolic patterns. Yet the separation of the play from the theatrical context has its dangers, not least the danger of over-interpretation. A critic, like C. H. Smith, who tells us that she is 'not primarily concerned with an evaluation of Eliot's work by current theatrical standards' may have, and, indeed, has many valuable insights to offer about the ritualistic overtones, but she is also liable to move a long way from stage or any other kind of reality, as she does in her account of Harcourt Reilly: 'Sir Henry's ritual identity is suggested by his continual drink of gin with a drop of water (he is adulterating his spiritual nature with a drop of water, representing time, flux, and humanity).'[6]

II

Eliot has, of course, invited symbol-hunting of the Thurberish kind by his ubiquitous dropping of clues, followed up by the answer in his next lecture.

The critical reception given to *Sweeney Agonistes* is a case in point. This piece has attracted much scholarly attention as a source of theme and symbol. But its stage inventiveness was scarcely given credit until the production of 1965 in the memorial programme, 'Homage to T. S. Eliot', at the Globe Theatre, with jazz accompaniment by John Dankworth, Cleo Laine as Doris and Nicol Williamson as Sweeney. Audience and reviewers were astonished on this occasion by the force and freshness of the piece; far from seeming a precious literary experiment, it was felt to be as alive as the sculpture by Henry Moore which preceded it on the stage. To one reviewer it seemed 'in the same class as the Berlin classics of Brecht and Weill', to another it 'uncannily' foreshadowed the British *avant garde* drama of the fifties.[7]

Literary critics, on the other hand, have tended to see it as a dead end, an experiment of limited interest, or even as the wrong turning which it seems to Grover Smith: '. . . the farcical music hall style, without any indication that Sweeney is deliberately talking down, is an improper vehicle for this serious theme'.[8]

The selection of a 'farcical music hall style' for the serious theme is in fact the best evidence of the acute theatrical sense with which Eliot was endowed at the start of his dramatic career. Nothing in his later development is more impressive than the instinct he showed then for recognising potentialities in popular and vulgar forms. In the waifs and strays of *Sweeney Agonistes* he hit upon just those types, derived from music hall and minstrel show, which thirty years later, in *Waiting for Godot*, were to be seen as the seed around which a modern drama could crystallise.

Fascination with music hall, circus, revue, and the ritualistic interpretations of them offered by scholars like F. M. Cornford, was of course, a feature of *avant garde* movements in the 1920s. Paris was then, as later, a breeding-ground. e. e. cummings, another young American, like Eliot at home in literary Paris, produced his own highly original blend of ritual and burlesque, *Him*, in New York, only two years after Eliot's Aristophanic fragments had appeared in the *Criterion*, and Cocteau's voice was frequently heard in that journal, prophesying the future role of 'le cirque, le music hall, le cinématographe'. The ideas were in the air, but no one saw further into them than Eliot.

The ambiguity of his attitude towards the music hall experience largely accounts for the originality of the form he drew out of it. He was greatly struck by the possibilities it offered for a ritualistic drama: 'Little Tich, George Robey, Nellie Wallace, Marie Lloyd . . . provide fragments of a possible English myth. They effect the Comic Purgation'.[9] These possibilities are no doubt uppermost in his mind when he emphasises what might to most people seem the quality least characteristic of music hall, the 'pure and undefiled detachment' which he found in performers of the supreme class. It sometimes seems that Eliot was attending the Islington Empire with a cold eye, seeing in the grotesqueness of some of the turns an approximation to that ideal, inhuman drama of masked beings which visited his imagination as it did that of Yeats.

Yet if we see for ourselves, even in the imperfect record of early film, a performance by one of Eliot's favourite artists, Little Tich, it becomes apparent that in stressing the detachment and impersonality of the great performers Eliot was making a profoundly imaginative judgement. It is easy enough now, after *Waiting for Godot* and *The*

Caretaker, to see how the figure of Little Tich, a solitary, inscrutable dwarf, patiently manipulating his Brobdingnagian boots, was pointing the way for the modern theatre. But in the 1920s it took an Eliot to see it, to recognise in Little Tich the qualities he found in Massine, of whom he said, 'Massine, the most completely unhuman, impersonal, abstract, belongs to the future stage'.[10]

Yet his awareness of the impersonal quality in the art of music hall did not prevent him from responding to its human warmth, as his loving essay in the first number of the *Criterion* on the occasion of Marie Lloyd's death shows very clearly. He admired the unself-consciousness, the proletarian vitality and, above all, the sense of human solidarity felt in the close collaboration between artist and audience. Some of this 'normal' human warmth comes through in *Sweeney Agonistes*, giving the fragments a quality which none of the later plays capture, even when Eliot is trying hard for it. The unsentimental, matter-of-fact relationship between Doris and Dusty projects a real sense of human closeness, a closing of the ranks against Pereira and the other menacing facts of their existence.

The special quality of the piece, however, springs from the skilful turning of elements derived from a warm, popular art to effects of isolation and disorientation. It is an exercise in black comedy whose success depends upon the sustaining of the popular note just long enough for the distortion to register. Heavily syncopated rhythms suggest sexual excitement passing into a state of hysteria and spiritual panic. The jovial nightmare song from Gilbert and Sullivan takes a sickening lurch into real nightmare, conveying in musical terms the experience Sweeney cannot find words for, the swallowing up of the known by an unknown world:

> You dreamt you waked up at seven o'clock and it's
> > foggy and it's damp and it's dawn and it's dark
> And you wait for a knock and the turning of a lock
> > for you know the hangman's waiting for you.
> And perhaps you're alive
> And perhaps you're dead
> Hoo ha ha
> Hoo ha ha
> Hoo
> Hoo
> Hoo

This is 'physical' theatre, where the poetry combines with the actors' bodily movements to draw primitive responses from the audience. Eliot may have been encouraged in his experiment by seeing the performance of Yeats's *At the Hawk's Well*, in Lady Cunard's drawing-room, to which Ezra Pound had taken him in 1916. Although he later dismissed the *Plays for Dancers* as more decorative than dramatic, he was at the time of that performance struck by a modern quality in Yeats which he had not perceived before. It took an acute sense of theatrical possibilities to recognise this 'modernity' in *At the Hawk's Well*, with its legendary hero, hawk goddess for heroine, and choral interludes from a group of musicians on the stage. But Eliot may well have had in mind Yeats's use of drum, gong and zither when, in 1924, he outlined to Arnold Bennett a project for a drama of modern life, 'perhaps with certain things in it accentuated by drum beats'.[11]

In *Sweeney Agonistes* he catches the drum beat in the verse: it plays upon the nerves, assaults the audience physically, suggesting meanings below the line which can only be apprehended in the beat. The play offers an experience of almost total alienation. The borrowings from music hall 'turns' like the soft-shoe number, heighten the sense of isolation: as characters go into their routines, they convey the essential solitariness of the music-hall performer before he makes contact with his audience, an idea later to be taken up by John Osborne in *The Entertainer*. There is a sustained threat in the verse rhythms, balanced as they are, and as the Dankworth production well brought out, on the edge of a great jazz explosion, which powerfully suggests the emotional explosion to which the action must move. That this explosion was to take the form of murder, real or 'acted out' is shown in early drafts of the play.[12] As the action stands, all the detail points to a slow moving together of Doris, the predestined victim, who has already turned up the coffin card, and Sweeney, the man obsessed with the thought of violence:

> Any man has to, needs to, wants to
> Once in a lifetime, do a girl in.

A play about spiritual 'lostness', expressed in the vocabulary of the jazz age, moving towards a symbolic act of violence, *Sweeney Agonistes*, even in its fragmentary state, was a very long step in a new theatrical direction. That it remained unfinished because, as Hugh Kenner says,[13] 'there was nowhere for it to go' has been disproved by the whole course of post-war theatre. Eliot's abandonment of the fragments may have been due to something in the subject-matter which he was not yet able to get under artistic control, or it may have been, as C. H. Smith suggests, the result of his conversion and reception into the Church of England which followed shortly after the publication of the piece.

The effect of this change in his life on his dramatic writing was great and in some ways damaging. From *The Rock* onwards, much of his energy went into an effort to extend his range, so as to accommodate, within the drama of alienation natural to him, the opposite experience of communion. The strain involved in this attempt creates the 'second voice', the voice of 'myself addressing, even haranguing an audience', which dominates the choruses for *The Rock* and is strong in *Murder in the Cathedral*.

Religious influences may have been reinforced by the didactic drama of Auden and Isherwood, who, perhaps inspired by the printed version of *Sweeney Agonistes*, were pursuing the direction indicated in it during the years when *The Rock*, *Murder in the Cathedral* and *The Family Reunion* were being written. The Group Theatre who produced their plays were dedicated to the exploration of popular techniques; they envisaged a new drama, 'analogous to modern musical comedy or the pre-medieval folk play', and in pursuit of this curious-sounding goal they explored the possibilities in dance, jazz effects and visual shock tactics such as masks.

'We should like less prancing and bad dancing' was Geoffrey Grigson's comment on the Group Theatre style, a remark which perhaps Eliot might have endorsed if, as Professor Isaacs tells us,[14] he was 'puzzled' by the production the theatre gave *Sweeney Agonistes* in 1935. He may well have considered that the notion of putting his characters into full or half masks destroyed the delicate tension he had built up between a commonplace surface and a profoundly disturbing under-pattern. Yet, in giving him a production of his play, and in drawing his attention to Auden and Isherwood in performance, the Group Theatre were encouraging him to continue his exploration of the possibilities in revue techniques. Certainly, *Murder in the Cathedral* owes a good deal of its theatrical life to flamboyant changes of rhythm. Its contemporary political flavour, too, in the totalitarian apologetics of the Knights, seems to point to the engaged drama of Auden and Isherwood, as later *The Family Reunion* was to show some striking similarities to *The Ascent of F6*.

If there was then this influence operating in *Murder in the Cathedral*, it is not likely to have lessened Eliot's difficulties in dealing with ordinary people like the Women of Canterbury and showing them in a convincing human relationship with Becket, or, indeed, with anyone else in the play. The characteristic hero of Auden and Isherwood, in all his high-minded liberalism, has as little real contact with the 'people' whose cause he espouses as has Ransom of *The Ascent of F6* with the suburban Mr and Mrs A, isolated in their stage boxes.

The isolation in that instance is deliberate. But in *Murder in the Cathedral* the isolated elements are meant to coalesce, Chorus and Saint to come together in the redemption of one by the death of the other. That there has been an interior happening of this kind is declared poetically with such skill as almost to convince that it has happened dramatically too. But it has not. The Chorus are not involved in any human relationship with Becket real enough to move belief in his having power to affect their lives. They are only a collective voice, not living people with a stake in the action. Becket addresses them, typically from a physical height above them, in the pulpit, but hardly speaks to them. Whether his awareness of them affects his own inner development is extremely debatable. Production could certainly make it seem that when he has his moment of illumination –

> Now is my way clear, now is the meaning plain:
> Temptation shall not come in this kind again–

it comes to him through listening to the entreaties of the Chorus,

> O Thomas Archbishop, save us, save us, save yourself
>   that we may be saved;
> Destroy yourself and we are destroyed.

But the recognition could with equal, if not greater theatrical plausibility, be shown as self-generated, coming out of the deep trance of self-communion in which Becket is engaged for most of the play.

Eliot admitted to having difficulty in imagining the chorus; it seems that he was able to imagine their thoughts, but not what they were actually doing, particularly at the crisis of the murder. If they are present at this event, it can only be as mute spectators, like the Priests who, as the director of the film version, George Hoellering, pointed out, 'do not lift a finger to come to his aid'.[15] No attempt is made to express their helplessness as a dramatic element, nor is any notice taken of Chorus and Priests by the Knights, who, after the murder, address the audience directly, giving them the orders which, if given to the Chorus would have helped to involve them as human beings in the situation: 'I suggest that you now disperse quietly to your homes. Please be careful not to loiter in groups at street corners, and do nothing that might provoke any public outbreak.'

The various changes made in the film version were in the first place a response to the demands of the different medium; the Knights could not address a cinema audience at such length, so they had to be shown speaking to a crowd outside the cathedral. But some of these changes would, as Hoellering suggested, improve stage versions too; he saw the need for 'tightening' the action by integrating the Women of Canterbury more closely into it and for increasing credibility by some quite simple rearrangements such as the dismissal of the Priests to vespers before the murder. Eliot accepted these alterations as 'improvements' in a statement of some ambiguity: the play worked in the Chapter House at Canterbury, he implies, because it was not really trying to be a play there: the film version 'made the meaning clearer, and in that way is nearer to what the play would have been, had it been written for the London theatre and by a dramatist of greater experience'.[16]

In failing to come to life as a play about the interaction of people, *Murder in the Cathedral* fails to become the new kind of play Eliot's religious belief compelled him to attempt. It is weakest in those areas where themes of Christian redemption and brotherhood are being worked out, as the precarious attachment of the Chorus to the action shows. Where it has strength is in precisely that territory already shown in *Sweeney Agonistes* to be Eliot's own. The central action is, indeed, curiously close to the action outlined in the earlier play. Eliot himself points to its extreme simplicity: 'A man comes home, foreseeing that he will be killed, and he is killed' (*PP* p. 79). Anticipation of, and preparation for, an act of violence generates the greatest dramatic excitement felt anywhere in the piece. Becket is most fully realised as a human character when he is involved with the idea of death, in the preparatory clearing of conscience with the Four Tempters and in the murder scene itself, where the intimacy of his relationship with his murderers, usually stressed in production by the doubling of Tempters' and Knights' roles, goes far beyond the degree of intimacy he achieves with anyone else in the play.

The Chorus, too, finds the most dramatic of all its functions in

winding up the suspense as the murder approaches, then releasing it in
a great outburst which in its exultingly violent rhythms, conveys a
Maenad-like impression of ecstasy in the sacrificial consummation:

> Clean the air! clean the sky!
> wash the wind! take the
> stone from the stone . . . Wash
> the stone, wash the bone . . .
> wash them wash them!

They may not be able to communicate as personalities, but they do,
though with some monotony, convey a state of mind with which Eliot
is, dramatically speaking, at home; a state of 'panic and emptiness'.
'The sense of disgust in the chorus', says Stevie Smith, 'is the most
living thing out of all the play.'[17] The word 'living' is correct here;
their 'disgust' grows out of the action, moves with it and is finally
appeased in the ritual killing.

Fascination with violence as a cleansing, therapeutic process is
strongly felt in *Murder in the Cathedral*. Virginia Woolf once said, 'If
you are anaemic as Tom is, there is a glory in blood'; without accepting
her explanation of the cause, we may agree with her findings. There is
a kind of glory in blood and violence in the plays, violence as a means
of opening the doors of perception. Sudden death, often in shocking
forms, is a recurring feature. The death of Celia was originally designed
to be still more horrible than it appeared in the final version of *The
Cocktail Party*,[18] and Stevie Smith is surely right in saying of *Murder
in the Cathedral* that 'the poetry mounts at each touch of pain'. Eliot
often seems to be on the verge of creating 'the theatre of cruelty', but
in the process gets into dramatic difficulties, since he is obliged by his
didactic intentions to represent the cruelty as somehow leading to an
advancement of human well-being all round. The unsatisfactory solutions of *The Family Reunion* and *The Cocktail Party* are the results of
this internal contradiction.

Yet *The Family Reunion* (1939), despite its flawed ending, is more
deeply satisfying than any other of the plays, more nearly a complete
expression of his dramatic vision. Eliot's severe criticism of its stage-
craft in *Poetry and Drama* is, in my view, one of his most misleading
accounts of his own plays. He underestimates and even distorts, dismissing two of the most moving scenes, the 'lyrical duets', between
Harry and Mary, and Harry and Agatha as 'remote from the necessity

of the action' and giving up as a bad job the notion of representing in stage terms 'those ill-fated figures, the Furies'.

It would be interesting to know, and this is another of the questions with which future criticism might well be concerned, how far these curious judgements spring from experience of inadequate productions, how far from the need under which he seems to have laboured, to apologise for, or turn away from, what is most alive and disturbing in his dramatic experiments. *The Family Reunion* has had some effective productions on stage and television since Eliot wrote so depreciatingly of it, notably, in my experience, by Michael Elliott, with a student cast, in 1966.[19] He successfully disregarded Eliot's injunction against making the Furies visible, contriving, with the aid of beautifully controlled modulations of light into darkness, spectacular incarnations for them as towering black shapes, alarmingly materialising between the audience, who sat round a skeletal framework enclosing the haunted room, and the characters. Harry made his entrance through the room where the audience sat, pausing with them for a long look at the family exposed to view a few yards away in the lighted framework before stepping into it and exchanging the watcher's role for the actor's. By this simple arrangement, an experience which can seem private and obscure in the far distances of the picture-frame stage was brought nearer and made comprehensible. Indeed, Harry's awareness of the eyes upon the house seemed to an audience made conscious of themselves as watchers more natural than the blank incomprehension of the family when he tells them they are being watched:

> How can you sit in this blaze of light
> for all the world to look at?
> If you knew how you looked, when I saw you
> through the window!
> Do you like to be stared at by eyes through
> a window?

This physical involvement of the audience in Harry's experience was completed when the Eumenides materialised between him and them, overlooking both, forcing them out of their safe role as watchers into the protagonist's situation of vulnerability to the inquisitorial eye. In appearance, these Furies were essentially shapeless, bundles of old clothes which might or might not contain life. They conveyed the fundamental ambiguity of Eliot's Furies, black and malign to view in the first shock of their appearance, yet perhaps to be seen differently, as soaring, upward-pointing beings. The question remained open: the movement toward an orthodox Christian solution at the end was not strong enough to obliterate the disturbing impression made by the strong physical impact of these Eumenides.

Imaginative staging of this kind makes it clear that in *The Family Reunion* Eliot had worked out a technique of special interest to the modern theatre, a method of dealing with metaphysical questions in a drama of contemporary life. He was pointing in a direction later to be taken by Beckett and Pinter: *The Birthday Party* has some striking likenesses to both *The Family Reunion* and *The Cocktail Party*, while the symbolism of the spiritual eye connects Eliot's play in an interesting way with the spotlight in *Play* which indicates to its victims the possibility that they are being 'seen'. The claustrophobic Wishwood interior, menaced by mysterious visitants, has, indeed, become a theatrical commonplace of our time.

The maintenance of a degree of ambiguity is an important element in the success of the play. Some strain is put upon it by the orthodox turning given to Harry's 'conversion' at the end. The faint suggestion of an emerging missionary motif strikes a discordant note which would have quite upset the dramatic balance had it been developed along the lines indicated to Michael Redgrave when he pressed Eliot for more definition in the ending: 'Oh yes, I think he and the chauffeur go off and get jobs in the East End.'[20]

If there is, as Eliot suggests, a 'failure of adjustment between the Greek story and the modern situation', this is where it lies, not in the confrontation of the Oresteian Harry with his Furies, a situation well within his dramatic range. But *The Family Reunion* is more than the characteristic ghost-play; it is also, and uniquely in the dramatic canon, a deeply moving play about human relationships, not only in their aspects of bitterness and failure, which are well captured in other plays, but also in aspects of tenderness and real intimacy.

One main reason for the much fuller human quality of this play is Eliot's acknowledgement of imperfection in all the characters, including, and especially in, the spiritually sensitive. That he was not altogether in conscious control of the process is suggested by his dismay on discovering that Harry was 'an insufferable prig'. It is understandable that he, who criticised D. H. Lawrence's people for their 'insensibility to ordinary social morality',[21] should find the prominence of this trait in his own heroes an embarrassment. For their indifference to social morality is a striking feature of their behaviour: in sexual matters especially, they are airily amoral. Even the gentle Celia feels no qualms of conscience over her adultery with Edward, while Agatha, an eminently ruthless being, glories in her special relation with Harry, described by Eliot himself as 'ambiguous', which is the fruit of her liaison with his father.

The strength of *The Family Reunion* consists in the recognition of these ambiguities, the admission that there is a neurotic element in the spirituality of Harry and Agatha, that Amy's 'human' criticism of them has validity. As a result, the spiritual climax, Harry's private illumination, becomes also a human climax, involving three people, Harry, Agatha and Mary in a delicate emotional consummation which depends for its effectiveness upon an awareness of them as deeply wounded, even crippled, human beings. That 'crippled' is not too strong a term is indicated by Eliot's own account of his intentions.[22] Harry was meant to show 'the attraction, half of a son and half of a lover, to Agatha, which she reciprocates in somewhat the same way', while in his relation with Mary he was to convey the 'conflict inside him between . . . repulsion for Mary as a woman, and the attraction which the normal part of him that is left, feels toward her personally for the first time'.

In the face of such emotional difficulties, the achievement of even a transient human contact should be felt as a touching achievement, as indeed it was in Michael Elliott's production, which avoided the trance-like, inhuman effect often seen in performance, by moving the characters towards each other as the verse mounted to its climax. The embrace in which they met, sexless, yet touched with sexual tenderness, delicately suggested a real human communion at some deep level of being. Far from being undramatic, 'beyond character', as Eliot puts it, these 'duets', in which poetic rhythm and imagery are put to intensely theatrical use, take us deep into character, communicating below the level of conscious thought, offering, indeed, a means to the only kind of communication in which the modern theatre really believes.

III

This study has been chiefly concerned with the earlier plays, in an attempt to show Eliot's range, theatrical originality and real achievement.

To do any sort of justice to the later plays would require a separate study, but one aspect of them may, perhaps, reasonably be considered in brief space, the comic or farcical forms in which they are cast.

Eliot's adoption of a Coward–Wilde formula has sometimes been thought the cause of the drying-up process in these plays, a sacrifice for the sake of acquiring an audience, to the gods of the West End theatre, and a useless sacrifice, since the formula had already lost its theatrical vitality. It seems unlikely that his acute sense of the contemporary had so completely deserted him. The choice of farce is, rather a proof of his continuing sensitivity to formal necessities. It offered him the withdrawal he needed to make, for whatever reason, from the emotional intensity of earlier work. That it was the right form, in offering a measure of control over the sentimental tendencies of the later phase, may be seen by comparing *The Confidential Clerk* with *The Elder Statesman*, a neo-Ibsenite structure in which sentimentality is allowed full play.

Coward's comedy offered patterns of separation and estrangement which could easily be adapted to Eliot's purposes. Coward too has his 'elect' and his 'damned'; on one side of the deep divide are the 'ordinary moral, high-thinking citizens', on the other, the amoral but honest and therefore more admirable Bohemians.[23]

This Calvinistic world, in which the elect remain the elect, no matter what they do, offered Eliot an escape from the need which had always proved so troublesome to him of translating spiritual experiences into terms of ordinary social morality. He takes advantage of this new freedom in *The Confidential Clerk* to explore, through the fantastically amoral situations of the play, various kinds of ambiguity. The skill with which the ambiguity is sustained, so that even after the oracular pronouncements of Mrs Guzzard, the question of Colby's identity remains central, is something new in Eliot's drama. It shows him still very much in the mainstream, offering an original means for handling themes which were to preoccupy the Pirandello-conscious theatre of the mid-century.

The Cocktail Party also has this kind of relevance. It hints the possibility of a 'black' theatre coming out of the Coward formula. One of the most impressive features of the play is the extraction of grim significance from the fussy detail, the seemingly empty chatter, the farcical poppings in and out of the party scene in the first Act. The effect of a remorseless machine at work is very well done. The frivolous, banal context brings out the chilling quality in lines like Julia's 'I like to manage the machine myself', and heightens the horror of the last Act in which Reilly smoothly describes his vision of poor, murdered Celia, and Alex makes his grotesque jokes about monkeys and mutilated Christians.

The Cocktail Party convinces when it is being a play about hell, the characteristic hell of Eliot's drama, an unhappy marriage. It was as such a play that it first came into his mind.[24] When contemplating the Alcestis legend and wondering what kind of life would have been possible for Admetus and Alcestis after her return from the 'death' wished upon her by her husband, he was thinking along lines which make fully explicable in formal terms his choice of the Coward convention for his Alcestis play. His view of the story and its 'happy' ending was more deeply sceptical even than Euripides', who provided his dramatic model. Where the Euripidean version, in reducing the legend to unheroic proportions, had allowed Alcestis at least some heroic virtue, Eliot made her and her Admetus equal in selfishness. He removed the selfless qualities of her classical prototype from the married woman, Lavinia, to give them to the unmarried Celia, the woman who will have no truck with domesticity. This pointed distinction, and the sardonic representation of married domesticity as a long waiting for a cocktail party, have the effect of going beyond criticism of individual characters, to raise doubt about the viability of marriage as a way of life. Despite the formal contradiction of the proposition in the last Act, it is nevertheless this doubt, so well established in stage terms, which emerges as a major theme of the play.

To make central a subject clearly so painful to him, Eliot probably needed the distancing devices of artificial comedy. Coward's frivolous anti-marriage plays offered suitably stylised expression. Eliot takes over their conventional assumptions – marriage is a joke and adultery a game – and sets out to show, not that Coward is wrong, but that the joke is a very black one, the game a sour business. The scenes of recrimination between Edward and Lavinia are done with a bitter intensity recalling the Strindbergian dance of death. As in Strindbergian drama, too, the onus is placed rather more upon the wife than the husband. Both are involved in extra-marital affairs – and seldom in stage history can there have been drearier ones – but Edward's situation allows him opportunities which are denied Lavinia for showing some emotional complexity. He is permitted to make a bid for sympathy in his account of his wretchedness:

> What is hell? Hell is oneself,
> Hell is alone, the other figures in it
> Merely projections.

6

Lavinia is more firmly entrenched in the cool, passionless Coward world, where 'love' is a word used with conscious mockery: 'I love you. You love me. You love Otto. I love Otto. Otto loves me. There now! Start to unravel from there!'

'Unravelling', for Coward a purely comic process, turns in Eliot's hands into the unwinding of a labyrinthine thread leading through dark places. The thread is firmly held by the Guardians, that menacing trio of watchers and manipulators, through whom he gets his blackest comic effects. They begin by seeming feeble imitations of lovable eccentrics in the Coward–Wilde tradition, a rather tame joke. But the joke is on the audience. The imitation is not meant to convince, only to sketch a half-mask, which draws attention to the real faces underneath, faces of alarming power. Again, as in *The Family Reunion*, the force controlling the action, whose agent the Guardians are, is represented by a watchful eye; in this play it has a disquieting likeness to the omnipresent Orwellian eye which haunts the modern mind. The likeness is strengthened by the image of the single eye shared by three, an image pointing to the legend of the Gorgon and her petrifying stare. Whether or not the audience catch such allusions, they cannot miss the oppressive watchfulness of the Guardians, the ostentatious contriving of exits and entrances to ensure that an eye is being kept on the movements of the 'patients'. Nor, one would think, can they miss a suggestion of gratuitous cruelty in Celia's death, the account of which is so loosely tacked on to the main action that it amounts, as Eliot suspected, to no more than an epilogue, in which form, in fact, he had originally written it.

What makes *The Cocktail Party* finally unsatisfactory is not of course the unpleasantness of its characters, nor the blackness of its jokes, but the insistence that all this is not so, that it is a play about heaven as well as about hell. Here, of course, the Coward formula works against Eliot's intention, rather as do the Wilde mannerisms against the pious conclusion of *The Confidential Clerk*. For though the formula allows for a good deal of oddity – it can accommodate an unprofessional psychiatrist, a son choosing his parents from a plethora of candidates, even a 'suburban Pallas Athene',[25] granting wishes all round – what it does not allow are situations of domestic snugness and sweetness, such as *The Cocktail Party* offers. Ideas of conversion and reform are alien to it; when Eggerson predicts a future for Colby as a chapel organist reading for orders the effect is as grotesque as though *Design for Living* were to end with Gilda taking up welfare work.

In selecting a form giving splendid opportunities for exploring conditions of alienation but none at all for solutions in terms of 'ordinary,
social morality', Eliot followed his theatrical instinct, though only by
making things difficult for himself as a moralist. It has been the object
of this study to suggest how strong that theatrical instinct was, however
fitfully it worked. Future criticism, it may be hoped, will explore more
thoroughly in theatrical directions, finding answers to some of the
perplexing questions raised by the many changes of Eliot's dramatic
style.

The plays can stand such scrutiny; uneven, flawed, though they may
be, they remain an achievement of great interest, not merely to admirers
of Eliot the poet, but to lovers of the living theatre, and it is in the
context of the living theatre that the kind of dramatic interest they have
shows most clearly.

NOTES

1. T. S. Eliot, 'Poetry and Drama', in *PP* p. 79.
2. M. C. Bradbrook, *English Dramatic Form* (1965) p. 173.
3. C. H. Smith, *T. S. Eliot's Dramatic Theory and Practice* (1963) p. 214.
4. D. E. Jones, *The Plays of T. S. Eliot* (1960) p. 215. The most thoroughly
documented account of the plays: an indispensable work of reference.
5. K. Tynan, *Tynan on Theatre* (Penguin, 1964). Kenneth Tynan's reviews,
for instance, call attention to the stage effectiveness of the 'chilly scenes', and
suggest new ways of looking at the plays.
6. C. H. Smith, *Eliot's Dramatic Theory*, pp. ix, 179.
7. A recording of this production is available in 'Homage to T. S. Eliot',
produced by Vera Lindsay (E.M.I. Records). Reviews in the *Guardian* and
The Times, 14 June 1965.
8. Grover Smith, *T. S. Eliot's Poetry and Plays: a study in sources and meaning*
(1956) p. 118.
9. Cited in J. Isaacs, *An Assessment of Twentieth-Century Literature* (1951)
p. 146.
10. T. S. Eliot, 'Dramatis Personae', in *Criterion*, I (1923) iii 305.
11. The relevant passage from *The Journals of Arnold Bennett* is quoted in
Jones, *Plays of Eliot*, p. 27.
12. A manuscript draft, reproduced in the programme of 'Homage to
T. S. Eliot', has stage directions for the entry of Mrs Porter after the chorus
'The Terrors of the Night'; a debate with Sweeney; her murder and, finally,
the 'Return of Mrs Porter'.
13. H. Kenner, *The Invisible Poet: T. S. Eliot* (1960) p. 186.
14. Isaacs, *An Assessment*, p. 147.
15. T. S. Eliot and G. Hoellering, *The Film of Murder in the Cathedral* (1952)
p. 10.
16. Ibid. p. 13.
17. This and the following comment on *Murder in the Cathedral* occur in

Stevie Smith's essay 'History or Poetic Drama?', in *T. S. Eliot: a symposium for his seventieth birthday*, ed. N. Braybrooke (1958) pp. 172–3.

18. See E. Martin Browne's account, in *The Making of a Play*, p. 22. See also his *The Making of T. S. Eliot's Plays* (1969).

19. Michael Elliott's production was given on the floor of the rehearsal room at the Central School of Speech and Drama, Swiss Cottage, in 1966.

20. Michael Redgrave's account of his conversations with Eliot is given in R. Findlater, *Michael Redgrave* (1956) pp. 49–50.

21. *ASG* p. 39. Lawrence's characters are said to be 'unfurnished with even the most commonplace kind of conscience'.

22. The relevant passage is quoted in F. O. Matthiessen, *The Achievement of T. S. Eliot* (1935) pp. 167–8.

23. Gilda, in *Design for Living*, when she apologises to her deceived husband, not for deceiving but for 'using' him – 'I've made use of you, Ernest. I'm ashamed of that' – seems to point to Celia making her similar apology to Edward. Other echoes abound, Eliot, in customary sly style, drawing attention to their source in his choice of Teddington, Coward's birthplace, as the home of Mrs Guzzard, and the place where the babies are hopelessly mixed up.

24. In an interview with Donald Hall, printed in the *Paris Review*, XXI (Spring/Summer 1959), 48–70, Eliot says of Lavinia and Edward: 'Those two people were the centre of the thing when I started and the other characters only developed out of it.' This interview is reprinted in *Writers at Work: The Paris Review Interviews*, Second Series (1963) pp. 77–94.

25. See Alison Leggatt's 'A Postscript from Mrs Chamberlayne and Mrs Guzzard', in Braybrooke's *Symposium*, pp. 79–80.

2

Eliot and F. H. Bradley: an account

RICHARD WOLLHEIM

And I am accustomed to more documentation; I like to know where writers get their ideas from.

– letter in the *Egoist*, IV xi (Dec 1917), from Charles Augustus Conybeare, the Carlton Club, Liverpool, presumably composed by the Assistant Editor, T. S. Eliot.

I

SINCE 1916 there has reposed, first in the Eliot House, Harvard, then in the Houghton Library, the typescript of a dissertation submitted by Eliot for the doctorate of philosophy under the title 'Experience and the Objects of Knowledge in the Philosophy of F. H. Bradley'. When Eliot agreed to publish this dissertation,[1] along with two related articles which originally appeared in the *Monist* for 1916, he spoke of his early academic philosophising as 'a curiosity of literature',[2] 'a curiosity of biographical interest' (*KE* p. 10), the curiosity of the work lying in its remoteness from the contemporary concerns of philosophers, let alone those of the poet himself, and its interest (according to Eliot, that is) in the evidence it furnished about the formation of his prose style. 'My own prose style', Eliot asserted in the preface,[3] 'was formed on that of Bradley': a style which he had already[4] described as 'perfect', perfect, he was careful to explain, in its match with content, in the way it was 'perfectly welded with the matter' (*SE* p. 445).

It is possible – in fact, not hard – to disagree with Eliot's comparison of his style to Bradley's. However, with the dissertation now in print, criticism is unlikely to confine itself to the problem that Eliot himself isolated: the stylistic problem will be only one amongst many, for the sake of which students of Eliot will resort to *Knowledge and Experience*.

Even before the text became publicly available, attempts had been made
to trace ideas, both in Eliot's poetry and in his criticism, to their origins
in his philosophical education.[5] It might seem as though now such a
project can enter into a co-operative, and hence more progressive, phase.

At the outset – it must be said – optimism on this score needs to be
heavily qualified. One immediate reason is the density, indeed the
obscurity, of Eliot's philosophical writing. Whether this is inherent,
residing in the prose itself, or whether time has not done as much as
Eliot to cloud his meaning from us, we must accept that *Knowledge and
Experience* is a painfully obscure work. Criticism that sets out to understand Eliot's work as a poet and as a critic by reference to it is likely,
fairly soon, to admit bewilderment, or else, overtly or covertly, to reverse
the enterprise and to use the poetry and the criticism as a gloss on, or
as a key to, the philosophy.

II

Poetry, we know, was amongst Eliot's earliest interests: from the age
of sixteen he wrote it,[6] and about this period circulated it amongst his
friends and family. However, there was a time when philosophy
appeared to challenge poetry in Eliot's esteem, and even led him to
suspend poetical work. Eliot's doctoral thesis, for instance, is not only
a highly competent work, but it reveals an acquaintance with the
contemporary American, English and continental literature far in excess
of what might reasonably be expected in a graduate student.[7]

Eliot entered Harvard in 1906.[8] Though as an undergraduate he
attended classes of Santayana and G. H. Palmer, it was only during his
stay in Paris in the year 1910–11, where he listened to Bergson,[9] and
again after his return to Harvard, that he became absorbed in philosophy.
Eliot enrolled as a graduate in the philosophy department in the
autumn of 1911, though, as was the practice, he did not embark on his
dissertation for another two years.[10] From 1912–14 he was an Assistant
in the Department.

In the spring of 1914 Russell,[11] who was at Harvard as Lowell
lecturer, gave a seminar on symbolic logic. Amongst a number of
indifferent students, he singled out two for their ability: Raphael Demos
and Eliot.[12] However, of the state of Eliot's philosophical development
at this period we have recently been afforded an illuminating, if somewhat intermittent, picture in the published transcript[13] of another

seminar which Eliot attended in this same year. This is Josiah Royce's famous seminar, which, officially listed as 'A Comparative Study of Various Types of Method', in fact ranged over as many topics as Royce's own energetic and capacious mind. Even from the somewhat staccato notes, taken down by Costello, the 'recording secretary' for that year, it is possible to reconstruct the animated discussion that followed on the reading of a paper, and that made 'Philosophy 20c', as it was generally known, the centre of Harvard philosophy.

Eliot produced four papers for Royce's seminar. Two were mere notes: one on 'description and explanation', read on 24 February 1914, and another on Causality, read for Eliot by another graduate, Sen Gupta, on 17 March. Of the two more substantial papers, the first, on the role of interpretation in the social sciences, is of interest largely for what it shows of Eliot's absorption even at this date in issues that were later to colour *The Waste Land*: primitive religion and ritual. Basing himself on Durkheim and Lévy-Bruhl, he also refers to Frazer, Jane Harrison, Max Müller, Tyler and Lang. His problem is this:[14] If we study primitive ritual, it is not enough to attend to the mere outward behaviour of those who participate in it. We must also attend to the interpretation they put upon it. But in doing so we have to rely upon our interpretation of what this is. So instead of the classical view, according to which scientific advance is always an increasing approximation to the truth – a view championed by Royce, who spoke of interpretation as 'a self-correcting process' – Eliot maintained that each new interpretation merely adds to the facts by introducing a new point of view: and he chose to see here support for the Bradleian thesis that no judgement is 'more than more or less true'.[15]

The second paper that Eliot read was ostensibly on the subject-matter of psychology, and it was presented on 5 May. Since the paper is, in detail as well as in substance, very close to the central part of *Knowledge and Experience*, it will be better to postpone discussion of it until the next section. Here I shall merely indicate the topic, which was, as Eliot was well aware,[16] a problem much in the air.

The problem is perhaps best seen as consequential upon the break-up of the empire of traditional empiricism. For the empiricists, everything that constituted the life of the mind – where this stretched from imagination through memory and perception to thinking and under-standing – could be analysed in terms of ideas presented, either singly or in complexes, to the mind. These ideas were, by and large, conceived

of as image-like phenomena. However, throughout the nineteenth
century it became increasingly evident that this account was inadequate,
at any rate to the totality of mental life. The objections were varied,
but the underlying criticism was that this account could not properly
exhibit the element of meaning or reference that was inherent in all
species of experience: that every mental event is (in an appropriate
sense) *of* something or other. To make good this deficiency what was
required was to substitute an account in which the mind stands in a
certain relation to things other than itself for one in where there is a
mere contemplation of its own ideas. But the question arose, How far
is this substitution to go? If we are to consider the *objects* of mental
events and not merely their *contents*, what place, if any, is left for
content? Does it have a residual role to play, or is it totally swallowed
up, or (another view) are object and content really the same thing viewed
from different perspectives? Now, to ask what is the subject-matter of
psychology is a convenient, if oblique, way of raising this question.
For it is evident that if there is anything left over to content after the
necessary subtractions have been made, then this will be studied in
psychology. Costello's notes suggest that already Eliot's view on this
subject were very negative, going well beyond Bradley in the direction
of Realism. But before taking up this point I shall complete the biographical picture.

In the summer of 1914 Eliot won a Sheldon Travelling Fellowship.
He went first to Germany, then, when war threatened, to Oxford, to
Merton, Bradley's own college. Bradley by this time was a total recluse,
and Eliot worked with his pupil, Harold Joachim, with whom he read
Aristotle and from whom he gained, as he put it, 'an understanding of
what I wanted to say and of how to say it' (*KE* p. 27). In 1915 Eliot
left Oxford, but was determined to stay in England. The thesis was
completed in April 1916 and despatched. Attached to the original
typescript is the carbon copy of a letter sent to Eliot from Professor
J. H. Woods, saying that Royce had spoken of it as 'the work of an
expert' (*KE* p. 10). But Eliot never returned for the viva, the degree
was not awarded, and it was only in 1932 that the poet revisited his
university, as Charles Eliot Norton Professor.

III

It was a likely choice[17] on Eliot's part to base his study of Bradley on
a study of Bradley's account of Immediate Experience. For the notion

of Immediate Experience is, according to Bradley, at the base of his own philosophy. That there is such a condition is for him an 'ultimate fact':[18] and elsewhere he says that no one is likely to go far in understanding his metaphysical theory who 'makes a mistake as to the given fact from which in a sense it starts'.[19]

The significance of Immediate Experience (or Feeling, as he also calls it) is for Bradley twofold.[20] In the first place it is important because it constitutes the foundations upon which all the higher forms of knowledge or consciousness are grounded. At no point do we ever get beyond what is given. Everything that we know, or will, or feel, is already implicit in the condition of immediacy, and moves into prominence as this condition breaks up or resolves itself into different elements. And it is important to see how broadly this is to be taken: for (to persist for a moment in a terminology that this view ultimately makes absurd) it is not merely the 'content' of any higher form of consciousness, but also the mental 'act' itself, that is contained in the fused-like condition of Immediate Experience. Secondly, Immediate Experience is important because it provides us with a model of the kind of whole that we encounter again at the very peak of human knowledge – or, perhaps better, would encounter again if that peak were not unattainable; the non-relational immediate felt unity, which is Immediate Experience, prefigures the supra-rational unity of the Absolute, in which thought and its object are united to form Truth, and the difference between the two stages is that, whereas at the former, divisions and relations have not yet emerged, at the latter they have been transcended, they merge again in the highest experience.

By and large, Eliot would seem to have accepted this general estimate of the significance of Immediate Experience for any sound philosophy. Nevertheless, there are, roughly, four reservations that he thought it necessary to enter, or four respects in which he thought that the Bradleian metaphysic was in need of supplementation or elaboration.

In the first place, Eliot was critical about the kind of priority to be attached to Immediate Experience. Is it logical, or temporal? Does it relate to the life-history of the individual or of the species? Since, however, it is far from clear what either Bradley or Eliot (*KE* pp. 16–18) concluded on this problem, and since the problem itself is only marginal, I shall not treat of it further.

Secondly, Eliot suggests – and this is definitely in the nature of a criticism – that Bradley is insufficiently radical in his account of what happens when Immediate Experience resolves itself, as it does, into its constituents. Thirdly, it is part of Eliot's thesis to suggest that this process would be better understood if we examined in great detail, or with more emphasis laid upon the peculiarities of each, the different kinds of 'object' into which Immediate Experience is, at any rate partially, resolved: in other words, those elements into which Immediate Experience breaks up on its objective or non-self side. Finally, Eliot would appear to be of the opinion that in one important respect at least Bradley had underestimated the (theoretical) difficulties of re-absorbing everything into a higher whole: he had taken insufficient account of the recalcitrance of 'finite centres' as Bradley calls the units into which experiences group themselves. In the second *Monist* article Eliot goes so far as to compare Bradley's finite centres to Leibniz's monads, the basic units of what is generally conceived to be (though perhaps not by Eliot) one of the most uncompromisingly pluralist philosophies ever devised.

The strategy I shall employ will be to try to analyse *Knowledge and Experience* by working through it in the light of my second and third points. I have, however, said enough about the difficulty of Eliot's thought to hold out no more than a partial hope of success.

A good way of introducing the criticism that Eliot makes of Bradley apropos of the resolution of Immediate Experience into its constituents would be to go back to an argument that Bradley himself employs in order to refute the suggestion that Idealism, or the thesis that everything is, or is constituted out of, experience, leads to Solipsism: the argument occurs in chapter XXI of *Appearance and Reality*. Bradley argues that such a suggestion derives from a misconception of the nature of Immediate Experience. It would be plausible to think that Idealism led to Solipsism, if, but only if, one also believed that the original form of experience was always my experience, or your experience, or X's, or Y's: if, in other words, the Self was a datum in immediate experience. But it is not. For immediate experience is essentially undifferentiated. It is only by a process of abstraction, or 'ideality' (where this means, roughly, filtering experience through 'ideas'), that we arrive at the notion of a Self: and when we do we simultaneously arrive, Bradley insists, at the notion of a not-Self, under which must be subsumed the notion of other selves.

Eliot clearly underwrites this argument. He accepts its premiss: 'We have no right except in the most provisional way, to speak of *my* experience, since the I is a construction out of an experience, an abstraction' (*KE* p. 19). And he accepts its conclusion: so much so that when he comes to write of Solipsism in chapter VI of the dissertation he uses the word to identify another problem, presumably on the assumption that the problem ordinarily so denoted has already been dealt with.

But Feeling is, as we have seen, unstable. In Idealist terminology, it is 'self-transcendent' (*KE* p. 21). Being neither 'complete nor satisfactory' in itself, it breaks up and develops into 'an articulate whole of terms and relations' (*KE* p. 21) within which the broadest division is that into Subject on the one side and Object on the other. It is necessary, Eliot insists, if we are to have a proper understanding of Bradley's philosophy, to realise that this process is just as important for the genesis of objects as it is for the genesis of the Self. We can readily accept the idea that there is initially a kind of indeterminate feeling, out of which self-consciousness, the awareness of a self, develops: that fits in with ordinary thought: but the philosophical point that Bradley makes, and in which Eliot concurs, is that *pari passu* with this, and logically of the same order, is the emergence of objects. And this is less readily conceded. 'It is easy to fall into the error', Eliot writes, 'of imagining that this self-transcendence of feeling is an event only in the history of souls, and not in the history of the external world' (*KE* p. 21). Why we should fall into this error so easily is, Eliot argues, not far to seek; and he gives two reasons. The first is that, in order for us to characterise the development or emergence of the subject, we have to assume the stability of external things, which are the objects of these subjective states. It is only by reference to these objects that we can identify the states. And, secondly, it is possible to ignore the fact that an object, too, depends for its existence on a continuity of feelings, because for the most part the feelings continuous with ours upon which its identity depends, will be concealed from us, being other people's: whereas those feelings upon which the existence of our soul depends are all open to us.

One point is worth noting here. In contradistinction to certain elements in German Idealism, Bradley rejects the idea that the transcendence of Immediate Experience can be regarded as the 'work' or 'construction' of the mind: for, of course, the mind and the external world are concurrent products of this process, so we must not attribute the latter to the agency of the former. Here Eliot obviously agrees with Bradley,[21] and indeed is quick to point out when Bradley, inadvertently, backslides from this position. So strong, however, is the terminological pull of this doctrine in the direction of asserting the workmanship of the mind that Eliot himself is not always able to retain consistency.

However, once the instability of Immediate Experience is conceded, there arises the problem to which, as we have seen, Eliot addressed himself, in the paper that he read to Royce's seminar on 5 May 1914. When Immediate Experience, or Feeling, develops into the two groups of Subject and Object, is there anything left over to the mind as its content, which can thus become the special subject-matter of a science of the mind? Eliot's position is that ultimately there is not: mental contents are at best a transient phenomenon: and Eliot develops at length, and obscurely, arguments concerning three possible confusions upon which a continued belief in their existence might depend.

By now we have arrived at criticism of Bradley. Bradley, it is true, maintained that, from a philosophical or logical point of view, we can (more or less) disregard the mere mental presentations that come before the mind. They lack, in themselves, the quality of meaning. Nevertheless, Bradley thought that there *were* such presentations, and he moreover believed that they formed the proper subject-matter of psychology, where they are studied without reference to their meaning. Such a position is not merely defended, it is also developed in certain characteristic Bradleian ways, in a paper significantly entitled 'A Defence of Phenomenalism in Psychology'[22] as late as 1900. And even Meinong, the philosopher who probably did most to influence Eliot in the direction of thinking of the mind as always conversant with objects, also postulated both object (*Gegenstand*) and content (*Inhalt*) for any mental state. What is distinctive about Meinong[23] is how he conceived content: by and large, as a kind of arrow which pointed, and pointed in a way that no one could mistake, towards the object. Though Meinong also allowed some presentational overtones to content.

The first confusion that, according to Eliot, perpetuates the myth of mental contents is the assimilation of feelings in the ordinary acceptance of the term – in which I fear X, or love Y – to feeling in the more metaphysical sense of Immediate Experience. In the first sense, a feeling is sometimes objective, to be observed and known in the same way as any other part of the world. This is confirmed by the fact, which we tend to slur over in philosophy, that 'often an observer understands a feeling better than does the person who experiences it.[24] However, the objectivity of feelings in this sense can get denied, because we tend to confuse them with the feeling of Immediate Experience, which has nothing objective to it. But Immediate Experience is not objective, only because, as we have seen, it anticipates the moment at which the objective–subjective classification begins to apply. 'So far as feelings are objects at all', Eliot sums up his position, 'they exist on the same footing as other objects . . . And so far as feelings are merely felt, they are neither subjective nor objective' (*KE* p. 24). Nevertheless, Eliot allows that it is comprehensible, though not condonable, that objectified feelings and the feeling of Immediate Experience should be confused, for they are continuous with one another, in that it is the latter that develops into the former.

Eliot's argument here is not as clear as one would wish. More specifically, the sense in which 'evolved' feelings are said to be objective suffers from a rather serious ambiguity. For is it Eliot's thesis that such feelings on examination simply *are* their objects: or, at any rate, are so intimately involved with them that they cannot without grave damage be considered apart from them? Is Eliot, in other words, assimilating feelings here to sensations as he treats them later as transparent or semi-transparent elements?[25] Alternatively, is it Eliot's thesis that feelings are objective merely in the sense that they can be studied scientifically, or as objects? If Eliot's thesis is the latter, then this does not establish that feelings are not mental contents. If Eliot's thesis is the former, then it is clearer why feelings are held to be non-mental or contentless: but the ground for the thesis is itself far from clear. We shall return later to this ambiguity.[26]

The second confusion that, according to Eliot, reinforces the notion of mental content is a running together of the two different points of view from which the life of the individual can be seen. From the point of view of the subject, an 'idea' or 'psychological event' (to talk generally) is something that is – with all the ambiguity that we have seen attaches to this term – objective: it belongs to the external world. From the point of view of the observer, however, a psychological event belongs to the history of the subject who experiences it: it is something personal. This theory of the two standpoints – which clearly bears upon it the influence of William James's neutral monism – can also be stated, according to Eliot, as a theory concerning the two different kinds of law in terms of which we can explain the event. We can explain a psychological event in terms of laws asserting 'connections of the real world': that is how the subject would explain it. Alternatively, we can explain it in terms of laws – and this is Eliot's tribute to the materialist psychology that was indigenous to Harvard – asserting 'physiological connections' (*KE* p. 75). 'The idea as you try to grasp it as an object, either identifies itself with the reality or melts back in the other direction into a different reality, the reality of its physiological basis' (*KE* p. 76).

It is, however, natural (Eliot goes on) to pass from one point of view to the other: Eliot uses a word of the period to characterise this transition, 'empathy'. And the ease of transition might then lead us, quite erroneously of course, to try and combine into a single description the attributes that psychological events present from these two different points of view. As a result we then postulate something that is at once experienced (as such events are, seen from the subject's point of view) and also subjective (as they are, seen from the observer's point of view). Eliot calls the objects of traditional psychology 'half-objects';[27] thereby suggesting the ambiguous way in which they are concocted, or what he refers to later as 'the psychologist's error of treating two points of view as if they were one' (*KE* p. 93).

The third confusion that, according to Eliot, sustains the belief in mental contents is a mistaken conception about reference: that is, what we are doing when we say or think something about reality. Now Bradley certainly would have agreed, indeed he had been amongst the first to insist, that to mean something cannot be equated, as the empiricists would claim, with having an image or representation of that thing: this is in large part the burden of Bradley's attack on 'the psychological attitude', in which, as he put it, we, that is, we English, 'have lived too long'.[28] Nevertheless, Bradley seems to have believed that the imagery of the mind plays some part in the whole process of reference. He puts it (obscurely) by saying that meaning consists in 'a part of the content, original or acquired, cut off, fixed by the mind, and considered apart from the existence of the mind'.[29]

But Eliot insists this cannot be right. For it assimilates (as Bradley intended it to) the relation that holds between an idea and its reference, or between meaning and reality, to that which holds between a fox and cunning or between a flower and some emotion which it has come to symbolise: ideas are assimilated to signs. But this is wrong. For, in the first place, a sign can be misinterpreted, or not recognised as a sign at all: secondly, we can identify that which is signified independently of the sign, the sign and its significance are heterogeneous. But neither of these characteristics hold good of meaning. A man could not think without knowing what he was thinking of, or, for that matter, that he was thinking at all: nor could he identify what he was thinking of without thinking of it.

How Eliot would have us see the matter is not so clear. We have, in his terminology, the following items to arrange: the idea, the mental content, the image, the concept, the (identical) reference (*KE* p. 42). In a piece of elaborate argumentation he disputes the equation of idea, which is what we predicate of Reality, with, successively, the image, the concept (here Eliot is criticising Moore), and the mental content. So there is left the relation of idea and reference, and for Eliot the idea is *almost* identical with its reference. What seems to prevent Eliot from totally identifying the two is a difference of aspect or function between them. For an idea is active, in that it has inherently an ostensive, or 'pointing towards' character. It points towards its reference.

But this way of putting the matter could itself easily be misunderstood, for it might mislead us into thinking that an idea points to something outside itself, which is its reference. But it doesn't. 'Every idea means itself' (*KE* p. 56). The conclusion that Eliot draws from this discussion he expresses by saying, 'Ultimately . . . ideality and reality turn out to be the same' (*KE* p. 57).

Eliot's position on the nature of the mind is radical: and he expresses his position with unaccustomed clarity. 'There is', he says at the end of chapter III,

> in this sense, nothing mental, and there is certainly no such thing as consciousness if consciousness is to be an object or something independent of the objects which it has. (*KE* p. 83)

Such a view undoubtedly circumvents certain problems both in the theory of the mind and in the theory of meaning. Yet a philosophy which adopts it thereby exposes itself to the no less serious dangers of Realism. For if the ultimate identity of ideality and reality, of consciousness and its object, is maintained, how can one avoid a monstrous overpopulation of Reality? Monstrous not only in its scale but for its character. Every supposition, paradox, error, self-contradiction, will spawn a corresponding inhabitant of the world: Ivanhoe, the present king of France, the golden mountain and the round square all exist. It was against such a vision of the world that Russell, about this period, invoked his 'robust sense of reality':[30] and it is worth recalling that the philosopher who aroused in Russell this vision was the very philosopher

whom Eliot appealed to in order to bring Bradley's philosophy of mind
more in accord with the ultimate presuppositions, as he conceived them,
of Bradley's metaphysic: Meinong.

Indeed, it is arguable that, even without the total replacement of
mental content by object, Bradley's later philosophy was similarly
exposed to the charge of a reckless proliferation of existences. In
Bradley's case the crucial paper was 'On Floating Ideas and the
Imaginary' of 1906,[31] in which he withdrew the thesis maintained in
the *Logic* that an idea could be 'held before the mind without any
judgement'.[32] Under protracted criticism from Bosanquet, Bradley had
come round to the view that every idea that is in the mind is *eo ipso*
employed. 'Every idea essentially qualifies Reality.'[33] There are no
floating ideas. At most an idea may not be referred to the limited section
of reality to which we might immediately or unreflectingly think it
relates: but that means only that it refers to another section.[34] However,
Bradley felt himself able to deal with at least the worst consequences
of this theory by appealing to a principle according to which the
offending incompatibilities or inner contradictions appear only if we
take too narrow a view of the groupings in which they are supposed to
be contained: if we widen our view, if we take the seemingly contra-
dictory elements as predicated of larger wholes, we shall find a point
of union or reconciliation. Eliot is amongst those students of Bradley
who have found this resolution of the problem intolerably brisk. For,
after all, when we do see the incongruous element in a larger whole, in
which it is said to be reconciled, this is because of a change in us, not
in it. It is we who have stepped back and altered our point of view. But
the element itself still remains. 'In the "transcendence" of error', Eliot
writes ('transcendence' being the Anglo-Hegelian word for the process
by which something is taken up in a larger whole),

> the error, as real object, is not got rid of. An object is not transcended,
> though a point of view is; and it is only as we consider the hallucina-
> tion not as an object, but as an element in a point of view, that it can
> be said to be 'transcended', 'transmuted', or 'dissolved'. Such a
> theory as that here outlined by Mr Bradley . . . appears unsatis-
> factory in that the unreality is merely pushed back and not done
> away with. (*KE* p. 119)

Nevertheless, for all the apparent clarity of what Eliot is saying here,
we could take his words in exactly the opposite sense from that which

he intended. For ultimately Eliot is not saying that Bradley's theory of the transcendence of error is wrong because it fails, despite its professions, effectively to spirit away recalcitrant objects in the world. Where it is wrong is in thinking that this is something to be done. Eliot's view might be expressed by saying that one has to address oneself to the problem of Realism, i.e. the overpopulation of the world, if, but only if, one accepts the assumption of Realism. This assumption, which is also called by Eliot the assumption of epistemology, is that 'there is one world of external reality which is consistent and complete' (*KE* p. 112): more succinctly, that the world is 'made up of objects' (*KE* p. 120).

But once we accept the full implications of equating, ultimately at least, ideality and reality, the problem transforms itself. For, in admitting the existence of an object, we are not (on Eliot's view) postulating the existence of something which reduplicates our experience. To every idea there does indeed correspond an object. 'So far as the idea "golden mountain" is a real idea', Eliot writes, taking up a provocative example of Meinong's, 'so far is it a real object' (*KE* p. 89). But that this does not induce a situation from which only 'a robust sense of reality' can save us follows from having a proper sense of what an object is. An object Eliot defines as a point of attention. 'An object is as such a point of attention, and thus anything and everything to which we may be said to direct attention is an object' (*KE* p. 99).

Nevertheless, the issue misleadingly debated within epistemology as to the existence or non-existence of objects, or of when we do and when we do not have knowledge, does for Eliot at least mark the site of a real problem: a problem that is better discussed, he maintains, in the familiar Bradleian terms of degrees of truth and reality. Objects, that is kinds of object, can be ranged according to the degree of reality that they possess, and this in turn is determined by the network of relations into which they enter. 'The reality of the object does not lie in the object itself but in the extent of the relations which the object possesses without significant falsification of itself.'[35] It is only under practical pressures, pressures which are unavoidable outside metaphysics and also make their mark inside metaphysics, that we abridge the scale of reality and start to pronounce, *tout court*, some objects to be real, others unreal.

What is required, Eliot thinks – and here I come to the third respect in which he appears to diverge from Bradley – is to categorise the various kinds of object into which Feeling can develop. This is in keeping with what Eliot says concerning the three traditional problems of epistemology. Of the problems of the genesis of knowledge, of the structure of knowledge, and of the possibility of knowledge, it is 'the position of all sound Idealism, and I believe it is the position of Mr Bradley that the only real problem is the second' (*KE* p. 84). Costello had already, in his summary of Eliot's paper of 5 May 1914, suggested that 'as regards the classification of objects, the paper was along the line of Meinong's proposed Gegenstandstheorie',[36] and it is evident that once more Eliot is employing Meinong to supplement Bradley.

In his scale of objects Eliot appears to encounter most difficulty at what we might reasonably think of as the top of the scale and the bottom. The top consists in those objects which are fullest in their relations, the bottom in those which are barest. At the top we can place material objects or 'things', at the bottom self-contradictions. The problem about things is that in order to have objects with that richness and permanence of property that belongs to thinghood we have to associate to the perceived and hence existent properties other properties which are unperceived or subsistent. Now these subsistent properties are universals, so we have the problem (which apparently appears everywhere to a greater or lesser degree) that a thing is 'a complex composed of universals and particulars' (*KE* p. 104). Not the least of the difficulties that arises here is how to fit these two elements into the same time-order. The other problematic case, from the bottom of the scale, is that of 'self-contradictory' objects like the round square. Eliot insists that, in so far as someone thinks of a round square, there is a round square, i.e. there is something that is both round and square. But we need to appreciate the very faint degree to which such an object has reality. For instance, it is not both round and not round, which is of course what would make it an 'impossible' object: for, on the level on which it exists, squareness does not imply not-roundness, though of course in other contexts it does (*KE* p. 130). And if this sounds an absurdly *ad hoc* way out of the difficulty there are two points we need to remember which may make it slightly more plausible. The first is that, for Eliot presumably as for Bradley (and, for that matter, for Hume), the relation of contrariety is something that we observe to hold between terms only on the basis of our experience: there are, in Bradley's words, 'no native contraries'.[37] Secondly, the link that holds between a word and its reference has, in Idealist thought, a closeness or intimacy that quite outstrips that between one word and another. What is of supreme importance for Eliot is the way in which any word merges with, and therefore necessitates the existence of, its reference.

However, by insisting more strongly than Bradley that we 'arrive at objects . . . by meaning objects' (*KE* p. 133), that every object that a finite centre apprehends is real, Eliot has, to a correspondingly greater degree, the problem how to unite the different points of view into a single world. For, since no reduction has been effected on the level of the individual, the dangers of conflict between the worlds of different individuals might excusably seem greater. This is the problem that Eliot calls Solipsism, and he treats of it in chapter VI. Solipsism, he says, 'has been one of the dramatic properties of most philosophical entertainers': but it 'rests upon a truth' (*KE* p. 141).

Eliot's argument on this point is hard to follow, but there seem to be roughly two different solutions between which he is indeterminate. One is that the different points of view fit together because we all intend a common reference. And Eliot seems to draw some support from the fact that in our own lives we are often able to transcend one point of view in favour of another; when we pass, that is, from one phase of thinking or feeling to another. For Eliot expressly rejects the equation of self with point of view: one self will contain many points of view.

To this solution, however, it might be objected, Yes, we may intend a common reference, but *is* there a common reference? At times Eliot seems to allow this objection, and thereby arrives at the second solution: which is that the metaphysics of a common world is based upon 'faith' (*KE* p. 163), a word which acquires a rather special sense in Bradley's metaphysic.[38] At other times, however, Eliot rejects this objection as too imbued with the assumptions of 'epistemology'. 'We ask', Eliot writes,

> in what the identity consists, beyond the 'identical reference'. Yet while the question is natural, I cannot admit that it is legitimate. . . . A reference to an identity . . . *is* the identity, in the sense in which a word *is* that which it denotes. An identity is intended, and it could not have been intended, we say, unless it was there: but its being 'there' consists simply in the intention, and has no other meaning. (*KE* p. 143)

Yet it is in keeping with the obscure and dialectical character of this whole philosophy that we find, only a page later, after the problem had seemed so finally settled, Eliot writing,

> When I say that there is one world because one world is intended, I have stated only half the case: for any explanation in terms of 'because . . .' can only be misleading unless we turn it about the other way as well. Let us say therefore, that we are able to intend one world because our points of view are essentially akin. (*KE* p. 144)

I do not think that this is quite the perversity of argument that it might at first seem to be. For in such a passage Eliot realised that identity of reference – where this means simply identity in the act of reference or an identity of intention – presupposes, if not a common set of objects where these are identified separately from the identity of reference, then at least a shared system of reference. But at the same time he failed correctly to appreciate the nature of this presupposition. He failed to see that the kinship required between points of view was the requirement that there should be a common language. Or rather he partly saw this: but partly – and here we have the influence of his old master Josiah Royce asserting itself – he thought that the requirement stretched beyond this and necessitated a community of souls upon which the individual was dependent for his existence. And here is the point at which a theory of Eliot's, which has many other roots as well, derives its philosophical support: I refer to his theory of tradition.

With the discussion of Solipsism Eliot brings to an end his account of what he regards as the one proper subject-matter of a theory of knowledge: as he puts it, in a poignant and dramatic phrase, 'the rise and decay of objects' (*KE* p. 156).

IV

Are we now in a better position to trace the influence of Bradley's thought upon Eliot?

Much depends on how we envisage such an inquiry to be undertaken. There is an evident invitation simply to spread Eliot's work out in front of one, and then try to trace this influence upon it in points of detail. But I doubt if this method could take us very far: more specifically, whether we can use it to advantage until we have first settled the very broad question of how Eliot envisaged the assembling of theoretical or speculative ideas inside literature. On this subject he was on a number of occasions no less than outspoken. 'A poet who is also a metaphysician', he wrote (and this is typical),

> and unites the two activities, is conceivable as a unicorn or a wyvern is conceivable: he is possible like some of Meinong's *Annahmen*; for such a poet would be a monster, just as (in my opinion) M. Valéry's Monsieur Teste is a monster.[39]

Eliot goes on to say that a poet might use philosophical ideas, but he has no need to think them.

It would be a subject in itself to study the irony of many of Eliot's pronouncements on literature in general or on his poetry in particular – of which this passage, in which Eliot simultaneously depreciates, and makes clear his own, philosophical culture, is a fine example. Nevertheless, there are reasons, over and above its reiteration by Eliot, why we should take this assertion seriously. Suppose, for instance, we begin our examination of Bradley's influence on Eliot at its most obvious starting-point – namely, the passage in *The Waste Land* to which Eliot associated a quotation from *Appearance and Reality* referring to Solipsism. Immediately we find ourselves in a difficulty of interpretation that is typical. For the lines to which the note relates,

> I have heard the key
> Turn in the door once and turn once only
> We think of the key, each in his prison
> Thinking of the key,

definitely express a solipsistic[40] thought: and so, it might be thought, does the passage from Bradley.* Nevertheless, as we have seen, Eliot did not think that Bradley subscribed to Solipsism: indeed, he thought, if anything, that Bradley underestimated the threat of Solipsism to someone whose philosophy starts from Immediate Experience. Moreover, the passage that constitutes the note had already been quoted by Eliot in a more extended form in the second of the two *Monist* articles

---

* 'My external sensations are no less private to myself than are my thoughts or my feelings. In either case my experience falls within my own circle, a circle closed on the outside; and, with all its elements alike, every sphere is opaque to the others which surround it. . . . In brief, regarded as an existance which appears in a soul, the whole world for each is peculiar and private to that soul.' (*Appearance and Reality*, p. 346.)

(*KE* p. 203): there to illustrate not Bradley's solipsism but rather his ambiguity or ambivalence on the subject of 'the common world'. So, why the note?

Taking this as a warning, I shall confine myself to suggesting three very general tendencies of thought that are to be found in Eliot's writing, particularly his critical writing, and that also occur in Bradley: so we can say of them that, even if they were not transmitted from Bradley to Eliot, they would have been reinforced in Eliot by his reading of Bradley.

The first is what might be characterised, very broadly, as a peculiarly empty or hollow way of conceiving the mind. As we have seen, in Bradley's philosophy, and even more in Eliot's emended version of it, everything that would usually be held to constitute an element or content of the mind either tends to reach out towards, or is itself, an object: so that, whereas from one point of view it belongs to the subject, to the history of a soul, from another point of view it can be easily detached from the subjective side and placed firmly on the side of the external world. And the paradox is that the point of view from which mental contents are subjective is the outsider's point of view: from the point of view of the person who experiences these feelings, sensations, desires, whatever, they fall on the objective side. It is not hard to see that we have here the background to Eliot's notorious 'impersonal theory of the poet' (*SW* pp. 46–53): or, for that matter, the dissociated way in which the experiences of *The Waste Land* stand to Tiresias, 'the most important personage in the poem, uniting all the rest'.

Nevertheless, there is a difficulty here, which is connected with how precisely the word 'background' is to be understood. For the conception of the mind that Eliot took over from Bradley, and added to, is philosophical in character, not psychological or ethical. In other words, we would expect it to hold at a higher level than, or be neutral between, the descriptions or prescriptions relating to the mind that occur in critical theory or a poetic programme. And there is, indeed, some ambiguity or uncertainty in Eliot's essays concerning the extent to which, say, the thesis of the impersonality of the poet derives support from any philosophical 'disproof' of commonsense notions of personality. Is the 'escape from personality', which is the poetic vocation, a direct logical consequence of the dissolution by Idealism of faulty and ultimately incoherent notions of the self or personality – or is it a mere analogue in critical theory to what in metaphysics is a necessary truth?

To put it crudely: Does the poet not express personality, because there is no such thing as personality, or because he shouldn't?

There is a great deal in Eliot to suggest the latter. But also there is enough not to rule out the possibility of the former. For instance, a natural philosophical corollary to the thesis that all states of consciousness are intrinsically connected with their objects is to deny substantiality to the self: and it is significant that, in criticising the theory of poetry as the expression of personality, Eliot writes, 'The point of view which I am struggling to attack is perhaps related to the metaphysical theory of the substantial unity of the soul' (*SW* p. 50). How expressive of Eliot is that use of the word 'perhaps'!

Once the metaphysical self is rejected, there is nothing to the self over and above 'a point of view': which is roughly the definition of 'finite centre' employed by Eliot in the dissertation.[41] If we wish to consider one point of view, we can do so only by adopting another. Our own point of view is, we might say, systematically elusive. 'To realise that a point of view is a point of view is already to have transcended it' (*KE* p. 148). It is an argument in favour of interpreting the impersonal theory of poetry 'philosophically', i.e. as a consequence of a philosophical thesis about the self, that we can observe the same connection between this new philosophical thesis and a further critical theory. And that is a theory which Eliot expounds in one place, but which we can assume to have been more widely operative with him, of the common roots of poetry and drama. For these roots lie in the continual shift we make inside our experience to take account of our point of view. 'In actual life', Eliot writes,

> in many of those situations in actual life which we enjoy consciously and keenly, we are at times aware of ourselves in this way [i.e. as dramatic figures], and these moments are of very great usefulness to dramatic verse. A very small part of acting is that which takes place on the stage! (*SW* p. 76)

Finally, in trying to determine the relation between the theory of poetic impersonality and the conception of the mind and its objects that we find in e.g. *Knowledge and Experience*, we should remember this: that in the philosophical doctrine the objective character of experience is, as it were, a late development. So, if Eliot argues, as he does at times, for impersonality as being true only or supremely of the poet, this is not conclusive evidence that the critical theory is not philosophical: it may rather indicate that for Eliot the poetic consciousness is peculiarly highly developed, and hence reveals consciousness in its purest form.

Now the question arises, Given that the emotions that enter into poetry are impersonal, how are they to be conveyed? And this leads us on to the second and third elements in Eliot's thinking that have a distinctly Bradleian character. For, if in Bradley's philosophy of mind emotions are only conventionally associated with what is ordinarily represented as the self that enjoys or experiences them, they are, in contrast, more intimately connected than they would be in common thought with two other aspects of the world: on the one hand, with objects, or their objects; on the other hand, with symbols or ideality. And Eliot in the development of his poetics, takes up both these connections.

The connection between emotions and their objects gives us the theory – if that is what we can call something so perfunctorily set out – of the 'objective correlative'. 'The only way of expressing emotion in the form of art', Eliot writes,

is by finding an 'objective correlative'; in other words, a set of objects, a situation, a chain of events which shall be the formula of that *particular* emotion; such that when the external facts, which must terminate in sensory experience, are given, the emotion is immediately evoked. (*SW* p. 92)

It will be appreciated that this critical theory derives from Eliot's account of the objectivity of emotions taken in the first of the senses I indicated: that is, that according to which emotions fall increasingly on the object-side, because of the way they coalesce around their objects. (It is irrelevant to the present discussion that the actual use Eliot makes of the idea of 'objective correlative' in his criticism of *Hamlet* is unwarranted on either conception of objectivity.)

The connection between emotions and ideality or, perhaps more simply, language, occurs in a theory that is generally asserted by Eliot in a historical form in which it is known as 'the dissociation of sensibility' (*SE* pp. 287–8). In the sixteenth century, when there was 'a development of the English language which we have perhaps never equalled . . . [s]ensation became word and word was sensation' (*SW* p. 117). Since then the falling apart of language and feeling, from which we have barely recovered, has made the poet's task intolerably difficult. In Swinburne we can see the disintegration at an extreme point: when we take to pieces his verse, we 'find always that the object was not there – only the word' (*SW* p. 134).

Once again there is some obscurity how this critical theory is to be connected with the philosophy that it seems to parallel: for instance, with such a view as that the symbol 'is continuous with that which it symbolises' (*KE* p. 132), or that name and object form 'a mystic marriage' (*KE* p. 135). The difficulty is the same as that which we encountered in connection with the thesis of poetic impersonality. For what in the critical theory is asserted as a perfection or something to be aimed at, in the philosophical theory is asserted as a necessary fact. So, for instance, in a critical writing of Eliot's we read, 'Language *in a healthy state* presents the object, is so close to the object that the two are identified' (*SW* p. 136; my italics): whereas in the dissertation we read, 'Idea and phrase both denote realities, but the realities which they denote are so far as idea or phrase denotes, identical with the idea or the phrase' (*KE* p. 129). How, we might ask, can it be a criterion of excellence in poetry to aim towards a certain condition of language that language necessarily or in its essence achieves? And here again the answer may lie in recognising that in idealist philosophy what is asserted to be the case is often, in effect, a terminal condition or condition of perfection: a condition which is realised when the phenomenon in question, say emotion or language, has become everything that it is in it to be. Feeling and language are inherently one, but it is only in poetry, in the best poetry at that, that the unity can be exhibited.

The 'dissociation of sensibility' theory contains the further suggestion that the proper development of language, as indeed of knowledge, requires that there should be a shared social context of some considerable stability, within which consciousness can evolve in an unhampered fashion. This, however, brings us once again up to the frontier of a large theory of Eliot's which, as I have already had occasion to say, is, I think, only marginally grounded in philosophy: his theory of tradition. For this reason, I shall once again pause upon this frontier.

v

To trace the influence of Bradley's philosophy upon Eliot any way beyond such generalities seems to me a most hazardous and uncertain undertaking: and for a reason that goes deeper than either the obscurity of Eliot's philosophical style or his habit of toying with ideas both in his poetry and his criticism. I refer rather to two dispositions of the psyche of which – as Eliot said apropos some speculations of his own concerning the Dante of the *Vita Nuova* – we become aware in reading the text: though the evidence for them is so fragmentary and elusive that (to take up Eliot's phrase) anything that we say about them must be confined to 'the unprovable and the irrefutable' (*SE* p. 272).

On the one hand, we may detect in Eliot a certain fear of the intellect: rather as though it were envisaged as something having the power to damage or dement those who used it in a literal manner. And alongside this, and at certain crucial points linked with it, there would appear to be in Eliot's make-up another disposition, which we may characterise by saying that it was only after he had made some kind of initial sub-mission to a force, felt in itself to be uncongenial or external, that he possessed the liberty to do something for himself or on his own account. Historically, of course, both dispositions have played a large part in the formation of art and its institutions. If we tend in Eliot's case to overlook or discount their operation, this (I suggest) is only because we are so seduced or beguiled by the highly evolved ironical manner, by means of which they are characteristically represented in his work, that we fail to appreciate the very real emotional tasks that this dis-charged for him. To see how the consistent self-depreciation masks but also reveals a sustained attack that Eliot made upon himself, we should perhaps divert our attention from its central manifestations and the way in which it conditions Eliot's achievement as a whole, and concen-trate rather upon the trivial or peripheral ways in which it betrays itself. In this connection a study of Eliot's inconsistencies,[42] of the way, we might say, in which he was compelled to deny an idea of his own once he had asserted it, might be very revealing as to his general temperament.

The effect of the two dispositions that I have tried to characterise might be put by saying that Eliot, in the pursuit of a certain kind of security or reassurance that we are in no position to define, was pro-gressively led to substitute, in his mind, on the one hand, ideas of less content for ideas of more content, and, on the other hand, poorer or softer ideas for better and stronger ideas. To cite Eliot's conversion to religious orthodoxy in this context might seem to some controversial: though certainly the dispiriting nature of the particular theological diet on which he fed is beyond disputation. A clearer case still is provided by the interest Eliot is known to have taken in a work of popular philosophy that enjoyed a considerable middle-brow vogue in the years preceding the last war: J. W. Dunne's *Experiment with Time*. It is no disparagement of the poetic quality of *Four Quartets* (though to some it may still be puzzling why it is not) to say that at this period of Eliot's life it is difficult to determine with any kind of accuracy when he was trying to express the doctrines of idealist metaphysics and when he was writing under the influence of what was the philosophical equivalent of *bondieuserie*.

NOTES

1. T. S. Eliot, *Knowledge and Experience in the Philosophy of F. H. Bradley* (1964). The two reprinted articles are 'The Development of Leibniz' Monadism', which originally appeared in the *Monist*, xxvi (Oct 1916) iv 534–56, and 'Leibniz' Monads and Bradley's Finite Centres', which appeared in the same number of the *Monist*, pp. 566–76. The text throughout was edited by Professor Anne Bolgan of the University of Alaska.

2. Letter of T. S. Eliot addressed to me, dated 22 Mar 1962.

3. *KE* p. 11. It is worth observing that there are at least two versions of this preface, one of which was set up in proof before it was also decided to reprint the *Monist* articles, the other being the published version. The change in tone between the two versions reflects the growing seriousness with which Eliot was prepared to take his philosophical writings. In the early version there is, for instance, whimsically inserted after 'a junior master at the Highgate Junior School', the phrase 'where a small boy in the lowest form, who had heard that the "American master" wrote poetry, submitted for my consideration a small sheaf of manuscript verse entitled *Best Poems of Betjeman*'.

4. Review of second edition of F. H. Bradley, *Ethical Studies*, in *Times Literary Supplement*, 29 Dec 1927; reprinted in *SE* pp. 444–55.

5. Eliot in the preface to *KE* says that Professor Hugh Kenner 'drew attention' to the doctoral thesis in a chapter in his *The Invisible Poet: T. S. Eliot* (New York, 1959). Kenner had received permission to examine the dissertation at Harvard. Reference to the dissertation is, however, also to be found in Kristian Smidt, 'Poetry and Belief in the Work of T. S. Eliot', in *Skrifter utgitt av det Norske Videnskaps-Akademi i Oslo* (II. Historisk-Filosofisk Klasse) (1949) no. 1; Grover Smith, *T. S. Eliot's Poetry and Plays: a study in sources and meaning* (New York, 1955); and E. P. Bollier 'T. S. Eliot and F. H. Bradley: a question of influence', in *Tulane Studies in English*, xii (1962) 87–111. These three studies depend for their knowledge of the dissertation on the far from luminous summary provided by R(alph) W(ithington) C(hurch), 'Eliot on Bradley's Metaphysics', in *Harvard Advocate*, cxxv (Dec 1938) 24–6. A more extended paraphrase of the dissertation is to be found in Eric Thompson, *T. S. Eliot: the metaphysical perspective* (Carbondale, Ill., 1963). Lewis Freed, *T. S. Eliot: aesthetics and history* (La Salle, Ill., 1962), which attempts to show that Eliot's theory of poetry derives from Bradley's philosophy of experience, subject to certain scholastic qualifications, reveals no knowledge of the existence of the dissertation. A detailed examination of the place of the dissertation in Eliot's thought is contained in an unpublished thesis submitted in fulfilment of the requirement for candidates for the Doctorate of Literature in English Literature

in the University of Patna by D. P. Singh entitled 'The Influence of F. H. Bradley on T. S. Eliot', dated Nov 1964. None of the published work throws any light on the questions discussed in this essay. I have not had the opportunity to consult J. Hillis Miller, *Poets of Reality* (Cambridge, Mass., 1965).

6. T. S. Eliot, 'Byron', in *From Anne to Victoria*, ed. Bonamy Dobrée (1937) p. 602.

7. In addition to Bradley and Meinong, who form the centrepiece of the thesis, Eliot shows familiarity with the ideas of Stout, Russell, Bosanquet, G. E. Moore, William James, Samuel Alexander, H. W. B. Joseph, Prichard and the American New Realists: he also quotes from Peirce, Messer, Sigwart, McTaggart, Jerusalem, Cook Wilson, Tichener and Witasek.

8. For the facts of Eliot's student life, the reader is referred to Herbert Howarth, *Notes on Some Figures behind T. S. Eliot* (1965) on which I have drawn heavily. Howarth has unfortunately almost nothing to say about Eliot and Bradley.

9. F. O. Matthiessen, *The Achievement of T. S. Eliot* (1947) p. 183. Matthiessen refers to a critical essay that Eliot wrote on the *durée réelle*.

10. These two years were intended for a more general study of philosophy. Eliot interested himself amongst other things in Indian philosophy. 'Two years spent in the study of Sanskrit under Charles Lanman, and a year in the mazes of Patanjali's metaphysics under the guidance of James Woods, left me in a state of enlightened mystification' (*ASG* p. 40).

11. Russell is, of course, recognisable in Mr Appollinax.

12. Alan Wood, *Bertrand Russell; the passionate sceptic* (1957) p. 94.

13. *Josiah Royce's Seminar 1913–14, as recorded in the Notebooks of Harry T. Costello*, ed. Grover Smith (New Brunswick, 1963).

14. I am, of course, relying here on Costello. Eliot gave his own account of his argument – a rather different one – in the introduction he provided to Charlotte Eliot, *Savonarola* (1926).

15. *Royce*, ed. Smith, p. 76.

16. To the corresponding section in the dissertation Eliot appends a footnote: 'I refer to the articles in *Mind* by Bradley, Prichard, Joseph, Stout, and Joachim; to the articles in the *Proc. Arist. Soc.* and in the British *Journal of Psychology* by Alexander; and articles in the *Proc. Arist. Soc.* by Stout, Hicks and Dumville. I shall also refer to writings of Meinong, Messer and Lipps (especially the latter's *Inhalt und Gegenstand*).' (*KE* p. 58.)

17. We do not know how or when Eliot came to make his choice of thesis subject. Eliot bought his copy of *Appearance and Reality* on 12 June 1913 (see Smith, *Eliot's Poetry and Plays*, p. 299 n. 3), but Bradley's ideas would already have been familiar to him. The term 'the Absolute' enters, ironically, into an undergraduate poem published in the *Harvard Advocate*, Jan 1910, and reprinted in *The Undergraduate Poems of T. S. Eliot* (Cambridge, Mass., 1938) p. 5. But the term is also central to Royce's version of Idealism.

18. F. H. Bradley, *Appearance and Reality* (2nd ed. 1897) p. 569.

19. F. H. Bradley, *Essays on Truth and Reality* (1914) p. 246.

20. From this and other points in Bradley's philosophy, which I have elaborated at greater length.

21. cf. 'I am as much my contruction as the world is' (*KE* p. 166).

22. F. H. Bradley, *Collected Essays*, 2 vols (1935) II 364–86. Eliot explicitly criticises this paper (*KE* pp. 76–7).

23. For Meinong's views the reader is referred to J. N. Findlay, *Meinong's Theory of Objects and Values* (2nd ed., 1963).

24. *KE* p. 24. Eliot returns to this point in the second of the *Monist* articles. 'My emotions may be better understood by others than by myself: as my oculist knows my eyes' (ibid. p. 204).

25. Ibid. pp. 65, 67–8, 71–3; e.g. 'Sensations are not separate objects which stand between us and the object.'

26. For the two senses in which Eliot appears to use the terms 'object' and 'objective', cf. 'The emotion is really part of the object, and is ultimately just as objective' (ibid. p. 80), and 'The attention to feeling presupposes that there is such an object present' (ibid. p. 26).

27. Ibid. pp. 81–3. The meaning of this phrase comes clearer later, where Eliot says of Meinong's content that it is 'only a half-object: it exists, that is, as an object only by our half putting ourselves in the place of the speaker and half contemplating him as an object' (ibid. p. 94).

28. F. H. Bradley, *The Principles of Logic*, 2 vols (2nd ed., 1922) I 2.

29. Loc. cit. (quoted by Eliot).

30. Bertrand Russell, *Introduction to the Philosophy of Mathematics* (1919) p. 170.

31. F. H. Bradley, 'On Floating Ideas and the Imaginary', in *Mind*, xx (1906) 445–72, reprinted in *Essays on Truth and Reality*, pp. 28–64.

32. *Principles of Logic*, pp. 76–7.

33. *Essays on Truth and Reality*, p. 28.

34. Ibid. pp. 35–6.

35. *KE* p. 91. Cf. p. 116. 'The difference between real bear and illusory bear is a difference of fullness of relations, and is *not* the sort of difference which subsists between two classes of objects.'

36. *Royce*, ed. Smith, p. 176.

37. *Appearance and Reality*, p. 572.

38. *Essays on Truth and Reality*, pp. 19–27.

39. Paul Valéry, *Le Serpent*, with a translation by Mark Wardle, and an introduction by T. S. Eliot (1924) p. 13. Other similar assertions are to be found apropos of Goethe and Blake in *The Sacred Wood* (1920) pp. 59 and 141–2 respectively, and apropos of Shakespeare, in *SE* pp. 134–9. It is important to distinguish this question from the question whether the reader has to share the beliefs of the poet in order to appreciate the poetry: which is discussed apropos of Dante in *SE* pp. 268–71, and more generally *passim*.

40. Here, I use the word 'solipsism' in the somewhat revised sense in which Eliot uses it in his thesis: to mean not that all experiences are mine, or that everything is my experience, but that everyone has access only to his own experiences.

41. e.g. *KE* p. 147. 'For Bradley the finite centre (or what I call the point of view).'

42. A small example would be the conflicting assessment of Charles-Louis Philippe, who is talked of in *The Sacred Wood* (p. 41) in a way that would not suggest that he aroused Eliot's intense admiration, both earlier on, when he was in Paris, and later (1932), when he wrote a preface to a translation of *Bubu de Montparnasse*. Or, again, contrast what Eliot usually says about the relation of a poet to ideas with the criticism he allows himself to make of Poe: 'All of his ideas seem to be *entertained* rather than believed' (*From Poe to Valéry* (New York, 1948) p. 19).

Authority and Personality in Eliot's Criticism

JOHN CHALKER

I

ELIOT frequently insisted that his criticism should be seen in relation to his creative writing. He described it as 'a by-product of my private poetry-workshop; or a prolongation of the thinking that went into the formation of my own verse',[1] which suggests that his early essays were largely written in order to clear his own mind. But this is a very modest account of his work, offering an engagingly amateur image which masks the element of commitment, even of ruthlessness, that appears in many of the early essays.

What strikes one particularly about them is their strongly rhetorical manner. The tone is immediately authoritative and magisterial, and there is a *gravitas* of syntax and phrasing, a studied 'placing' of writers that often recalls Johnson. This is Johnson on Addison's style: 'What he attempted, he performed; he is never feeble, and he did not wish to be energetic; he is never rapid, and he never stagnates.'[2] Writing on Seneca, Eliot pitches on exactly the same note:

> An essential point to make about Seneca is the consistency of his writing, its maintenance on one level, below which he seldom falls and above which he never mounts. . . . Seneca is wholly himself; what he attempted he executed, he created his own genre.[3]

This judicial style can be a little overpowering, particularly in combination with some of the casual references that Eliot includes in the essay. About the Elizabethan translation of Seneca's *Tenne Tragedies*, for example, we are told that 'their literary value remains greater than that of any later translations of Seneca's tragedies that I have examined

either in English or French', and the reader is scarcely left in a position
to admit, even to himself, that he has not up to this time sufficiently
pondered the question of French translations of Seneca. Similarly, the
tone of the writing forestalls a natural surprise when one reads that
'Few things that can happen to a nation are more important than the
invention of a new form of verse', or, elsewhere, that 'In one play,
Everyman, and perhaps in that one play only, we have a drama within
the limitations of art.'[4]

Sometimes the propaganda note is unmistakable. In discussing
Dryden and Pope, for example, Eliot quotes Arnold's comment that
'their poetry is conceived and composed in their wits, genuine poetry
is conceived in the soul', and he adds:

> Arnold was, perhaps, not altogether the detached critic when he
> wrote this line; he may have been stirred to a defence of his own
> poetry, conceived and composed in the soul of a mid-century Oxford
> graduate.[5]

The laugh against Arnold is strategic in that it supports a pattern of
attitudes that Eliot wished to foster, but it appears at first to be gratuitous and it works by insinuation. It is ironic that Eliot should immediately afterwards quote a remark of Walter Pater on Dryden (to the
effect that Dryden's distinction between poetry and prose came with
'diminished effect from one whose poetry was so prosaic') only to
dismiss it as 'cheap journalism'.

The most potent example of Eliot's propaganda tactics comes,
however, in 'The Function of Criticism'. The subject is the opposition
between authority and the individual conscience, and Eliot takes issue
with Middleton Murry, who had said that Englishmen 'inherit no rules
from their forebears; they inherit only this: a sense that in the last
resort they must depend upon the inner voice'. Eliot turns upon this
sentence with a positively forensic display of scorn:

> This statement does, I admit, appear to cover certain cases; it throws
> a flood of light upon Mr Lloyd George. But why *'in the last resort'*?
> Do they, then, avoid the dictates of the inner voice up to the last
> extremity? My belief is that those who possess this inner voice are
> ready enough to hearken to it, and will hear no other. The inner
> voice, in fact, sounds remarkably like an old principle which has
> been formulated by an elder critic in the now familiar phrase of
> 'doing as one likes'. The possessors of the inner voice ride ten in a

7

compartment to a football match at Swansea, listening to the inner
voice, which breathes the eternal message of vanity, fear and lust.

This is brilliant debating (it might have come well from the despised
Lloyd George), but it sounds an unexpected note in an essay called
'The Function of Criticism'. Strangest of all, it is remarkably close in
tone to some of Arnold's pieces of special pleading – his imputation,
for example, of 'a touch of grossness' in the British race from 'the
natural growth amongst us of such hideous names – Higginbottom,
Stiggins, Bugg', and his development of this, which works only on the
level of debate, that 'in Ionia and Attica they were luckier in this respect
than "the best race in the world" '.[6]

It is right to add to this discussion of Eliot's tone that as early as the
1928 preface to *The Sacred Wood* he confessed to finding in his early
essays 'a stiffness and an assumption of pontifical solemnity which may
be tiresome to many readers', and that much later, in 'To Criticize the
Critic' (1961), he continued to deplore what he now disarmingly called
'the braggadocio of the mild-mannered man safely entrenched behind
his typewriter'. But, deplorable or not, the tone is an inescapable
quality of the essays, and important in communicating, even at this
distance, an exciting sense of active commitment and struggle.

The case that Eliot is fighting is a large one, and its nature is well
defined in a passage in *The Use of Poetry*:

> From time to time, every hundred years or so, it is desirable that
> some critic shall appear to review the past of our literature, and set
> the poets and the poems in a new order. This task is not one of
> revolution but of readjustment. What we observe is partly the same
> scene, but in a different and more distant perspective. . . . (p. 108)

It is towards a readjustment in this sense that the strategy of Eliot's
early critical work is directed, and it is this purpose which explains
much of the surface asperity towards Arnold. In many ways this attitude
is unexpected. It has been shown that Eliot's tone can be closely
paralleled in Arnold and there are many areas where their ideas are also
very similar. In both one finds a reverence for a free play of intelligence
which is said to be characteristic of the French mind; both are fond of
imagining cultural development as an organic growth towards maturity;
both insist on the importance of viewing the European tradition as a
whole. Nor do they necessarily disagree in their particular judgements:

Eliot returns more than once to praise one of the lines from Dante which Arnold had used as a touchstone of excellence –

In la sua volontade è nostra pace.

Yet despite these large similarities Arnold's position is constantly subverted, often in the most feline manner: 'Arnold was not Dryden or Johnson; he was an Inspector of Schools and he became Professor of Poetry' (*UPUC* p. 110).

What is being attacked in the person of Arnold is the view of English literature that he had established in which Milton and Wordsworth were central examples of the ultimate criterion of great poetry, the beautiful and profound application of ideas to life. And in undermining this position it is clear that Eliot is implicitly defending the kind of poetry that he himself was publishing. His ironical (yet compassionate) treatment of indecisive and unheroic figures demanded a new response, for it would scarcely be possible to find the 'accent', to use Arnold's words, 'of high seriousness' in the most celebrated lines of 'The Love Song of J. Alfred Prufrock':

> In the room the women come and go
> Talking of Michelangelo.

or

> I have measured out my life with coffee spoons.

To provide a critical justification for poetry of this kind new criteria had to be found, and it was in the two major essays, 'Tradition and the Individual Talent' and 'The Function of Criticism', that Eliot laid the foundations for a radical critical reorientation. His argument had two aspects: first, a discussion of the process of artistic creation; and, secondly, a definition of tradition and an assertion of the need for authority. It is an eclectic argument which contains some inherent contradictions (and some of its extreme positions were subsequently modified by Eliot), but it was none the less an argument of great value, which has had an enduring effect on subsequent criticism, and which above all provided the starting-point for his own criticism of other writers.

Although the definition of tradition takes first place in 'Tradition and the Individual Talent', it is the discussion of poetic creation and the theory of the depersonalization of the artist that is the most significant part of the argument, the part most fruitful in establishing a new attitude to the past, and with most bearing on our reading of Eliot's own poetry.

Towards the end of the first section of 'Tradition and the Individual Talent', which originally appeared in the *Egoist* in the issue of September/October 1919, Eliot suggests that as the poet develops an awareness of the past he will be forced to make 'a continual surrender of himself as he is at the moment to something which is more valuable'. Depersonalization is necessary to mature artistic creation. The first part of the essay ends on a note of suspense with an enigmatic and now famous image:

It is in this depersonalization that art may be said to approach the condition of science. I therefore invite you to consider, as a suggestive analogy, the action which takes place when a bit of finely filiated platinum is introduced into a chamber containing oxygen and sulphur dioxide.

The riddle element gives the image an air of impressive depth, but in the second part of the essay, which appeared in the November/December issue, the analogy is developed suggestively rather than precisely. The catalyst precipitates a reaction, but remains itself unchanged: the poet also, Eliot suggests, is, in a sense, passive. His mind is a 'more finely perfected medium in which special, or very varied, feelings are at liberty to enter into new combinations'. The catalyst works, in fact, less as an argument than by its unexpectedness as an analogy, by its aura of scientific precision, which opens the mind to Eliot's crucial point, namely that poetic quality does not depend on great themes and grand emotions, but on the intensity with which varied emotions are fused together to form new wholes.

The wider implications of this exposition begin to clarify when Eliot says:

If you compare several representative passages of the greatest poetry you see how great is the variety of types of combination, and also how completely any semi-ethical criterion of 'sublimity' misses the mark.

Arnold's criteria were 'semi-ethical', and it is his whole position that is here being called into question. More specifically, Eliot subverts common assumptions about the nature of poetic creation by turning to Wordsworth's definition of poetry as 'emotion recollected in tranquillity', and concluding that this formula is inexact:

For it is neither emotion, nor recollection, nor, without distortion of meaning, tranquillity. It is a concentration, and a new thing resulting from the concentration, of a very great number of experiences which to the practical and active person would not seem to be experiences at all; it is a concentration which does not happen consciously or of deliberation. . . . it is not the expression of personality, but an escape from personality.

The image of the catalyst as an analogy of poetic creation is interesting for its rhetorical success in the context: it also points, in its attempt at finding a scientific basis for discussing artistic phenomena, at the influence of one of Eliot's most frequently and warmly acknowledged sources, Remy de Gourmont.[7]

II

In the first essay of *The Sacred Wood*, 'The Perfect Critic', Eliot had written that 'of all modern critics, perhaps Remy de Gourmont had most of the general intelligence of Aristotle'. Gourmont's 'general intelligence' ranged not only over languages and over the related disciplines of psychology and philosophy, but also over zoology and physiology, and it is the informing presence of this last study in his discussion of literary style that is particularly important for Eliot.

In *Le Problème du style* Gourmont characterizes as absurd the idea that style can be learnt by the imitation of models. When an author writes he should not be concerned either with models or with his style. Style is not a quality that can be isolated in the process of creation or that can be cultivated for its own sake: 'c'est de sentir, de voir, de penser, et rien de plus.'[8] It is determined by the physiology of the writer; it is the product of the brain structure itself: 'On ne se donne pas son style; sa forme est déterminée par la structure du cerveau; on en reçoit la matière des faits avec qui l'on est en commerce.'[9] It is this recognition of the inescapable part played by the physiology of the writer that underlies Eliot's objection in the essay on 'The Metaphysical Poets' to those who tell us 'to look into our hearts and write'. That, he says, is not looking deep enough. 'One must look into the cerebral cortex, the nervous system, and the digestive tracts.'

Again Gourmont had expressed in physiological terms the idea that what is important is a strong visual memory, strengthened and supported by a richness of sensory experience which can only come with maturity:

Un style sensoriel, un style d'images n'est jamais précoce; il s'affirme à mesure que les sensations s'accumulent dans les cellules nerveuses et font plus denses, plus riches et plus complexes les archives du souvenir.[10]

Sensory experience provides a 'réservoir d'images où puise l'imagination pour de nouvelles et infinies combinaisons'.[11] This conception of artistic creation as dependent on organic processes and taking place apart from the conscious will of the artist is in its essentials close to Eliot's view of the poet's mind as a 'medium in which . . . feelings are at liberty to enter into new combinations'. And it is the same view which is applied specifically to the Metaphysicals when Eliot defines the quality of Donne's mind as an ability to form new wholes from the disparate facts of existence, and says that the 'poets of the seventeenth century . . . possessed a mechanism of sensibility which could devour any kind of experience', and through which thought could be apprehended as immediately as sensation.[12]

The idea of poetic involuntariness continued to be important for Eliot. Some fifteen years later he quoted with approval Housman's thoroughly organic image of poetic inspiration – 'I should call it a secretion' (*UPUC* p. 144); and later still (1953) he said that the poet is oppressed during composition 'by a burden which he must bring to birth in order to obtain relief from acute discomfort'.[13]

The implications of this position are far-reaching. For if the mind is a mechanism which devours experience it also transmutes it. The catalyst presides over a chemical change so that the work of art which emerges from the experiment is not simply a distillation. It is not the communication of truths intellectually conceived, nor can the artist fulfil in any exact way Arnold's requirement that he should express the best that has been thought and felt in the world. Eliot deals with this question directly in *The Use of Poetry* where he supports Maritain's assertion that poetry needs to be saved by religion from the absurdity 'of believing itself destined to transform ethics and life'. The poet cannot operate directly in the moral sphere, because a work of art is a new creation and only to a limited extent within his control:

> The 'experience' in question may be the result of a fusion of feelings so numerous, and ultimately so obscure in their origins, that even if there be communication of them, the poet may hardly be aware of what he is communicating; and what is there to be communicated was not in existence before the poem was completed. 'Communication' will not explain poetry. (*UPUC* p. 138)

And just as the work of art is a new creation, independent of the experiences from which it has been formed, so our appreciation of it must be uncluttered by the ordinary emotions of life: 'The end of the enjoyment of poetry is a pure contemplation from which all the accidents of personal emotion are removed . . .' (*SW* pp. 14–15); and the critic should have 'no emotions except those immediately provoked by a work of art' (*SW* p. 12).

This insistence on a radical divorce both for the author and the reader between literature and life derives from symbolist aesthetics, and it carries with it an inherent paradox. Art may not be self-expression, and Eliot may be justified in deploring elements of unresolved human experience in literature (as he does most notably in the essay on *Hamlet*), but although the conscious will may have little or no part to play in the writing of poetry it is not easy to escape from the idea of personality altogether. Gourmont had said, in a passage quoted by Eliot in the essay on Massinger, that 'la vie est un dépouillement. Le but de l'activité propre d'un homme est de nettoyer sa personalité.'[14] Man must cleanse himself from all the stains left by education and by adolescent enthusiasms until he emerges thoroughly scoured. It is something of this sort that Eliot seems to have in mind in 'Tradition and the Individual Talent' where he writes of the need to 'escape from personality', to escape, perhaps it would be better to say, from the self-conscious display which is an abuse of personality. But the result of a scouring is actually to reveal the true personality more completely. Flaubert, in one sense the pattern of impersonality, is none the less completely revealed by the very transparency of his style, by his success in transmuting his life completely into art. And this kind of revelation of personality, Eliot suggests, is found in Marlowe or Jonson, but not in Massinger whose 'personality hardly exists'.[15] This represents a signal modification of the apparent rigour of the original theory.

It is perhaps the problem posed by personality that leads Eliot always to be very cautious in his approach to symbolist idealism. In *The Use of Poetry* the difficulty is posed very clearly, but Eliot seems determined to avoid anything beyond the most tentative conclusion:

> Why, for all of us, out of all that we have heard, seen, felt, in a lifetime, do certain images recur, charged with emotion, rather than others? The song of one bird, the leap of one fish, at a particular place and time, the scent of one flower, an old woman on a German mountain path, six ruffians seen through an open window playing

cards at night at a small French railway junction where there was a
watermill: such memories may have symbolic value, but of what we
cannot tell, for they come to represent the depths of feeling into
which we cannot peer. (*UPUC* p. 148)

This is an unexpectedly retiring statement for a man whose later work
uses so powerfully the kinds of experience that are referred to here.
But the central problem of symbolism is that while the poet claims to
be in touch with a profound world of ideal truth, he must ultimately
rely absolutely on the individual sensibility to explore this world, and
to express its truths in symbolic form. For Eliot, with acute tempera-
mental doubts about the validity of individual judgement, it is impossible explicitly to trust such explorations except fleetingly and in
individual cases. The value of Gourmont was that he located poetic
experience so firmly in the tangible facts of physical existence, and made
poetic value spring, not from arbitrary apprehensions of the absolute
expressed through the individual interpretative consciousness, but
from the complete objectification of combinations of acute sensory
experience.

But even though Gourmont's analysis is the basis for some of Eliot's
most important assumptions, it is evident that these assumptions did
not provide sufficient support against the dangers of individualism.
Eliot's quest for literary authority is developed further in his discussion
of tradition, and this has troubled many people. Wellek says, for
example, that his 'classicism is a matter of cultural politics rather than
literary criticism'.[16] There is certainly a political element in it, related
to the need to establish a new and non-Arnoldian order, but an equally
important motive seems to be the need for psychological reassurance
and a defence against the unrestrained personality. Eliot has an acute
distrust of 'palpitating Narcissi',[17] a distrust which, even when it is
more fully formulated than in this phrase, is still informed with a strong
current of emotion, as in the following passage from *After Strange Gods*:

> . . . when morals cease to be a matter of tradition and orthodoxy –
> that is, of the habits of the community formulated, corrected, and
> elevated by the continuous thought and direction of the Church – and
> when each man is to elaborate his own, then *personality* becomes a
> thing of alarming importance. (p. 54)

'Men cannot get on', he says in 'The Function of Criticism', 'without
giving allegiance to something outside themselves', and that authority

is to be found in 'tradition and the accumulated wisdom of time'. The essential problem is one of order, and this can only be solved by regarding literatures as ' "organic wholes", as systems in relation to which . . . individual works of literary art, and the works of individual artists, have their significance'. Eliot finds it disastrous when a writer can be cherished 'not in spite of his deviations from the inherited wisdom of the race, but because of them' (*ASG* p. 33). Obviously this general standpoint is one with extremely wide implications and its religious and political tendencies are hinted at, although not developed, as early as 'The Function of Criticism' in references to Catholicism and Whiggery. But this aspect of Eliot's thought, in which the influence of Charles Maurras and Julien Benda played an acknowledged and important part, is not at issue here. The controversies aroused by Eliot's defiant right-wing assertiveness belong, in any event, to a historical situation which awakens fewer and fewer emotional commitments.

Eliot's specifically literary traditionalism has been shown to derive particularly from Irving Babbitt whose Harvard course on 'Literary Criticism in France with Special Reference to the Nineteenth Century' he attended, and whose insistence on the importance of valuing originality only so far as it relates to a vital tradition he developed.[18]

If a man wishes to grow beyond poetic adolescence, Eliot says, he must develop an awareness of tradition, and 'a perception, not only of the pastness of the past, but of its presence'. A historical estimate, as Arnold had said, is not enough: it is no good judging Pope in terms simply of the eighteenth-century cultural situation. The poet must be aware of which poets are particularly alive and significant for his own age. He will think of the past not as something static and completed, but as a sort of slow-moving kaleidoscope which throws up new patterns for each generation. The whole of past literature has 'a simultaneous existence and composes a simultaneous order', but the order itself changes under the pressure of new literature:

> The existing order is complete before the new work arrives; for order to persist after the supervention of novelty, the *whole* existing order must be, if ever so slightly, altered; and so the relations, proportions, values of each work of art toward the whole are readjusted; and this is conformity between the old and the new.[19]

One significance of the new writer, as Eliot said much later in 'The Social Function of Poetry', is that it is 'through the living authors that the dead remain alive' (*PP* p. 22): there is a continuous process of reabsorption and reinterpretation.

One of the interesting things about this theory is that, although it is developed in part as a barrier against the expression of unrestrained personality (Whiggery) in art, the values which it can sustain in practice are very far from absolute. It leads, almost despite itself, towards a practical relativity of judgement. The immediate call is for a reassessment of the tradition: 'The poet must be very conscious of the main current, which does not at all flow invariably through the most distinguished reputations.'[20] But the limited validity of any reassessment that may be made is clear when one turns to the work of past critics. Johnson was among those who reviewed the past and 'set the poets and the poems in a new order'. But as Eliot was to show so well in 'Johnson as Critic and Poet' (a lecture delivered in 1944 and an effective counter to those who see a decline in Eliot's critical powers as he grew older) he was inevitably subject to historical and personal limitations which other ages may be able easily to correct. Johnson 'took for granted a progress, a refinement of language and versification along definite lines . . . which implied a confidence in the rightness and permanence of the style which had been achieved', and this, Eliot suggests, 'we can hardly see . . . as anything but a blemish upon his critical ability' (*PP* p.165). Eliot's own judgements are obviously no less limited.

Indeed the inevitability of our reassessments is clear in Eliot's changing treatment of Milton. This change springs from the idea that literary history sees an alternation between 'times for exploration and times for the development of the territory acquired',[21] and from an assumption (at odds with the authoritarianism of 'The Function of Criticism') that the critic should be pragmatic in the direction he chooses to take. Eliot, feeling in 1936 that Milton was a bad influence upon modern poets, attacked his work for displaying a damaging predominance of 'the auditory imagination'. By the Academy Lecture of 1947, however, Eliot had diagnosed a different poetic situation.[22] By then he felt that the struggle to establish colloquial rhythms and idioms and to use modern and non-poetic subject-matter had been won, that poetry might be entering on a phase of expansion rather than discovery. In this situation the poet might 'have much to learn from Milton's extended verse structure; it might also avoid the danger of *servitude* to colloquial speech and to current jargon'. It follows that Milton's place in the kaleidoscope of tradition has changed. But the Inner Voice itself

could hardly be more unpredictable than to call for a radical reassessment of a major poet within so short a time, and this shift represents a
practical abandonment of the claim for order as an authoritarian concept.
The inevitability of a personal interpretation of tradition becomes
apparent.

The final development in the search for permanence is to be seen in
the later essays in the use of a concept of cultural maturity which brings
Eliot again close to Arnold. In asserting that Chaucer had not the
'classic' status of Dante, Arnold had said that this status was out of
reach of any poet in 'the England of that stage of growth', and the whole
discussion in 'The Study of Poetry' rests upon the idea of a literary
growth which is related in its stages to organic development. As early
as 'The Function of Criticism' Eliot introduced, rather enigmatically,
a similar idea. The question whether the French were in the year 1600
Classical or the English Romantic is dismissed as relatively trivial: 'A
more important difference, to my mind, is that the French in the year
1600 *had already a more mature prose*' (*SE* p. 28). In 'What is a Classic'
(1944), however, the idea of maturity is fully developed and is used as
a touchstone. A classic (in the sense in which Virgil is a classic) can
only occur 'when a civilization is mature; when a language and a literature are mature; and it must be the work of a mature mind' (*PP* p. 55).
These conditions elevate immensely the importance of impersonal
historical forces, and enable the genres to be thought of almost in
allegorical terms: 'Our prose was ready for some tasks before it could
cope with others: a Malory could come long before a Hooker, a Hooker
before a Hobbes, and a Hobbes before an Addison' (*PP* p. 57).

But they lead also to judgements which depend inevitably on the
semi-ethical criteria that Eliot had earlier rejected, and in establishing
these criteria the critic must, once again, be forced back to a subjective
position. For,

> To define *maturity* . . . is almost impossible . . . if we are properly
> mature, as well as educated persons, we can recognize maturity in a
> civilization and in a literature, as we do in the other human beings
> whom we encounter. (*PP* p. 55)

The concept of maturity, like those of tradition and impersonality,
provides a framework of objective authority which, while it remains
valid for many stages of the argument, is in the last resort illusory.

Eliot, then, has an exceptionally acute distrust not only of the limitations of individual judgement, but of the danger to civilization posed by the uncontrolled personality. It is fitting that the butt of the early poems should be Apeneck Sweeney, a nightmare embodiment of the complacent, vulgar, overdeveloped self. In his literary theory Eliot explores concepts which run counter to the idea that art is a 'turning loose' of personal emotions, and he constantly seeks to establish the objectifying nature of poetic creation. But objectivity proves extremely elusive. In each major area of discussion personality is left behind defeated, only to reappear at a later stage and in a different form. The characteristic movement is circular, and the reader may be led to believe that a search which so often ends in frustration is directed at a chimera.

II

Yet from the standpoint of most readers the importance of Eliot's theoretical arguments does not depend on their ultimate validity (one may be sceptical about the possibility of a permanently valid literary theory), but rather upon the nature of their influence.

Dr Leavis has pressed home the reservations which most people must have, for example, about the theory of impersonality in artistic creation:

> In contemplating the work of one of the great creative powers we don't find ourselves impelled to think of the pressure of the artistic process as something apart from the pressure of the living – the living life and the lived experience – out of which the work has issued; for that the work *has* so issued, deriving thence its sustenance and the creative impulsion, we don't question.[23]

One may – without paradox – sympathize fully with this position and yet be grateful for Eliot's discussion, for, nearly fifty years after they appeared, the ideas of 'Tradition and the Individual Talent' cannot be considered in isolation any more than those of Wordsworth's Preface to *Lyrical Ballads*. Both essays prepare for the appreciation of a new kind of poetry; in both this leads to the stating of extreme positions; and in both the value of the essay must be discussed in terms of its contribution to forwarding a radical re-examination of the nature of poetry. Very few people will take literally Wordsworth's remark that, 'there neither is, nor can be, any *essential* difference between the language of prose and metrical composition', but nonetheless it is an important remark, not least because it provoked Coleridge to discuss Wordsworth's theories. Eliot's remark that 'poetry is an escape from personality' has a similar importance: it introduced a fresh current of ideas, and it provoked among other things the very trenchant attack that we see in Dr Leavis's essay. It is only through this sort of dialectic that the nature of poetry can be discussed. As Eliot himself said about I. A. Richards (whether ironically or not it is hard to say): 'Even if his criticism proves to be entirely on the wrong track . . . [he] will have done something in accelerating the exhaustion of the possibilities' (*UPUC* p. 123).

Another kind of influence, analogous to the influence of Wordsworth's description of poetry as 'the spontaneous overflow of powerful feelings', was achieved by Eliot's phrases, the distillation of his theory of impersonality, 'dissociation of sensibility' and 'objective correlative'. These have been so thoroughly absorbed into modern criticism that it is impossible to know where we should stand without them, or at least without the discussion behind them which determines so much of our thinking, especially about seventeenth-century poetry. A passage like that in which Eliot says that 'a thought to Donne was an experience; it modified his sensibility' has permanently modified the sensibility of all subsequent readers. Its effect, to adapt a Wordsworthian phrase, is 'not individual and local, but general and operative'. And it is at this point that the influence of Eliot's poetry is most closely related to that of the criticism. For the effect of the phrases could hardly have been so powerful without the poetry for which they are, in one sense, an explanation. To experience the 'amalgamation of disparate experience' in reading 'A Game of Chess' is both to feel the truth of Eliot's discussion on the pulses, and to have illuminated one's whole reading of the metaphysical poets. In discussing this aspect of Eliot's influence it is impossible to separate the criticism from the poetry. The criticism deals with problems that have arisen because Eliot is creating a particular kind of verse, but the poetry would, on its own, have demanded a special critical response, and it consequently encourages the acceptance and development of his critical ideas.

Finally, there is the influence of Eliot's theories upon the conduct of his own discussion of other writers. And here comparison moves from the achievement of Wordsworth to that of Johnson. Johnson is a great critic because the acute sensibility and good sense that informs all his work operates within a framework of established principles that gives a coherent over-all structure to his discussion of individual works.

Moreover his principles act so as to sharpen his perception and make possible discoveries that are of permanent value. Without the assumptions so dogmatically expressed in the tenth chapter of *Rasselas* Johnson's examination of the metaphysical poets would scarcely have been possible: it is his absolute clarity about what he expects from poetry that enables him to define the characteristics of work even of an alien kind and to give a sense of continuity to the most diverse material.

Similarly Eliot's theory secures a hearing for the discussion of problems that otherwise might not be heard at all, and provides an astonishing coherence in a collection of work that is, for the most part, strictly occasional in origin. Most of the *Selected Essays* were book reviews, yet, because of the precision with which he has established his theory, Eliot is able to present a continuing argument.

One of the major areas, for example, where Eliot's critical contribution – a permanently valuable one – derives directly from the theory is his study of the diction and syntax of dramatic verse. The hypothesis of the ideal order which may be modified by the appearance of a new work of art provides a model of development against which the achievement of the Elizabethan and Jacobean dramatists can be tested, and through which new insights can be achieved. A characteristically exciting Eliot perception in this field is the comparison between Jonson and Marlowe.[24] This insight is established through a comparison of the verse when Eliot points to the similarity between the expansiveness of Sir Epicure Mammon and the orotundity of Marlowe's tragic heroes. In this kind of critical comparison the theory is completely justified, not in the sense that it is proved true, but in that its application to a specific field has led to a valuable statement about the nature of two works of art, and has enabled them to be seen afresh, stripped of the veneer of conventional acceptance and categorization. 'Romantic' tragedy and 'realistic' and classical comedy have been brought into a useful relationship.

This constant awareness of tradition and originality in the handling of words provides much of the most exciting work in *Selected Essays*, but the development of Eliot's preoccupation in modern criticism makes it easy to forget how important his own contribution was. He said, in *The Use of Poetry*, that he wished

. . . that we might dispose more attention to the correctness of expression, to the clarity or obscurity, to the grammatical precision or inaccuracy, to the choice of words whether just or improper, exalted or vulgar of our verse. (*UPUC* p. 25)

In 1932, when this was written, Eliot had been making precisely that kind of critical discrimination for fifteen years. An example of this aspect of Eliot's criticism at its best occurs in his treatment of the lines from Tourneur which he echoes in 'Gerontion':

> Does the silk worm *expend* her *yellow labours* . . .
> Why does yon fellow *falsify highways*
> And lays his life between the judge's lips
> To *refine* such a one? keeps horse and men
> To *beat their valours* for her?

Eliot has never over-emphasized his explications (showing a slight disdain for what he calls the 'lemon squeezer' school of critics),[25] and all he does here is to italicize the significant words, and then to comment that

> These lines . . . exhibit that perpetual slight alteration of language, words perpetually juxtaposed in new and sudden combinations . . . which evidences a very high development of the senses, a development of the English language which we have perhaps never equalled.[26]

The extreme economy of this comment is possible only because there lies behind it the whole weight of a theory of order which lends its strength to the valuation. In attempting to evaluate Eliot's criticism one will inevitably think first of passages of this kind, and only secondly of the theoretical discussions, yet this is a false distinction. Here the two sides of Eliot's work are completely fused, the theory controlling the very nature of the critical inquiry and providing the standard of judgement.

And although this may be a by-product of Eliot's poetry workshop (to return again to his own description), it is not so in any limiting sense. At its best Eliot's criticism has a value which is likely to endure and which is independent of the particular historical circumstances that gave rise to it.

NOTES

1. 'The Frontiers of Criticism', in *PP* p. 106.
2. See the conclusion of the Life of Addison.
3. 'Seneca in Elizabethan Translation', in *SE* p. 75. The next two quotations are from pp. 66 and 101.

4. 'Four Elizabethan Dramatists', in *SE* p. 111.

5. 'John Dryden', in *SE* p. 309.

6. Matthew Arnold, 'The Function of Criticism at the Present Time'.

7. For a detailed and valuable study of Gourmont and of his influence on Eliot, see Glenn S. Burne, *Remy de Gourmont; his ideas and influence in England and America* (1963).

8. Remy de Gourmont, *Le Problème du style* (16th ed., 1907) p. 32.

9. Ibid. p. 81.

10. Ibid. p. 73.

11. Ibid. p. 35.

12. 'The Metaphysical Poets', in *SE* p. 287.

13. 'The Three Voices of Poetry', in *PP* p. 98.

14. *Le Problème du style*, p. 104.

15. 'Philip Massinger', in *SE* p. 217.

16. René Wellek, 'The Criticism of T. S. Eliot', in *Sewanee Review*, LXIV (1956) 432.

17. 'The Function of Criticism', in *SE* p. 27.

18. See Herbert Howarth, *Notes on Some Figures behind T. S. Eliot* (1965) pp. 127–35.

19. 'Tradition and the Individual Talent', in *SE* p. 15.

20. Ibid. p. 16.

21. 'The Music of Poetry', in *PP* p. 35.

22. Both studies of Milton are reprinted in *PP*. The next quotation is from 'Milton II', in *PP* p. 160.

23. F. R. Leavis, T. S. Eliot's Stature as a Critic', in *Commentary*, XXVI (1955) 401.

24. 'Ben Jonson', in *SE* pp. 153–5.

25. 'The Frontiers of Criticism', in *PP* p. 113.

26. 'Philip Massinger', in *SE* p. 209.

Continuity and Coherence in Eliot's Religious Thought

ADRIAN CUNNINGHAM

WHATEVER the aim or approach, almost every evaluation of Eliot's work has at some point to consider the problems of continuity or discontinuity, consistency or inconsistency in his development. The majority opinion seems to be that between roughly 1928 and 1934 there was a major shift in his centre of interest. For some the declaration of classicism in literature, royalism in politics and Anglo-catholicism in religion marks the first stage of a progressive decline in critical and poetic power; others find a continuity in poetic development with a shift or decline from literary to social and religious criticism. These questions matter beyond the importance of Eliot himself. For if his work can be shown as a progressive and coherent development the arguments about whether or not it underwent a radical transformation would appear in a very different light. I am not suggesting that if you take any Eliot you must take all, but that if Eliot is consistent then his critics may not be; or, in other words, that those who wish to reject Eliot's later positions and identify with the earlier work are evading its real significance.

The present essay seeks to establish general characteristics of continuity and coherence in what I think is the most neglected aspect of Eliot's work: his religious position as set out in the prose writings, and the light it throws on his views on tradition and culture. A study of the whole body of Eliot's writings soon reveals its almost palimpsest nature. Ideas, phrases, analogies, recurrent preoccupations are consciously and unconsciously developed, refined, dropped and readopted in new forms in the many different areas of his interests and over long periods of time. This quality and range of thought, and the enormous diversity of criticism make some limitation imperative. Thus, there is a general distinction between the religious attitudes represented in the drama and poetry (more properly theological, even mystical) and those represented in the prose writing which deal almost exclusively with the social and cultural features of religion. The reason for this division, the absence of any critical theological or religious argument, is a subject for investigation in itself but I think it is initially legitimate to consider separately the prose writing on religious topics, and in view of the palimpsest nature of Eliot's mind to proceed chronologically. For my present purpose this implies some consideration of Babbitt, Bradley, Hulme and Maurras, the study of whose formative influence on Eliot still, surprisingly, leaves much to be desired. This is especially so of Maurras. The perfunctory attention which is given him has led to serious gaps in the understanding of Eliot's development.

I

A first reading of Babbitt's work – garrulous, repetitive, *simpliste* and obsessive – makes it hard to understand the impact he made on a whole generation of students. His attacks on Romanticism and the debilitating cult of personality have now been modified and assimilated to our habitual assumptions, and the appeals to the 'inner check' and the 'higher self' seem to belong to the mid-nineteenth rather than early twentieth century. As Eliot sharply remarks, in retrospect the New Humanism appears as 'a by-product of Protestant theology in its last agonies' (*SE* p. 475). Yet it was the intensity of his attack on the modern age, the vast range of his knowledge and the imaginative poverty of his offered solutions which made for demanding reactions in his pupils.[1]

Babbitt's whole effort was an attack on the 'incomplete positivism' nurtured by Romanticism, and in particular by Rousseau to whom he constantly returns. Against the ubiquitous Rousseauist 'in perpetual adoration before the holy sacrament of himself' he urged that man's deepest need is for genuine communion which means a genuine escape from his ordinary self. 'Man is not only a stupid animal in spite of his conceit of his own cleverness, but we are here at the source of his stupidity . . . moral indolence',[2] the dodging of ethical effort. The ideas of the primacy of personality, emotion and instinct led to a perversion of human standards and a dissipation of human energies. Ethical effort, the submission of one's impulses to the 'inner check' f the ethical imagination, constituted the human as distinct from he natural law, and offered the only alternative to the world of the >rutal imperialist and the self-admiring humanitarian, full of 'brother-ood' and the loveliness of his own soul. Civilization itself consisted above all in the orderly transmission of right habits secured chiefly hrough education. Barbarism could only be avoided by a return to noral responsibility. Since societies always decay from the top, higher :ducation must be recalled to its true function of producing leaders uled by the ethical imagination, and exemplary to the multitude. The >ervasive results of the unsound rupture with traditional wisdom that •ccurred in the eighteenth century could only be met by a classical esurgence 'consecrated to the service of a high, impersonal reason'.[3])emocracy was incapable of producing sufficient numbers of sound ndividualists who look imaginatively to standards set above their •rdinary selves.[4] The point was reiterated, and, as the years passed, vith desperation: an American Mussolini might be needed to prevent he emergence of an American Lenin, the Catholic Church might end is the only institution in the Occident to uphold civilized standards.

The similarities between Babbitt's teaching and central strands of Eliot's thought are clear – as are the differences, and most notably in the :ase of Babbitt's confusion about the relation between humanism and eligion. But another and underlying connexion between the two men teeds to be suggested. 'The by-product of Protestant theology in its ast agonies' might be further defined by seeing the New Humanism is the final product of the New England voluntaristic tradition, and hus the inner check as a late expression of the voluntaristic belief that norality is arbitrary and incomprehensible.[5] Such a pointer to Babbitt's ntecedents helps illuminate the only genuinely philosophical basis of iis teaching, almost completely overlooked by those who have written .bout him and of some importance, I think, with regard to Eliot.

Characteristically seeking to reduce the history of post-Greek >hilosophy to the clashes of the metaphysicians of the One – following ³lato, establishing a world of essences above the flux of life – and the netaphysicians of the Many – intoxicated by the element of change .mong whom James, Bergson, Dewey and Croce were the latest epresentatives – Babbitt finds this history largely a monstrous logo-nachy. 'Life does not give here an element of oneness and there an lement of change. It gives a *oneness that is always changing*.'[6] Admission •f the inseparability of oneness and change means that such reality as

can positively be known is inextricably mixed up with illusion. 'Man i
cut off from immediate contact with anything abiding and therefor
worthy to be called real and condemned to live in an element of fictio
or illusion.'[7] Yet civilization must rest on the recognition of somethin
abiding. Abstractly and metaphysically insoluble, the problem ca
only be solved, practically and in terms of actual conduct by recours
to imaginative symbols which convey those truths upon which th
survival of civilization rests. The root error of naturalism lay in it
intoxication with the everlasting flux in which the human law c
righteousness, restraint, and certain moral standards was dissolved
it denied, that is, 'the duality of human nature'. It is at this level,
would suggest, that Babbitt's influence was most profound an
enduring. It is around the preoccupation with the duality of order an
relativity, the dual nature of man, the problematic continuity of th
human through wide cultural change that both men develop thei
ideas of classicism, tradition, impersonality and the necessary relatio
between humanism and religion. It is within this prepared contex
that Eliot's engagement with Bradley, Hulme and finally Maurra
takes place.

Between 1911 and 1913, Eliot was reading Bradley and some indica
tion of how this affected his development is provided by Costello'
notes on his contributions to Royce's seminar in December 1913. Elio
was interested in the relationship between description and interpretatio
and took primitive religion as an especially apposite example.[8] He argue
that in studying religious behaviour we also study both our ow
interpretation of it and the participants' interpretation of what they ar
doing, the primitive mind's interpretation of its behaviour being
significant part of that behaviour. In a later comment on the paper h
stresses that in many cases *no* interpretations of a rite could explain it
origin. 'For the meaning of the series of acts is to the performer
themselves an interpretation.' Thus new interpretation adds to an
falsifies the facts, creating further problems. In fact, 'interpretation i
the other fellow's description'.[9] As Costello commented, the theor
seems to allow no escape from endless relativity, and it might we
appear that in his study of Bradley, Eliot had tended towards th
metaphysicians of the Many whom Babbitt had so insistently denounced
Moreover, the problems raised by the paper would obviously complicat
Babbitt's sweeping generalizations about tradition and the past. Th
problem of interpretation was also raised with reference to the questio

of social or religious evolution. Natural evolution *can* be considered from our point of view and with our values, but the evolution of society or religion clearly cannot. In his very subtle analysis of Eliot's thesis on Bradley, Professor Wollheim has already noted its connexions with his theory of tradition, but I would like to add three further comments. The first is to emphasize a continuity with the philosophical problem at the root of Babbitt's social and cultural criticism: the irreducibility between oneness and change, reality and illusion. It is part of my argument that the problems of relativism raised in totally different ways by Babbitt and Bradley are central to an understanding of Eliot's work; and, more generally, that his whole development is governed by an overriding preoccupation with the conditions for the unification of experience. Secondly, if 'no absolute point of view' is possible, then 'we can only discuss experience from one side and then from the other, correcting these partial views'.[10] This theory of partial truth, the fluidity of object and subject in their definition by context and relationship, indicates a pervasive characteristic of Eliot's processes of thought, the fairly consistent and deliberate evasion of precise definition, every point seeming to overlap with the next until imperceptibly the two emphases of a single conception stand in apparent opposition. Eliot's writing is often at the most crucial points simultaneously dense, allusive, elliptical, the meaning suggested only in the organization of a particular context. This stylistic feature sits closely with his philosophical preoccupations and suggests that many alleged inconsistencies and contradictions in his critical theories might be re-examined for their substantial coherence. Beyond the almost symmetrical balance of mutual correction between conflicting statements, the dialectical movement engendered by the theory of partial truth gives one a guideline to that pervasive project of unification by antithesis that is indicated in the individual talent and tradition; the individual and society; the nation and the region; the national and the universal church; the christian society and its rulers; class and *élite*. In fact the continuity with the work on Bradley is even closer if we note that the antitheses are rather symbiotic relationships. The concepts are dialectical polarizations of the same phenomenon: tradition and the individual talent are different but inseparable terms in constant interaction. This symbiotic form is fundamental to Eliot's exposition and criticism of Bradley; at various points, mind and external world, the genesis of the object and the genesis of the self are seen as concurrent products of the transcendence of Immediate Experience. The permanency of dichotomy, the impossibility of an absolute view, may find relief in a religious and more specifically christian incarnational belief which suggests some direct mediation of, or access to, an absolute point of view, but outside this belief and its specific applicability the tendency to connect and the resistance to connexion remain constant. We can only argue from this side, and then from that side, indefinitely – the final possibility of unification is unattainable outside faith.[11]

Thirdly, attention to this pattern can clarify one of the difficult features of 'Tradition and the Individual Talent' which has often been seen as Eliot eating his literary cake and having it too; the apparent inconsistency, that is, between the given nature of the tradition and its constructed nature established through individual choice. 'The mind of Europe' seems to be an entity existing prior to, and independent of, the individual to which he must submit himself, yet the past cannot be taken as 'a lump, an indiscriminate bolus', it cannot be inherited but obtained only at the cost of great labour. And the two positions run together; the main current of tradition does not invariably flow through the greatest reputations – the main current is there as a 'given' beyond the interference of private taste, yet the reputations it comprises are a matter of selection. This problem of the selected and the given has been related to Eliot's problematic combination of cosmopolitanism and vigorous attachment to English culture. While this combination may certainly influence Eliot's conception of tradition, the main trend of the argument is coherent in itself as a development of the problems of cultural evolution, partial truth, and the constancy of dialectical movement between points of view: 'the line between the experienced, or the given, and the constructed can nowhere be clearly drawn. . . . There is no absolute point of view from which real and ideal can be finally separated and labelled . . .' (KE p. 18). But if no absolute separation can be made, the very process of interconnexion can itself function as a kind of vague absolute. In engaging with the past, a partial surrender of his own particular perspective may enable a man to enter a common and impersonal realm of subjectivity, a 'collective idealism'. The apparently fragmentary consciousness can be enriched, paradoxically by an act of self-renunciation, to find its place within a collective consciousness. This strain is clear in the distinctly idealist tone of the original version of the essay:

We suppose . . . writers who are not only connected by tradition in time, but also are related so as to be in the light of eternity contemporaneous, from a certain point of view cells in one body . . . We suppose a mind which is not only the English mind of one period with its prejudices of politics and fashions of taste, but which is a greater, finer, more positive, more comprehensive mind than the mind of any period. And we suppose to each writer an importance which is not only individual, but due to his place as a constituent of this mind.[12]

The process of continuity in culture is the shifting and mutual modification of the tradition and the individual, but what finally validates or guides the individual's assertion that *this* is the tradition or that this or that author is to be excluded is not clear. At this further reach the question of relativism remains and it is not easy to see how the 'mind of Europe' as described could be located or employed outside directly literary problems. It is this, perhaps, which impels Eliot increasingly to strip the individual or contingent qualifications from the concept, as he moves towards Maurras where the given and limiting totality of tradition is the central truth to which the individual definitely submits.[13]

Before Maurras, the last important figure in the developing refinement of central problems and presuppositions in Eliot's early phase is Hulme. The general lines of connexion with Eliot and the modern period are generally available and accepted,[14] but given the features of the background already established his influence on Eliot seems to be the summarizing and emphasizing of elements already present rather than the contribution of anything fundamentally new or different. The one vital area where tensions in Eliot's thought were confronted and forced by Hulme is that of religion. Perhaps precisely because Hulme's position is a rational justification for the senselessness of the world rather than for any specifically theological or religious commitment, it would tend radically to undermine, or rather break beyond the limit of Eliot's collective idealism as the solution of the problems he had long been pondering. Hulme's anti-romanticism goes far beyond Babbitt's for it is also an uncompromising anti-humanism. The duality of human nature in Babbitt and the irreducible nature of the gaps in experience in Bradley are totally inadequate to Hulme's insistence on the discontinuity of levels in man – evidenced in the well-known statement on original sin cited by Eliot.[15] Hulme's classicism demands at its centre

the assent to some form of transcendental certainty of ethical validation
it is this assent which, I think, plays a part in Eliot's realization of the
inadequacy of previous systems of resolution and raises the question
of religious belief[16]. This does not mean that Eliot's growth towards a
religious position reverses any previous assumptions: the notably
bloodless tone of his religious writings suggests that the religious
question is posed by the insufficiency of the pattern already established
and that the religious answer does not cancel or radically alter that
pattern but validates it at the points where it would otherwise break
down.

II

Although minor points in the relation of Eliot and Maurras like the
adaptation of a passage from L'Avenir de l'Intelligence in 'Triumphal
March' are generally known, the major point – Maurras' political and
religious position – is less well understood; and the more clearly one
can grasp Maurras' thought the clearer the continuity in Eliot's own
thought becomes.[17] The first point to dispose of is that Maurras was a
fascist. In the loose sense of the term this may be roughly true – Eliot
himself remarked, 'most of the concepts which might have attracted
me in fascism I seem already to have found . . . in the work of Charles
Maurras' (Criterion, VIII 288). However, despite the association of the
Action Française with specifically fascist organizations, its main concepts were different and require separate treatment.

   In his opposition to the Renaissance, Romanticism and the Republic,
Maurras was completely monarchist, and this monarchism was distinguished from fascism by being rational rather than irrational, anti-State
rather than pro. The hereditary monarchy, Maurras never tired of
repeating, was the natural, rational, the only possible constitution of the
central authority; an authority that was one, independent and undivided.
When society was unified in the king, politics was endowed with all
the advantages of a human personality – conscience, memory, reason,
will. But if the monarchy was to be traditional, hereditary and anti-
parliamentary it was also to be decentralized, at once representative
and corporative, eliminating all democratic, parliamentary and republican institutions from politics, and the State from the social life of the
nation. Representation and government were to be strictly distinguished.
Besides diplomacy, conduct of the armed forces and national police,

high justice and other matters reserved to the sovereign, France would be left to organize itself in a multitude of small, decentralized groups: local, professional, moral, religious republics, freely associated in self-governing federations. The wedding of a form of Proudhonian mutualism to monarchism was to guarantee the maximum weight to both unity and diversity. Absolutism was not arbitrary rule; with freedom from the rule of money, political factions and the politico-cultural dictatorship of the Jews, with the restoration of the natural freedoms and functions of the family, the corporation and the province, a kind of open aristocracy would be possible.

It is not difficult to see the appeal of this to Eliot, especially when combined with a distinguished literary reputation and powerful advocacy of classicism: 'England is a "Latin" country' (*Criterion* II 104) was an early and rather naïvely enthusiastic indication of this. Although Eliot invariably qualified his remarks on Maurras with a note on his exasperating or deplorable aspects, his admiration for him is continuous from 1911 when he first read him to 1955 when he addressed the London Conservative Union.[18] Maurras' influence is not only directly reflected in Eliot's own writing on royalism, his attitude towards Pétain,[19] his adoption of the theory of the *moment privilégié*,[20] the preoccupation with unity and diversity, the difference between uniformity and unification, the state of social stasis akin to classicism in literature, with order, hierarchy, tradition. It appears in the separation of functions described in *The Idea of a Christian Society*, more stridently and directly in *After Strange Gods*, and underlies also many of his reflexions on education.

In a sense, one might see the Maurrasien monarch as the incarnation of that collective idealism which lies behind the conception of an intellectual fraternity and temporal and timeless cultural tradition, giving it a stable and embodied focus, a concrete centre of authority beyond the realm of universal subjectivity. The Bradleyan unification is given shape and roots. The king, as Eliot says, incarnates the idea of a nation, and something of a similar order is later transferred to the stress upon unconscious collective habits and blood-kinship in tradition and 'that mysterious social personality which we call our culture' (*PP* p. 23).

Yet the picture is very incomplete without mention of Maurras' religious position. The key to the religious problem of the *Action Française* is that Maurras was not himself a Christian but saw the

Catholic Church as the essential embodiment of the classical hierarchic tradition. For Maurras the Church had no theological content at all, it was supremely a cultural institution.[21] Maurras was, and still is, accused of Gallicanism, the autonomy of the patriotic national Church, but – and this is important for Eliot – he insisted that 'the Roman attachment is precisely that which conserves for Catholicism in France its double character, ordered and French'. The unification of the nation in the monarch balanced by the diversity of the region and the corporation is part of a wider European cultural unification in which Rome is balanced by the particularity of the French Church.

Eliot replied to Leo Ward's accusation that Maurras' intention was to pervert his disciples and students away from Christianity, 'I have been a reader of the work of Maurras for eighteen years; upon me he has had exactly the opposite effect.'[22] He implicitly rejects the merely politic adoption of Catholicism: 'I say only that if anyone is attracted by Maurras' political theory, and if that person has as well any tendency towards *interior* Christianity, that tendency will be quickened by finding that a political and religious view can be harmonious' – a rejection that in other contexts will prove of great significance.

The search for that external authority, that something beyond the individual to which the name truth may be given, which would finally validate the calculus of unification, led Eliot beyond Maurras; Hulme's absolutes providing a major irritant. If in Maurras the idea of tradition was available as fact and institution and not just as ideal or collective mind, at the limit of its concreteness the Bradleyan problem is raised again, complementary to that raised earlier by Eliot's dissatisfaction with Babbitt's humanism. Just as humanism is parasitic on Christian tradition so Christian tradition must be more than a human fact if it is to be guaranteed against mere relativism. Just as individual subjectivity is located in a common realm of universal subjectivity and this in turn embodied in a literary and then politico-cultural tradition, so this latter is to be located in the reality of Christian belief. This progressive sublimation of the constituent elements is the logic of Eliot's development. 'Among other things, the Christian scheme seemed the only possible scheme which found a place for values which I maintain or perish (and belief comes first and practice second), the belief, for instance, in holy living and holy dying, in sanctity, chastity, humility, austerity.' And the abiding lesson of Hulme completes this, 'it is in favour of the Christian scheme from the Christian point of view, that it never has and never will work perfectly. No perfect scheme can work perfectly with imperfect men.'[23]

III

In January 1926 Eliot assembled the texts representing the 'tendency' with which the *Criterion* was associated – Sorel, Maurras, Hulme, Babbitt, Maritain, Benda – 'We must find our own faith, and having found it, fight for it against all others' (*Criterion*, IV 5–6). But that very year was one of the key dates in recent Catholic history, for it saw the Vatican's condemnation of Maurras and the *Action Française*. Its effect on Eliot's religious position and on his development as a whole was, I think, crucial.[24] For just when, via Maurras, he came closest to that group of Catholic intellectuals who were decisive for his thinking, they moved into an intransigent opposition to Maurras.

The condemnation of the *Action Française* involved the Catholic assertion of the primacy of the spiritual, of the transcendence of culture by religion, and a fierce emphasis on the primacy of Rome. The hardening of lines between a formal and ultramontane Catholicism and the loose coherence of a primarily cultural Catholicism which could leave unexamined the question of particular loyalties raised immediate problems for Eliot. Whilst post-Maurrasien Roman Catholic writers like Maritain and Dawson ran into grave problems on the immanence and transcendence of religion, Eliot's position was even more difficult. Although areas of agreement were possible, a rift developed between those who followed a Roman and firmly European tradition and those who could find room within this for the Anglican and English cultural traditions, and for Eliot, with his continued loyalty to Maurrasien principles, this rift made for particularly severe difficulties. In the period of confusion following 1926 three major effects on Eliot's work are to be noticed: a continual qualification of Maurrasien ideas to safeguard the primacy of the spiritual while leaving the basic orientations unchanged; a complex rethinking of the concept of tradition which results in *Notes towards the Definition of Culture*: and a finally unresolved attempt to harmonize the Catholic and European and the Anglican and English traditions.[25]

The most quoted phrase of Maritain's famous apologia for the condemnation of the *Action Française*, 'the restoration of order will be wholly Christian or an utter failure'[26] is a point which Eliot increasingly stresses. In hoping that Babbitt might come to see that humanism is subordinate to religion, that religion means Christianity and that Christianity implies the Church, Eliot thought Babbitt's influence might then join that of Maurras and correct the latter's extravagances. The references to the primacy of the contemplative life over the active, and of the supernatural over the natural life become more frequent. But the Maurrasien emphasis is pervasively present in *After Strange Gods*, especially in the notes on the *métèque*, and though Professor Cameron finds it wholly absent in *Notes*[27] he must have overlooked Eliot's description of culture as being 'essentially the incarnation (so to speak) of the religion of a people', and of religion and culture 'being when each is taken in the right context, different aspects of the same thing' (*NDC* pp. 28–9). The influence of Maurras, that is, remains predominant.[28]

The second major effect of the 1926 crisis on Eliot was his reformulation of the concept of tradition. In so far as the two can be separated, it was the condemnation of Maurras rather than Eliot's conversion to Christianity which spurred him to go beyond the world of literary criticism. His commentaries in the *Criterion* had from the outset shown concern for social and political matters, but while these followed an increasingly Maurrasien line the remarks on tradition and classicism were the only extended indications of his position. In his controversy with Middleton Murry the idea of tradition as an inter-subjective literary totality is already qualified as 'generally a problem of order' (*SE* p. 23); by 1934 the problem is not such a simple one 'nor could I treat it now as a purely literary one' (*ASG* p. 15). For the pondering on Maurras and his condemnation had raised wider problems:

> [Civilization] seems, on the face of it, to mean something definite; it is, in fact, merely a frame to be filled with definite objects, not a definite object itself . . . if you mean a spiritual and intellectual co-ordination on a high level, then it is doubtful whether civilization can endure without religion, and religion without a church. (*SE* pp. 478–9)

And although from the side of poetic creation the original idea is maintained – the process of artists' originality is 'towards a finding of themselves by a progressive absorption in, and absorption of, and rejection (but never a total rejection) of other writers'[29] – the more general use of the term has changed:

Tradition is not solely, or even primarily, the maintenance of certain dogmatic beliefs; these beliefs have come to take their living form in the course of the formation of a tradition. What I mean by tradition involves all those habitual actions, habits and customs, from the most significant religious rite to our conventional way of greeting a stranger, which represent the blood kinship of 'the same people living in the same place'. (*ASG* p. 18)

There is much in the whole passage from which this is taken that is essentially continuous with the essay of 1919; the presence of even dogmatic beliefs as secondary is new, but in the longer perspective the second half of the paragraph is even more important, for it clearly relates to the sense of culture later given in *Notes:* 'the way of life of a particular people living together in one place' (p. 128).

But there is a further stage in the development, for in *The Idea of a Christian Society* this 'tradition' has become 'political philosophy', the dogmas have become conscious formulations:

. . . what I mean by political philosophy is not merely even the conscious formulation of the ideal aims of a people, but the substratum of collective temperament, ways of behaviour and unconscious values which provides the material for a formulation. What we are seeking is not a programme for a party but a way of life for a people. (p. 18)

The interesting thing is that, though Eliot must by now have been perfectly familiar with Christopher Dawson's use of 'culture' for such an idea, he failed to use it himself. And this, I think, is to be explained partly by the general difficulties facing the Maurrasien Eliot and partly by another part of the *Idea* where commenting on (and I think misreading) some remarks of Dawson on the organization of culture, he says:

. . . isolating culture from religion, politics and philosophy we seem to be left with something no more apprehensible than the scent of last year's roses. When we speak of culture, I suppose that we have in mind the existence of two classes of people: the producers and the consumers of culture – the existence of men who can create new thought and new art (with middlemen who can teach the middlemen to like it) and the existence of a cultivated society to enjoy and patronize it. (p. 77)

The sense of culture here seems to me to indicate that, while Eliot has adopted the substance of Dawson's idea of culture first as tradition and then as political philosophy, he himself still thinks of culture as referring primarily to artistic creations. By the time of *Notes* all these earlier and slightly differing terms are correlated as the three aspects of culture: the development of the individual, the group or class, and the whole society.

The Catholic writers of whom Dawson and Maritain are representative also complement Eliot's thinking on another aspect of the concept of tradition, the reconciliation of unity and diversity which, as we have seen, is one of the earliest themes in his development and had especially attracted him to Maurras. They stress the importance of the family and the region as basic elements in culture, and the importance of the rural community as the repository of cultural continuity in an age of urbanization. Unity and diversity are reconciled not in a Maurrasien monarchical scheme but at a higher level of integration in the Church:

> Since a culture is essentially a spiritual community, it transcends the economic and political orders. It finds its appropriate organ not in a state but in a church, that is to say a society which is the embodiment of a purely spiritual tradition. . . . (*ICS* p. 262)

In Eliot (cf. the postscript to *Idea*), however, this theme undergoes a Maurrasien change of emphasis. For the Catholic critics the reconciliation of unity and diversity in the Church reaches beyond particular societies to a global conception of christendom, as when Maritain speaks of 'a new ideal . . . in which an entirely moral and spiritual activity of the Church shall preside over the temporal order of a multitude of politically and culturally heterogeneous nations . . .'[30] Eliot takes this up, again eschewing the Roman implications, when he writes that

> The only positive unification of the world, we believe, is religious unification; by which we do not mean simply universal submission to one world-wide ecclesiastical hierarchy, but cultural unity in religion – which is not the same thing as cultural uniformity.[31]

This idea reaches full development six years later as a central theme in *The Idea of a Christian Society*.

Behind this vague spiritualized hierarchy of levels which preoccupy the Catholic critics it is not difficult to see the reaction to the *Action Française*, with which Maritain had been actively engaged; the stress upon the universal and spiritual nature of order against Maurras' identification of the nation, Church and political order is constant. And this pressure of reaction is to be found also in Eliot, as a reluctant though genuine qualification rather than a substantial conviction.

The tension implicit in this differing emphasis in the reaction to Maurras becomes explicit in the third major effect of the events of 1926 on Eliot, the relation between the Roman–European and Anglican–English traditions. The reaction of the Catholic critics to those events was a unanimous and fierce assertion of the European tradition as essentially Catholic and fully intelligible only from a Roman Catholic position: the tone of embattled ultramontanism is caught in the titles of their leading reviews, *Colosseum* and *Arena*. The effect of this on Eliot is that the group of thinkers to whom he feels closest implicitly exclude him from a complete grasp of the tradition which is at the centre of all his work. Eliot first refers to this tension in 'Thoughts after Lambeth': 'if the Church of England was mutilated by separation from Rome, the Church of Rome was mutilated by separation from England. If England is ever to be to any appreciable degree converted to Christianity, it can only be through the Church of England.'[32] And he goes on to speak of the Church of England as a branch of the Catholic Church, and of that interdependence of the Universal and the National Church which runs through his work. For the Roman Catholics this appeal could not have any substance, Eliot's Universal Church being merely nominal, an idea or a gesture. This exclusion is made most provocatively explicit in an article by G. M. Turnell in 1934, which is worth quoting at some length, for Turnell was the only Catholic critic really equipped to approach Eliot at all on the grounds of literary criticism. Having challenged Eliot's criticism of Hopkins in *After Strange Gods* he goes on,

We cannot read the criticism in this volume without realising that it is a highly conscious operation, the deliberate application of standards from without. The reason is evident. Mr Eliot does not belong to the European Tradition. He is neither possessed of a European consciousness nor does he feel as a European. This means that in his hands the principles underlying Tradition become mere counters completely divorced from the spiritual life which produced them. Thus concepts like order and authority, emptied of their positive content, cease to be creative and life giving and become sterile and deadening. . . . The difficulty of Mr Eliot's position comes from the fact that while belonging to one tradition, he is constantly trying to apply the standards of a different one. . . . It is

not simply a case of national characteristics dominating the European
characteristics. It is that an antipathy has grown up between the
English and the European traditions, so that we have not merely two
distinct traditions, but two traditions that are definitely hostile to
one another. . . .

Supporting his argument with references to Herbert and Crashaw
Turnell concludes,

The difficulties are only cleared up when we come to ask about the
foundations of the English tradition. When Mr Eliot speaks of
dogmatic theology, he means the dogmatic theology of the English
not the Catholic Church. It seems to me that theological differences
are ultimately responsible for most of the differences between the
two traditions. . . . Denunciation will not change the English
tradition into the European. That can only come about through
religious transfiguration. . . . *After Strange Gods* is in a sense the
epitaph of the generation of the men over forty – the generation for
whom compromise is still possible.[33]

I would suggest that this line of attack is one of the factors which lies
behind Eliot's inconclusive preoccupation with unity and diversity in
religion, and, more tentatively, one of the reasons why the development
of the idea of tradition towards that of culture was delayed longer than
might have been expected. So far as I know Eliot never replied to this
attack on his own position, and in this very difficult issue of religion
and culture he was always vulnerable not only to criticism from the
Catholics, but, as the controversy between C. S. Lewis, George Every
and S. L. Bethell obliquely revealed, from important members of his
own communion.[34]

In the light of the gradual evolution of his thinking sketched here it
is difficult to see how the problem could have been resolved.[35] Indeed,
that the antitheses in terms of which his whole development takes place
posit the impossibility of a conclusion is suggested if one goes back to
one of our starting-points, Bradley. As Richard Wollheim notes, in
Bradley's scheme religion is essentially practical, a feeling or attitude
which demands an object to relate to; but all relations are self-contradictory, only appearances: 'The only solution would be for God
and that which is set over against him, for the two terms of the religious
attitude, to be fused into one whole.'[36] But to do this is clearly contrary
to the central religious tradition. And Wollheim adduces Bradley's

'short of the Absolute, God cannot rest, and having reached that goal, he is lost and religion with him.'[37] It does not seem to me fanciful to suggest a connexion between this problem posed by Bradley and Eliot's inability to bring the emphasis on belief and transcendence, and that on religion as a cultural fact in his own work into the same perspective, especially if one keeps in mind the parallel difficulty raised in quite different terms by Maurras and Maurras' condemnation.

Returning to the outset in another way, we can take up again the more general question of Eliot's continuity *vis à vis* his critics. In that part of his writing considered here, though the variations and digressions are complex, the continuity of the project of the unification of experience is quite clear, especially in the development over almost thirty years from tradition to culture. Attention to the work of Bradley and Maurras suggests that although concern with the ultimate validation of experience becomes explicit only after 1926 (and is never consistently resolved) there are good grounds for seeing its existence from the very beginning of Eliot's writings. If this is the case, then two related general problems are raised for further examination, which cannot be undertaken here. First, if in Eliot's own work the concepts of tradition and organic culture originate in idealism, then the implications for conceptions derived from his work or even those of a parallel nature require careful scrutiny. For example, it is worth investigating the degree of relationship between idealism and the concept of organic culture in the nineteenth century, and possible contemporary and current forms of this. Secondly and relatedly, if Eliot's development is far more consistent (he would presumably have assumed it to be irreversible) than his critics have often suggested, then the connexions between the earlier critical work and the later need to be re-examined. In such an examination one would have to see how far his was a reasonable development of the critical assumptions he had established, indicating that the terms of resistance to this development (in itself without coherent conclusion) on the part of the majority of critics may, in fact, be the locus of a far more important discontinuity. Seeing Eliot in this perspective might, in ironic conformity with the principle we inherit from him, lead us to see current literary criticism and the cultural analyses derived from it in a different and disturbing perspective.

NOTES

1. 'His best students . . . could not help going beyond him, where only some deep privation of imagination, some paucity of sympathy, some racking poverty

of sensibility, kept him from going himself. It was as if he taught music, and taught it magnificently, but only in the written score. . . . His Humanism, by acting as if it were complete, as if it were itself the unity of what it saw, became in effect a methodology of pre-judgement, a barrier between the mind and the sensibility in which it lodged, between the score of the music and its performance.' (R. P. Blackmur, *The Lion and the Honeycomb* (1956) pp. 146–51.)

2. *Rousseau and Romanticism* (1919) p. 278.

3. *Literature and the American College* (1908) p. 35.

4. *Democracy and Leadership* (1924). According to Eliot (*Criterion*, XIII 118), 'his single most important book', although its theocratic implications were not lost on the original *Criterion* reviewer, Herbert Read (III 129–33). Eliot too noted that '. . . for others who had followed him hungrily to the end and had found no hay in the stable, the collapse might well be into a Catholicism *without* the element of humanism and criticism, which would be a Catholicism of despair' (*SE* p. 479).

5. Cf. Yvor Winters, *In Defence of Reason* (1937) pp. 151–344.

6. *Rousseau and Romanticism*, p. 7.

7. Ibid. p. 8; cf. pp. 278–9.

8. *Josiah Royce's Seminar 1913–14: as recorded in the notebooks of Harry T. Costello*, ed. Grover Smith (New Brunswick, 1963) pp. 73–85.

9. Introduction to Charlotte Eliot's *Savonarola: a dramatic poem* (1926) p. viii.

10. In particular see Fei-Pau Lu, *T. S. Eliot: the dialectical structure of his theory of poetry* (Chicago, 1966); Eric Thompson, *T. S. Eliot: the metaphysical perspective* (Illinois, 1963); J. Hillis Miller, 'T. S. Eliot', in *Poets of Reality* (Cambridge, Mass., 1966).

11. Compare the following passages:

Bradley's universe . . . is only by an act of faith unified. Upon an inspection, it falls away into the isolated finite experiences out of which it is put together. Like monads they aim at being one; each expanded to completion, to the full reality latent within it, would be identical with the whole universe. But in so doing it would lose the actuality, the here and now, which is essential to the small reality which it actually achieves. (*KE* p. 202)

. . . an explanation of what makes modern poetry would have to be an explanation of the whole modern world; to understand the poet we should have to understand ourselves – we should have, in fact, to reach a degree of self-consciousness of which mankind has never been capable, and of which if attained, it might perish. (Preface to *A Little Book of Modern Verse*, ed. Ann Ridler (1941).)

To judge a work of art by artistic or religious standards, to judge a religion by religious or artistic standards should come in the end to the same thing; though it is an end at which no individual can arrive. (*NDC* p. 30.)

. . . it is ultimately the function of art, in imposing a credible order upon reality, and thereby eliciting some perception of an order *in* reality, to bring us to a condition of serenity, stillness, and reconciliation; and then leave us, as Virgil left Dante, to proceed toward a region where that guide can avail us no farther. ('Poetry and Drama', *PP* p. 87.)

12. 'Was there a Scottish Literature?' *Athenaeum*, 1 Aug. 1919, p. 680.

13. So much of our present understanding of the relations between society and the individual, past and present, and of the origin and continuity of culture depends upon an understanding of the role of language that it is worth noting the early presence of the elements of this idea in Eliot's work: the essay on 'Tradition', the record of the Royce seminar on the relations between expression,

description and communication, the shared system of references presupposed in *Knowledge and Experience*, the insistence that the writer concern himself with the traditions of his own language, rather than his nation or race offer seminal insights. The fact that Eliot never developed them probably arises both from his concentration on *literary* language, and from the instability of his idealist concept of Tradition, which leads directly to Maurras and an emphasis precisely upon the nation and the race.

14. See especially Hugh Kenner, *The Invisible Poet* (1959), and Frank Kermode, *Romantic Image* (1957).

15. *Speculations* (1924) p. 71. Cited by Eliot in 'Second Thoughts about Humanism', in *SE* pp. 490–1.

16. Cf. 'If truth is always changing, then there is nothing to do but sit down and watch the pictures. . . . I should say that it was at any rate essential for religion that we should have the conception of an immutable object or Reality the knowledge of which should be the final object of the Will; and there can be no permanent reality if there is no permanent truth.' (From a letter to Bonamy Dobrée, 12 Dec 1927, cited in *T. S. Eliot: the man and his work*, ed. Allen Tate (1966) p. 75.)

17. Materials for a full study of Maurras are now available: E. J. H. Greene, *T. S. Eliot et la France* (Paris, 1951); Samuel M. Osgood, *French Royalism under the Third and Fourth Republics* (The Hague, 1960); Michael Curtis, *Three Against the Third Republic: Sorel, Barras, and Maurras* (Princeton, 1959); Herbert Tint, *The Decline of French Patriotism 1870–1940* (1964); Eugen Weber, *The Action Française* (Stanford, 1962); E. R. Tannenbaum *The Action Française* (New York, 1962).

18. 'The Literature of Politics', in *CC* pp. 142–3; cf. 'The Literature of Fascism', in *Criterion*, VIII 280–90.

19. 'The device Liberté, Egalité, Fraternité is only the memorial of the time of the Revolution; Famille, Travail, Patrie has more permanent value' (*Christian News Letter*, 3 Sept 1941).

20. Cf. Herbert Howarth, *Notes on Some Figures behind T. S. Eliot* (1965) p. 176.

21. The importance of the Church as a cultural institution for the spiritual reorganization of society and the simultaneous hostility to its doctrine and admiration for its organization stem originally from one of Maurras' masters, Auguste Comte. Cf. *The Positive Philosophy of A. Comte*, (1875) II 252.

22. 'The *Action Française*, M. Maurras and Mr Ward', in *Criterion*, VII 202.

23. 'Christianity and Communism', in *The Listener*, 16 Mar 1932. Certainly the ultimate transcendence of religious belief is present in Eliot's drama and poetry, but the gap between this and his prose writings remains. Failing to see the connexions between Maurras and Bradley, both J. Hillis Miller and Dr Lu overstate Eliot's religious orthodoxy, and miss the significance of the problems of the 1930s. Dr Lu stresses that 'Never for a moment does Eliot lose sight of the larger frame of reference of the unity of human beings in the Kingdom of God' (*Dialectical Structure*, p. 72), but this is because he follows the development of the *poetic* criticism, which culminates in the passage of 1951, quoted in note 11. Attention to this social and cultural thinking would modify this view. Miller, who briefly connects Eliot's idealism with the problems discussed in his cultural writings, oddly places his comments *before* his account of 'the reversal which transforms idealism into Christianity' so that only 'traces of idealism remain in his later prose'. Both the chronology and the detail of Eliot's prose reveal a different picture.

24. 'Only from about the year 1926 did the features of the post-war world begin to emerge clearly – and not in the sphere of politics. From about that date one began slowly to realize that the intellectual and artistic output of the previous seven years had been rather the last efforts of an old world, than the first struggles of a new.' (*Criterion*, XVIII 271.) For an account of the crucial significance of the *Action Francaise* and its connexion with English Catholic history see the present writer's 'Culture and Catholicism: an historical analysis', in *From Culture to Revolution*, eds. T. Eagleton and B. Wicker (1968) and 'Aspects of Distribution', in *Newman*, IV 1 (Jan. 1969).

25. A fourth area is the relation between literature and religion, a matter requiring separate and extensive treatment. Eliot's supposed confusions and contradictions involve not one problem, as most writers on the subject appear to think, but two. There is the relation between poetry and belief on the part of the poet in the process of poetic creation; and on the part of the reader or critic responding to the completed work. Taken separately, Eliot's writing on these topics is remarkably coherent, even if rather vague on the latter.

26. *The Things that are not Caesar's* (1930) ch. 3.

27. Eliot implicitly disclaims a Maurrasien position in *The Idea of a Christian Society* (p. 58), but, as Professor Cameron notes, the book involves a basic confusion as to whether the idea of a Christian society is a sociological or a theological category. Basically, Eliot is still judging religion by its cultural fruits as he had done in *For Lancelot Andrewes* (cf. Cameron, *Night Battle*, p. 29).

28. Dawson makes this line of argument his main criticism: 'Yet in spite of these paradoxical consequences, Mr Eliot remains convinced that religion and culture are inseparable and that the traditional conception of a *relation* between them is fundamentally erroneous and unacceptable. Yet I believe that the idea of such a relation is inseparable from the traditional Christian conception of religion and that the paradoxes that are inherent in his view are gratuitous difficulties which are due to his ignoring the transcendence of the religious factor.' ('T. S. Eliot on the Meaning of Culture', in *The Month* (Mar 1949), reprinted in *Dynamics of World History* (1957) pp. 107–8.)

29. Preface to Harry Crosby, *Transit of Venus: poems* (1931).

30. *Religion and Culture* (1931) pp. 28–9, the first of *Essays in Order* (1931), a series edited by Dawson.

31. 'Catholicism and International Order' (1933), in *EAM* pp. 123–4.

32. *SE*, pp. 382–3. Earlier, however, he wrote, '. . . it seems almost inevitable that Canterbury should eventually be succeeded by Rome. . . . It is their own fault.' (Letter to Bonamy Dobrée, 15 Aug 1926, quoted in *T. S. Eliot: the man and his work*, ed. Tate, p. 69.)

33. 'Tradition and Mr Eliot', in *Colosseum*, I 2 (June 1934) 50–1, 53.

34. In *Theology*, Mar – Sept 1940. Lewis's contributions are reprinted in *Christian Reflexions*, ed. Walter Hooper (1967).

35. Towards the end of the 1930s, these particular divisions became of little practical importance in the face of international events, and Eliot and several of his Catholic critics united in the Moot, an 'Order' for Christian intellectual reconstruction led by J. H. Oldham. The sociologist Karl Mannheim was one of the most important members. *Idea* and *Notes* both owe something to the Moot, as does the *International Library of Sociology and Social Reconstruction* which still bears Mannheim's name. A study of this group will be the subject of a forthcoming paper by the present writer. One of Eliot's letters to another member indicates his inability to bring the problems we have outlined into a single perspective: 'I have still got nowhere near a satisfactory formulation of

my notions about the *unobserved accretions* of attitudes, beliefs, etc., which take place in the passage between "Christian thinking" and "Christian action". I am sure that these are legitimate – because they are inevitable: but the general law of this operation is very difficult to come by. What happens (to put it in terms of books, which is only a part of the story) for instance, when I pass from the Sermon on the Mount to Aquinas, and (more immediately to the point) at what moment, on the stage of my mind, does Burke make his entrance ? There may be some ambiguity in the adjective "Christian" which my instrument is not fine enough to detect: a difference between "purely-Christian" and "partly-Christian" such that in one sense almost no human act can be Christian, and in another, almost every act should be. The foregoing is only a kind of map of a fog, to indicate the area of ignorance in which my mind has been fumbling. . . .'
This was written, as nearly as I can judge, about 1942.

36. Richard Wollheim, *F. H. Bradley* (1959) p. 271.
37. *Appearance and Reality*, quoted in Wollheim, *Bradley*, p. 447.

'Of Clerical Cut': retrospective reflections on Eliot's churchmanship

MARTIN JARRETT-KERR

I

Waal Possum, my fine ole Marse Supial . . .
Sez the Maltese dawg to the Siam cat
'Whaaar'z old Parson Possum at ?'
Sez the Siam cat to the Maltese dawg
'Dahr he sets lak a bump-onna-log.'[1]

WHEN in 1927 T. S. Eliot announced that he had become a member of
the Church – and the Anglican Church at that – one might have expected
an explosion from his old friend Ezra Pound. There does not, however,
seem to be a single reference to the event in Pound's published letters
of the time; though later he makes occasional quips about Eliot's
allegiance. In 1935, for instance, he says in a letter

A couple of bawdy songs from father Eliot wdn't go bad with the
electorate. I see he has written a play. Mebbe a few lyrics sech az:

When I was only a slip of a girl
Wot couldn't eat more'n a couple of chops . . .

or of course 'Bolo', which I am afraid his religion won't now let him
print.[2]

No doubt he adopted the same attitude to Eliot's allegiance that he
adopted towards some of his Roman Catholic friends, which was, in
effect, 'leave them there – don't stir them up: they'd do *much* more
damage outside the Church'. Indeed, as time went on it seems that

Pound's gravamen was not so much that Eliot was a Christian, but that he did not as Anglican come out sufficiently vigorously in favour of the traditional Catholic condemnation (echoed by some of the Caroline divines) of usury. Or, as he put it in another way in 1937, 'During the past 20 years the chief or average complaint against the almost reverend Eliot has been that he exaggerated his moderations.'[3]

This is, as one would expect of Pound, acute criticism. Most other voices took on a different tone: the tone of 'high hopes disappointed'. In 'Thoughts after Lambeth' Eliot specifically refers to this tone:

> When . . . I brought out a small book of essays, several years ago, called *For Lancelot Andrewes*, the anonymous reviewer in the *Times Literary Supplement* made it the occasion for what I can only describe as a flattering obituary notice. In words of great seriousness and manifest sincerity, he pointed out that I had suddenly arrested my progress – whither he had supposed me to be moving I do not know – and that to his distress I was unmistakably making off in the wrong direction. Somehow I had failed, and had admitted my failure; if not a lost leader, at least a lost sheep; what is more, I was a kind of traitor; and those who were to find their way to the promised land beyond the waste might drop a tear at my absence from the roll-call of the new saints. (*SE* p. 368)

I do not recall having seen this review in the *Times Literary Supplement* reprinted anywhere, so it may be of some interest to see what the reviewer said. (It would be of even greater interest to know who the reviewer was.) It occupied nearly two columns and was entitled 'Mr Eliot's New Essays'. It starts off on a tone (remarkable for the date) of great respect.

> Mr Eliot owes his eminence in the world of modern literature to something more than his possession of a critical and poetic mind of an high and original order; even those who have never been able to accept his point of view have always recognized and paid tribute to the seriousness and integrity displayed in his unremitting quest for a philosophy, or at least a mental attitude, which might square with the complexities, the realities and, in particular, the scepticisms of contemporary living.

It goes on to discuss the possible directions of this quest.

It is now some years since it was first suggested by an acute critic*
that Mr Eliot would find it possible to reconcile his principles with
his practise only 'by an act of violence, by joining the Catholic Church'.
A drawing nearer to Anglo-Catholicism is the step his new book
announces.

The reviewer then takes the essays in turn, and pays generous tribute
to their quality.

> The essay on Andrewes reveals him [Eliot] almost at his very
> best. . . . The form of the essay is perfect, the expression (but for
> one or two harsher outbursts) almost exquisite in its unemotional
> purity.

True, the reviewer dissents from Eliot's view of Bramhall, considering
that Bramhall's refutation of Hobbes was by no means 'unanswerable',
as Eliot said. (His defence of Hobbes, however, seems very lame, as
Eliot no doubt observed with relish when he came to read the review.
All that the anonymous author can say, to support Hobbes' determinism,
is

> Have we really any right to go beyond the position of those who
> urge both free will and predestination as equally indisputable though
> incompatible facts? Admittedly we take free will for granted, but
> are we entitled to hold it as more than a working belief? . . .)

But it is in his comments on Eliot's essay on 'The Humanism of
Irving Babbitt' that the dispute really comes to the surface; and this is
the section that Eliot refers to in the remarks, quoted above, in 'Thoughts
after Lambeth'. The reviewer takes up Eliot's argument that humanism
cannot survive without a religion – and that means, here, the Christian
religion, and that in turn involves a Church.

> Here, certainly, is nothing new, but from the author of *The Waste
> Land* it is at first sight astonishing, to say the least. We ourselves can
> only conceive of Mr. Eliot's 'act of violence' as consequent upon a
> dynamic fusion of the need for an object of belief with the desire – the
> increasing desire – for a universal and continuous rather than a living
> tradition. He has discovered at once a respite and a continuity. But
> it is our view that by accepting a higher spiritual authority based not
> upon the deepest personal experience (for that we must still turn
> to the poems), but upon the anterior and exterior authority of revealed

* It would be equally interesting to know who that was.

religion, he has abdicated from his high position. Specifically he rejects modernism for medievalism. But most of us, like Mr Babbitt, have gone too far to draw back. It is in the country beyond the Waste Land that we are compelled to look, and many will consider it the emptier that they are not likely to find Mr Eliot there. Recently he recorded his conviction that Dante's poetry represents a saner attitude towards 'the mystery of life' than Shakespeare's. Not a saner, we would say, but simply a different attitude, and to the majority, the great majority, to-day no longer a vital one.[4]

It was worth digging up that old, forgotten passage, I think, for the light it throws not only upon Eliot's opponents of the time, but also indirectly upon Eliot's own reaction to them. For do we not feel today (admittedly with a deal of hindsight that could not be given to Eliot at the time) that something has gone awry with the argument on both sides ? Admittedly the accusation of 'medievalism' is a curious one to pin on Eliot; and the defence of Babbitt is a little shrill, giving the impression of a touchy, self-defensive kind of humanism. The uneasy 'let's pretend' kind of pragmatism, revealed in the defence of Hobbes, shows also an insecure stance to set beside Eliot's certainties. But the reviewer's suggestion that Eliot, in looking for tradition and continuity in a fluid and insecure world, had merely found a 'universal and continuous rather than a living tradition' is one which has to be taken seriously; and the final hint that what Eliot was opting for is 'no longer a vital' attitude is (we shall see) being echoed by critics of today, forty years after that original article.

II

The *Times Literary Supplement* reviewer should perhaps have shown less surprise. He admitted that an 'act of violence' by Eliot had been predicted years before. And the movement from the early detached attitude towards religious belief to the at least theoretical possibility of a necessary commitment could not have gone unobserved. In 1916 Eliot had observed that, though clearly a man's philosophy will affect his enjoyment of art, there seemed to be no reason why the latter

should be atrophied by a naturalistic philosophy or stimulated by a theistic one. . . . The feeling and the belief are different things in different categories of value. We enjoy the feeling, and we cannot rest content unless we can justify it by exhibiting its relation to the other parts of our life. Having made this attempt, we then enjoy the theory we have made.[5]

But by 1927 there had been not only the premonitions in *The Waste Land*, but the fairly specific discussion of the relation between Dante's belief and his poetry in *The Sacred Wood* (1920). And 'A Dialogue on Dramatic Poetry', written (presumably) in 1927, at about the same time as *For Lancelot Andrewes*, most clearly marked the frontier between a detached appreciation of Christian faith and practice, *qua* cultural fact, and their acceptance as truth. '*E*', it will be remembered, had argued that

> the consummation of the drama, the perfect and ideal drama, is to be found in the ceremony of the Mass . . . And the only dramatic satisfaction that I find now is in a High Mass well performed. Have you not there everything necessary!

But '*B*' questioned whether our cravings for drama are really fulfilled by the Mass.

> For I once knew a man who held the same views that you appear to hold, *E*. He went to High Mass every Sunday, and was particular to find a church where he considered the Mass efficiently performed . . . the Mass gave him extreme, I may even say immoderate satisfaction. It was almost orgiastic. But . . . he was guilty of a *confusion des genres*. His attention was not on the meaning of the Mass, for he was not a believer but a Bergsonian; it was on the Art of the Mass. His dramatic desires were satisfied by the Mass, precisely because he was not interested in the Mass, but in the drama of it. Now what I maintain is, that you have no business to care about the Mass unless you are a believer.

And '*B*' goes on to talk more generally about the nature of faith:

> We need (as I believe, but you need not believe this for the purpose of my argument) religious faith. And we also need amusement. . . . Literature can be no substitute for religion, not merely because we need religion, but because we need literature as well as religion. And religion is no more a substitute for drama than drama is a substitute for religion.[6]

Eliot had evidently moved across the frontier at this time, from the position of '*B*''s unnamed 'a man' to that of '*B*' himself. And it became specific in his preface to *For Lancelot Andrewes*, declaring himself 'a classicist in literature, a royalist in politics, and an Anglo-Catholic in religion'. We now know more about that famous announcement than did the reviewer in the *Times Literary Supplement*. For in the unfinished essay (1961) 'To Criticize the Critic' (included in the posthumous volume of that name) he has told us that

> The sentence in question was provoked by a personal experience. My old teacher and master, Irving Babbitt, to whom I owe so much, stopped in London on his way back to Harvard from Paris . . . and he and Mrs Babbitt dined with me. I had not seen Babbitt for some years, and I felt obliged to acquaint him with a fact as yet unknown to my small circle of readers (for this was, I think, in the year 1927) that I had recently been baptized and confirmed into the Church of England. I knew that it would come as a shock to him to learn that any disciple of his had so turned his coat, though he had already had what must have been a much greater shock when his close friend and ally Paul Elmer More defected from Humanism to Christianity. But all Babbitt said was: 'I think you should come out into the open.' I may have been a little nettled by this remark; the quotable sentence turned up in the preface to the book of essays I had in preparation, swung into orbit, and has been circling my little world ever since.

And Eliot took the opportunity to bring us up-to-date on his present position in the matter:

> Well, my religious beliefs are unchanged, and I am strongly in favour of the maintenance of the monarchy in all countries which have a monarchy; as for Classicism and Romanticism, I find that the terms have no longer the importance to me that they once had. But even if my statement of belief needed no qualification at all after the passage of the years, I should not be inclined to express it in quite this way. (*CC* p. 15)

It would be interesting to know in what other way he would have been inclined to express his belief in 1961. But we do know that the decision of 1927 had significant gradual results, marked by slow but steady shifts in emphasis. Not, it must be emphasised, a shift towards ivory-towerism.

A decade or so later Eliot was discussing quite concrete social problems in his lectures given in Cambridge in 1939, 'The Idea of a Christian Society'. What those lectures, and their more concrete sequel, the *Notes towards a Definition of Culture*, do reveal is a shift away from politics. In 1931 Eliot was still hopeful for a new Toryism, though even then he distinguished this from the kind of Conservatism that 'has been overrun first by deserters from Whiggism and later by businessmen'; rather it will have to 'erect its philosophy on a religious foundation'.[7] But by the time he wrote his 'Last Words' in the *Criterion*'s closing number, looking back over the previous eight years he admitted that 'For myself, a right political philosophy came more and more to imply a right theology – and right economics to depend upon right ethics: leading to emphases which somewhat stretched the original framework of a literary review' (*Criterion*, XVIII 272).

So, sceptical of any party-political solution of our social problems, Eliot was turning increasingly to a religio-cultural analysis of them. At the time of Munich he expressed the doubt whether our civilisation was now valid at all, whether we could 'match conviction with con- viction . . . [or] had [any] ideas with which we could meet or oppose the ideas opposed to us. Was our society . . . assembled round anything more permanent than a congeries of banks, insurance companies and industries' (*ICS* p. 64). But, however telling his critical analysis of modern society, the doubt remains whether his positive suggestions are anything like proportionate to the scale of the problems. Mr D. L. Munby, an economist who is himself a Christian, has devoted a book to disputing Eliot's theses, and some of his comments are weighty.[8] His two main contentions are, first, that we are further from a 'Christian Society' than Eliot thought, and, second, that a secular, neutral society can be a better context for the growth of Christian life and values than a uniform, 'Christian' one. I think that Mr Munby does not face Eliot's claim that, since debility in language reveals debility of soul, attention to a society's prose may be more important than tinkering with its economy. Further, Mr Munby does not, perhaps, fully appreciate that, far from having an aesthete's, highfalutin' notion of culture ('perpen- dicular Gothic and the music of Elgar', as Eliot puts it), for Eliot culture means also 'Derby Day, Henley Regatta, Cowes, the twelfth of August, a cup final, the dog races, the pin table, the dart board, a Wensleydale cheese, boiled cabbage cut in sections. . . .'[9] But Mr Munby's main challenge to Eliot's belief that 'we have a culture which is mainly negative, but which so far as it is positive, is still Christian' seems to me incontrovertible. What, in effect, Mr Munby was saying to Eliot was 'Today is no longer the time to appeal to Coleridge on Church and State: it's later than you think.' Indeed, he implied, a more Christian discernment of our society would value more the positive contribution of the liberal, open, secular elements in it to the life and happiness of man.

III

Mr Munby's sense that Eliot was failing to read the signs of the times finds confirmation in an episode which took place in 1948 in America. Eliot had been invited by the Episcopal Fellowship to address them in the Parish House of St Thomas', Washington. This was intended as a private, informal gathering; but news of the meeting got around (it was in the 'entertainment' columns of the *Washington Post*) so that instead of the usual group of two or three dozen parishioners the audience grew to some 150 to 200 – teachers, students, civil servants, diplomatic corps. Eliot was, naturally, taken aback; an extempore talk to a few church friends was hardly suitable to this gathering. Yet he had not prepared anything else, and Eliot was far too conscientious either to disappoint his hearers or to speak unprepared on some wider topic. So he gave them what he had come to give. It was not his fault that the result was disastrous. A journalist, Hans Meyerhoff, reported the meeting; and this is the digest of his report:

> Mr Eliot welcomed the opportunity of being an emissary for the Community of Episcopal Churches throughout the English-speaking world; but, alas, he was hesitant and unprepared 'for this specific situation . . . or any situation in general'.
>
> His was a strange performance. . . . There was a delicate, almost embarrassing element in it for those who came to hear the 'noted' poet T. S. Eliot. What they did hear was the recital of a rather private record, almost in the nature of a diary, of Mr Eliot's credentials as a guest-speaker before the Episcopal Fellowship. This is what they heard.
>
> For thirteen years Mr Eliot was a Vicar's Warden in an unspecified church in Kensington. There is much to be learned from performing such a church function in a residential urban community over such a long time. For instance, it appears that the Church of England (like so many other worthy organizations in the post-war world) suffers from a lack of funds. The urgent task of repairing or totally rebuilding bomb-damaged houses of worship is not an easy undertaking, partly because of the declining Church revenues, partly because of the unavailability of building materials and the ever-present maze of bureaucratic red tape. . . .

At this point there was a (perhaps welcome) diversion.

A lady in the audience, big-bosomed, gray-haired, and volatile, took this opportunity to denounce the Labour Government's encroachment on Church property. Mr Eliot explained patiently that, according to his knowledge, Church property had not suffered from the nationalisation of coal mines, but he recalled a letter to *The Times* according to which Church revenues had been affected by the nationalisation of the railroads which, it seems, caused a considerable decline in railroad stocks. . . . This did not entirely satisfy the lady questioner who seemed to have special sources of information according to which the Church did own coal mining property which the Labour Government had expropriated. Mr Eliot, pleading ignorance, did not indulge in a criticism of the Labour Government. Even when pressed for an affidavit on Mr Attlee's religious convictions (the lady asked: 'Isn't Mr Attlee some kind of a Quaker?') Mr Eliot hesitated long before replying cautiously: 'I really don't know.' This . . . was one of the rare occasions for an outburst of general hilarity among the audience. . . .

Repair of bomb damage and relations with secular authorities, however, are not the only concern of church wardens. Mr Eliot's church in Kensington, for instance, was undamaged by bombs except for a stained glass window which, as he added, was so ugly that it should have been replaced anyway; but there are other enemies attacking religious as well as secular buildings. In the Kensington church, the worst enemy was dry rot. On the subject of dry rot Mr Eliot (perhaps to no one's surprise) grew eloquent and emphatic . . . Since dry rot was not covered by the War Damage Insurance Act . . . the parish was compelled to raise funds by subscription. The raising of funds, however, was only the beginning. Next, applications had to be made to the Board of Works for a licence on building materials. In England the bureaucratic maze is further complicated by the fact that a special Church Board is set up in the Board of Works. To deal with these various channels of bureaucratic authority in a situation of material scarcity is time-consuming and, most people would agree, unsatisfactory in the long run. . . .

Eliot then moved from the 'dry rot in the rafters' to dry rot in the Church as an institution. Here he ranged widely over the sad tendency to secularise religious symbols and the intellectual poverty of religious education. He commented upon matters of Christian reunion, reasserting the thesis of his famous pamphlet[10] on the proposed United Church of South India that such a union could only be had at the unacceptable

rice of a sacrifice of principles. He also described his membership of a
Committee of theologians, one of the three appointed by the Archbishop
of Canterbury to report on the state of the Church –

> an Anglo-Catholic, a Liberal-Evangelical, and a Free Church
> committee; but the latter two either did not function at all or, if they
> did, did not deliver any goods. The Free Churches could not even
> agree on the composition of the committee. The Liberal-Evangelical
> committee met, but could not agree on any common principles which
> might be submitted. . . . It was different with the Anglo-Catholic
> committee. Mr Eliot, growing visibly warmer, was deeply stirred
> while recalling a long list of 'young, brilliant Anglican theologians'
> who had rendered 'brilliant' services. . . . Mr Eliot lingered long and
> affectionately over every one of them. They represented the galaxy
> of stars in the firmament of the English Christendom, eclipsing by
> their brilliance the two or three minor lights in the non-Catholic
> ranks which Mr Eliot credited rather condescendingly with at least
> good intentions and a certain degree of professional competence.

Late in the evening there was a slightly disrupting intervention.

> A young student from a local university rose . . . and asked im-
> patiently: 'Mr Eliot, why are you opposed to a secular, rationalist
> society?' Recovering quickly from the unexpected protest, Mr Eliot
> replied briefly, with an undertone of irony: 'I proceed on the
> assumption that the Christian idea is a true idea; and that it is better
> to embrace a true idea than any other. Of course, we might push the
> enquiry further back and question these assumptions; but I daresay
> this is neither the place nor the time for such an enquiry.' He was
> right. The Chairman called the meeting to an end and requested
> that the benediction be pronounced. The audience rose. Mr Eliot
> bowed low.

The journalist who gives us this account has his own comments on
Eliot's appearance at the meeting:

> tall, gaunt, of pallid hue, and tensely withdrawn from anything
> reminiscent of the flesh, did he not belong more rightfully in a
> monastic order than in the Fellowship of the respectable, upper-class
> citizens gathered in the Parish House of St Thomas' Church? In a
> monastic order there would be no irreconcilable conflict between
> mystic, poetic ecstasy and the practical pursuits of life, the tending

of flowers and bees, the manual tasks at the work bench, the accumulation of Church revenues . . . the repair of dry rot in the buildings ?[11]

This sort of language is enough to put us on our guard in accepting the
rest of the account. But, all allowances made for an unsympathetic
reporter, the occasion was revealing.

Revealing, I think, in several ways which link with what has been
said earlier in this essay. First, and perhaps less important, revealing
of a certain failure of judgement about people. Some of Eliot's favourite
runners turned out to be but moderate performers. The group to which
Eliot referred, which produced the report *Catholicity* presented to the
Archbishop of Canterbury, contained some distinguished older
theologians.[12] But the younger group to which Eliot referred was
composed of those with whom he also collaborated to produce the
volume *Prospect for Christendom* (1945), and that group contained some
members who did not fulfil the promise then shown; the picture of
them as a unique galaxy in the theological firmament looks rather silly
now. Certainly to dismiss the other two groups (both of which did, in
the event, produce their reports, contrary to Eliot's surmises) as merely
containing 'a certain degree of professional competence' was seriously
mistaken. Second, Eliot's predictions about the Church of South India
have been largely, if not wholly, falsified by events: a theoretical and
largely abstract, distant, judgement upon a historical movement, is the
characteristic judgement of a don, a publisher, a man of letters, and
must expect to be qualified by the concrete occurrence. But, third,
these both point to a deeper weakness – a failure in sympathy leading
to an underestimation of a particular tradition in English culture: the
Puritan. Eliot was fond of quoting Paul Elmer More's definition of the
Anglican position: 'not compromise, but direction'.[13] This may have
been a fair characteristic of seventeenth-century Anglicanism: though
even that was not the whole of English culture then. Eliot, after all,
came into the English scene from outside – and in reaction against an
image of Puritanism which he knew from the American Unitarianism
he had been brought up in. From his reading, especially in the seventeenth century, he formed a picture of what the English, and Anglican,
situation should have been like. When, ten or twelve years later, he
looked around for a specific materialisation of the tradition with which
he could identify himself, he thought he found it in Knightsbridge and
Kensington. One cannot but wonder how much of what he found was

eally there, how much merely envisioned. And the inability to appreciate he other tradition, or traditions, followed from this. As far back as 916 there is evidence for this lack of sympathy. Reviewing a philoophical work by A. J. Balfour, *Theism and Humanism*, in which the uthor attacked 'naturalistic' theories of morals and aesthetics (the ood' and the 'beautiful'), Eliot said, '. . . to say that any one type of hilosophy is hostile to art or to morals is manifestly unfair . . . no hilosophy can force us not to feel or value at all. A distorted puritanism, ndeed, is as fatal to values in art, an orgiastic mysticism as fatal to alues in morals, as any materialism can be.'[14] Addressing a group of Jnitarian clergymen in 1933 he said, pointedly, if not with a faint egree of tartness:

> To believe in the supernatural is not simply to believe that after living a successful, material, and fairly virtuous life here one will continue to exist in the best-possible substitute for this world, or that after living a starved and stunted life here one will be compensated with all the good things one has gone without: it is to believe that the supernatural is the greatest reality here and now.[15]

can recollect only one reference to Bunyan in Eliot's critical essays, nd that, though favourable, is not so much a discussion of Bunyan imself as a consideration of how Bunyan (and Shakespeare, mentioned rith him) came to be great writers with so little education: 'we have o ask, not merely what had Shakespeare and Bunyan read, but what ad the English authors read whose works nourished Shakespeare, and Bunyan?'[16] Part (though I think only a small part) of Eliot's animus gainst Milton was an animus against his politico-religious viewpoint. Ie admits that Charles I's opponents were not all 'of the flock of Zeal-of-the-land Busy or the United Grand Junction Ebenezer Temperance Association'; that they were gentlemen.

> . . . though they were . . . Liberal Practitioners, they could hardly foresee the tea-meeting and the Dissidence of Dissent. Being men of education . . . some of them were exposed to that spirit of the age which was coming to be the French spirit of the age. This spirit . . . was quite opposed to the tendencies latent or the forces active in Puritanism; the contest does great damage to the poetry of Milton.[17]

s it surprising, in view of all this, that Eliot and Dr F. R. Leavis should clash on the subject of D. H. Lawrence? It may seem unfair to dig out he notorious discussion of Lawrence in *After Strange Gods*, since it is

9

well known that Eliot did not allow this book to be reprinted; and ther
is evidence (which will no doubt appear if and when Eliot's letters a
published) that he modified his view of Lawrence towards the end.
But the book was evidence of what Eliot thought at that central par
(1934) of his career.

> . . . nothing could be much drearier (so far as one can judge fror
> his own account) than the vague hymn-singing pietism which seem
> to have provided her with any firm principles by which to scrutinis
> the conduct of her sons. (*ASG* p. 39)

Eliot was evidently unaware that Lawrence had drawn the distinctio
between the pietist, Methodist tradition and the Congregationalist, i
which he was brought up.

> The Congregationalists are the oldest Nonconformists, descendant
> of the Oliver Cromwell Independents. They still had the Purita
> tradition of no ritual. But they avoided the personal emotionalisr
> which one found among the Methodists. . . .[18]

It is an indication of Eliot's particular limitations that (one suspects
even if he had been aware of this important distinction of Lawrence*
he would not then have known what to make of it. And this gives us
concrete example of the one-sided reading of English cultural histor
which makes *The Idea of a Christian Society* now seem something of a
artificial exercise in social theorising.

IV

From about the fifties onwards there has been a reaction against Eliot*
dominance of the literary scene; and, though not always spelled out
I think this reaction was largely due to a sensing of the sort of limitation
of sympathy in Eliot which we have been illustrating. It is only fai
however, to acknowledge that the empirical, institutional church,
which Eliot idealised and often failed to see for what it was, has to b
thanked for at one moment coming in, like the plumber, and unblockin
the drains. Eliot once told an audience (before a reading from *The Rock*
that two years before writing it he had doubted whether he had an

---

* He told me (I think in 1960) that he hoped to re-read Lawrence, and writ
afresh about him.

† And, given an empirical, institutional church, its wardens have to deal wit
matters like dry rot.

nore poetry to write. 'When the London churches had asked him to collaborate in the pageant with E. Martin Browne he had agreed as an ct of conviction and obligation. In the result his numbed powers were evived by the exercise, and he was able to proceed to the second half f his creative life.'[19]

But it is precisely the word 'creative' that would be challenged as a lescription of much that he wrote in this second period – including nuch in *The Rock* itself.

> O weariness of men who turn from GOD
> To the grandeur of your mind and the glory of your action . . .
> Engaged in devising the perfect refrigerator,
> Engaged in working out a rational morality,
> Engaged in printing as many books as possible,
> Plotting of happiness and flinging empty bottles. . . .
>
> (*CP* p. 167)

The idiom is familiar: the vague, generalising idiom of the sermon. There is, unfortunately, quite a lot of this sort of writing, not only in *The Rock* but in some of the later plays. And when we look at the rather flaccid poetry right at the end we are disturbed by the uggestion that the graph from the beginning of the 'second period' o his last poem is simply a line descending at 45°. Certainly the poetry owards the end becomes almost embarrassingly improving: the kind ld uncle shaking his finger at us.

> The child wonders at the Christmas Tree:
> Let him continue in the spirit of wonder
> At the Feast as an event not accepted as a pretext. . . .
>
> ('The Cultivation of Christmas Trees', 1954)

Or the rather too intimate dedication of *The Elder Statesman*, 'To My Wife' (1959):

> To whom I owe the leaping delight
> That quickens my senses in our wakingtime
> And the rhythm that governs the repose of our sleepingtime. . . .

Must we say that as Eliot came nearer within reach of the ordinary hurchman in the pew he became less and less vital and vigorous as a oet?

This is certainly the view of most literary critics. Speaking of *The Cocktail Party* Mr Raymond Williams says that 'Eliot's Christian

action is not tragic redemption, but tragic resignation. . . . [He
abandons the Christian tradition of sacrifice and redemption. He
removes the action elsewhere, and to a minority. He replaces, as the
controlling structure of feeling, with a socially modulated resignation.'²
And Mr Williams contrasts the late Eliot with Pasternak, to the detri
ment of the former: 'To move from the world of Eliot's cocktail party
where the sound of human beings was heard as the rubbing of insects
legs, to the world of Zhivago, where a whole society is in known
torment, is to be reminded sharply of the true status of literature.'²
A few years early Mr Williams had spoken of *The Elder Statesmen*. He
admitted that there had been a time when Eliot did truly speak about
'experiences which, at great cost even in social thinking, most master
of the Left seemed to omit or not even to know'. Yet he held that now
this is no longer so.

> In 1950 Eliot's sensibility was still significantly directive in our
> literature, as it had been for the previous twenty years. In 1960 it i
> not directive at all. . . . Watching the last scene of *The Elder
> Statesman*, in which the cold, conscious love talk seemed to go on and
> on while Monica knew her father lay dying in the garden, it was
> finally and unmistakably clear that one was watching an alien
> world.²²

And Mr Williams found that this disillusionment brought by 'late
Eliot' begins to 'spread a long way back': that as a result he found
himself wondering why he, and other admirers, took so much on trust
from the earlier work.

Personally I agree with Mr Williams' judgement on the late work
without finding it spreading back. I agree that, as has been suggested in
discussing *The Idea of a Christian Society*, Eliot did not realise that
'it's later than you think'. But it has to be realised that the problem of
the later plays is one of the occupational hazards of the Christian (or of
any committed) artist. For, as Eliot's Christian understanding deepened
the early harsh, almost cynical laughter at man's stupidity and pride
gave way to compassion: compassion for the women of Canterbury
for the mediocre Edward and Lavinia as well as the exceptional Celia
in *The Cocktail Party*, and even for the middlebrow muddlers of *The
Confidential Clerk*. This compassion led to an unwillingness to castigate
But drama can only be made from conflict. To make allowances for
the villain is to weaken the drama: but the Christian is taught to love

the villain while hating his villainy. Therefore the protagonists in his later plays have had to be sought not in life – where charity is the rule for the Christian – but in the safe, invulnerable land of the cartoon (and not very lively cartoons at that). The conflict, the castigations and denunciations, occur now in the harmless area of generalisation where (so to speak) no libel suits can be filed, for there are no imaginatively living characters to bring them. Perhaps it was inevitable. Eliot's lyrical talent had bred with his wonderful intelligence and sensitivity to produce *Four Quartets*. But in his later plays (and slight poems) he failed in the different marriage – the marriage of charity with imagination. Perhaps it is the most difficult marriage of all, and how can we wonder that he failed?*

V

Four Quartets, however, is safe from criticism, early or late. It stands one of the supreme products of this century. And it is one of the great merits of the poem that, steeped though it is in Christian doctrine, imagery, mystical theology, it has an appeal far beyond confessional, let alone denominational, boundaries. The greatest living critic, himself not a Christian, has written as profoundly as anyone on this Christian poem. And he – Dr F. R. Leavis – specifically says that Eliot's poetry from *Ash-Wednesday* onwards doesn't say 'I believe', or 'I know', or 'here is the truth'; rather it is what he calls 'a searching of experience, a spiritual discipline, a technique for sincerity'.[23]

Eliot didn't often talk about himself, least of all about his religious quest; but he did once say, in 1932, that it was scepticism that brought him to Christianity. He spoke of 'the removal of any reason for believing in anything else, the erasure of a prejudice, the arrival at the scepticism which is the preface to conversion'. And he concluded with the characteristically modest and dry statement: 'It is in favour of the Christian scheme, from the Christian point of view, that it never has, and never will, work perfectly. No perfect scheme can work perfectly with imperfect men.'[24] It is this modesty – a permanent achievement though constantly having to be fought for since 'humility is endless' – that prevents Eliot at his best from writing doctrinaire propaganda-poetry

---

* I have developed this point at some length in an essay, 'The Pitfalls of the Christian Artist', in *The Climate of Faith in Modern Literature*, ed. Nathan A. Scott (Greenwich, Conn., 1964) pp. 177–206.

for Christianity. And so, in *Four Quartets*, there is no assertion of Christian dogma, though it is constantly there in the background and from time to time is directly appealed to. But there is room in the poem, too, for a Chinese jar and a Hindu religious classic (the *Gītā*); and the form of the poem is based on the least propositional of the arts – music, a string quartet, one of the late Beethovens, in five movements. If we have to find one word to characterise the poem it will be 'integrity'. The analogy for achieving integrity in life is the analogy of language. To fashion an essay or a poem (even a letter to the Press or a sermon) care is needed – in choice of words, eliminating cliché and waste, achieving honesty and balance,

> . . . where every word is at home,
> Taking its place to support the others,
> The word neither diffident nor ostentatious . . .
> The complete consort dancing together. . . .

And (he means) it needs this same discipline and discrimination, vigilance, to achieve order in life, to find significant moments in time. Indeed, it is not we who can make these moments significant: only a power outside can do this. For

> . . . to apprehend
> The point of intersection of the timeless
> With time, is an occupation for the saint –
> No occupation either, but something given
> And taken, in a lifetime's death in love,
> Ardour and selflessness and self-surrender.

Hence in each of the Quartets there is one section about language, and one which appeals to a particular Christian truth – the Temptation of Christ, Good Friday, the Annunciation, Communion, the Fire and the Dove of Pentecost. But that is why there is a vision in this poem also for those who cannot accept Christianity, for those who cannot go beyond 'hints and guesses'.

> For most of us, there is only the unattended
> Moment, the moment in and out of time,
> The distraction fit, lost in a shaft of sunlight,
> The wild thyme unseen, or the winter lightning
> Or the waterfall, or music heard so deeply
> That it is not heard at all, but you are the music
> While the music lasts.

One of Eliot's last writings was a critical study (1962), brief but just and delicate, of George Herbert. He contrasts Herbert with Donne. One of the differences, he says, between these two poets who shared the same faith and period, can be seen in two of their religious sonnets: Donne's 'Batter my heart . . .', and Herbert's 'Prayer (I)'. Eliot quotes the last lines of each. Of Donne's last line, 'Nor ever chast, except you ravish mee', Eliot says that it is, 'in the best sense, wit'. But of Herbert's last lines,

> Church-bels beyond the starres heard, the souls bloud,
> The land of spices; something understood,

Eliot says it is the kind of poetry which 'may be called *magical*'. Eliot himself has both kinds – witty and magical poetry. But the resemblance goes further. Eliot says that Herbert's poems are of value not only for Christians but for every student of English poetry, irrespective of religious belief or unbelief, because they 'form a record of spiritual struggle which should touch the feeling, and enlarge the understanding of those readers who hold no religious belief'. And, on the wider question of the relation of enjoyment to belief, he says,

> . . . even if the reader enjoys a poem more fully when he shares the beliefs of the author, he will miss a great deal of possible enjoyment and of valuable experience if he does not seek the fullest understanding possible of poetry in reading which he must 'suspend his disbelief'. (The present writer is very thankful for having had the opportunity to study the *Bhagavad Gītā* and the religious and philosophical beliefs, so different from his own, with which the *Bhagavad Gītā* is informed.)[25]

If we substitute 'T. S. Eliot' for 'George Herbert' in these passages, the application will remain just. For Eliot has made it possible for the unbeliever to read, and make something of, St John of the Cross as well as Virgil; and thus made it possible for the Christian to meet the sceptic in the auditorium where the four Quartets are being performed.

NOTES

1. To T. S. Eliot, 16 Apr 1938 (*The Letters of Ezra Pound*, 1907–41, ed. D. D. Paige (1951) pp. 401–2).
2. To Arnold Gringrich, 30 Jan 1935 (ibid. p. 354).
3. Ezra Pound, *Polite Essays* (1937) p. 98.
4. *TLS*, no. 1401 (6 Dec 1928) p. 953.

5. Review of A. J. Balfour's *Theism and Humanism* (the Gifford Lectures for 1914) in *International Journal of Ethics*, XXVI (Jan 1916) 284–9. This little-known piece of Eliot's is of some significance. Balfour's book represented the 'intuitionist' school of theistic apologetics: basing the argument for God upon a refutation of 'naturalistic' theories of value. But Eliot finds this only a disguised, and not very persuasive, form of naturalism. 'Mr Balfour's ethics are a sort of Tennysonian naturalism. If we find the explanation of history in a divine purpose, as yet but partially fulfilled, then we may feel sure that the best will survive; and between saying this, and saying that what survives is best, there is in practice very little to choose' (p. 287). Balfour, he says, holds that there are certain beliefs, e.g. in 'an external world', which are intuitive, immediate and highly probable. 'But', asks Eliot, 'is this belief actually held by any but philosophers? . . . The existence of an external world hardly seems to be a "probability" at all; it is either something which only a madman would doubt, or something which only a philosopher would assert. Do we know in the first place what we *mean* by an "external world"?' (p. 289) And he concludes this review – which might have been written by an A. J. Ayer of the time – by saying that in demolishing naturalism Balfour 'has demolished a very unsubstantial fabric'; but that Balfour's formulation of naturalism, 'it is to be anticipated, the majority of Mr. Balfour's readers will accept' (p. 289). The superior tone is already detectable.

6. 'Dialogue on Dramatic Poetry', in *SE* pp. 47–8.

7. Herbert Howarth, *Notes on Some Figures behind T. S. Eliot* (1965) pp. 255–6.

8. D. L. Munby, *The Idea of a Secular Society* (1963).

9. *NDC* p. 31. Cited in 'Cultural Forces in the Human Order', in *Prospect for Christendom*, ed. M. B. Reckitt (1945) p. 65.

10. *Reunion by Destruction* (1943), published by the now defunct Council for the Defence of Church Principles.

11. Hans Meyerhoff, 'Mr Eliot's Evening Service', in *Partisan Review Anthology* (1962) pp. 400–4. First published in *Partisan Review*, XV (Jan 1948) 131–8.

12. *Catholicity* (1947). The group consisted of E. S. Abbott (now Dean of Westminster), H. J. Carpenter (now Bp of Oxford), V. A. Demant, Dom Gregory Dix, A. M. Farrer (late Warden of Keble), F. W. Green, A. G. Herbert, S.S.M., R. C. Mortimer (now Bp of Exeter), A. M. Ramsey (now Archbp of Canterbury), A. Reeves, C. H. Smyth, E. R. Morgan, L. S. Thornton, C.R. They were certainly a distinguished body; but none of them, except the late Dom Gregory Dix, could have been called 'young' in 1947, and four of them are now deceased. The younger group to which Eliot was evidently referring was that which contributed to *Prospect for Christendom*, and also produced a series of twelve books in the Signpost series (1940). Not all the authors of these reached the eminence Eliot predicted for them.

13. P. E. More, *Anglicanism* (1935) p. xxxvii, published by the Society for Promoting Christian Knowledge.

14. *International Journal of Ethics*, XXVI 285. See note 4, supra.

15. *Christian Register*, 19 Oct 1933. Cited in Kristian Smidt, *Poetry and Belief in the Work of T. S. Eliot* (1949) p. 231.

16. 'The Classics and the Man of Letters' (1942), in *CC* p. 148.

17. 'Andrew Marvell', *SE* p. 294.

18. D. H. Lawrence, 'Hymns in a Man's Life', in *Assorted Articles* (1930) pp. 161 ff.

19. A speech at the Braille Centenary. Cited in Howarth, *Notes*, p. 294.

20. Raymond Williams, *Modern Tragedy* (1966) p. 166.

21. Ibid. p. 167.

22. Raymond Williams, 'Eliot and Belief', in *Manchester Guardian*, 9 Dec 1960, p. 6.

23. F. R. Leavis, *Education and the University* (1943) p. 89.

24. From a talk on 'Christianity and Communism', which appeared in *The Listener*, 16 Mar 1932. Cited in Smidt, *Poetry and Belief*, pp. 28 ff.

25. *George Herbert*, Writers and their Work series, no. 152, published by the British Council (1962) pp. 23–4. The two previous quotations occur on pages 18 and 19.

Note. Certain parts of this essay appeared in an obituary article in the *Expository Times*, March 1965. Acknowledgment is due to the editor for kind permission to reprint.

Eliot and the *Criterion*

JOHN PETER

ANY editorial performance can be seen as overt, or covert, or as a combination of both. Addison's and Steele's, for example, has to be considered overt: it took the form of essay after essay in which the editors' views were directly conveyed, and beyond that there is little to suggest any editorial function worth the name. In the case of someone like Ross of the *New Yorker*, on the other hand, all the overt signs of editorship seem to be missing: we realize that this editor's achievement is not to be measured in his own contributions, still less in manifestos, but in the unseen persistence that held a brilliant staff together on the same magazine year after year. The one kind of performance is public and recorded, and therefore relatively easy to assess; the other is so invisible that it needs the testimony of a Wolcott Gibbs, an A. J. Liebling, or better still a James Thurber to remind us that the editor did any work at all.

These are extreme cases. Most editors prefer to combine their back-stage labours, often very arduous, with discreet personal appearances before the footlights, and in his management of the *Criterion* Eliot was no exception. Over the sixteen-year run of the journal his 'Commentaries' occupy more than three hundred pages, a fair-sized book. Undue concentration upon these pages, merely because they are plain and accessible, will admittedly misrepresent a performance which must have consisted of many other things besides; but they are bound to provide the primary focus for attention when we try to map out, roughly, the place of the poet's editorship in the rest of his literary life.

I

For the first third of the magazine's existence Eliot's commentaries average three per volume, and from the start of volume VIII in September

1928 they became a regular feature in every issue. Writing of this sort, obliged to meet successive deadlines over an extended period of time, is not likely on the face of it to be especially homogeneous; but there is a consistency and continuity about his editorials which a little browsing will soon disclose. In many ways, of course, their consistency has to be regarded as admirable. Here is no journalizing weathercock swung to a new position with every passing gust, but a mind that is more like a windmill, using the shifting currents of opinion to grind its convictions pure and fine. In another way, however, the obligation to occupy and then defend a particular position probably worked to the editor's disadvantage. A task conceived of as mildly insurrectionary could easily reverse itself when the insurrection had seemed to fail, becoming a rearguard action instead, and this chance was all the more likely when the chief strategist the *Criterion* relied upon happened to have been dead for thirty-four years when it began.

I mean Matthew Arnold, the somewhat unlikely spirit glimpsed in motion again and again behind the editor's commentaries for the first decade. Today we seem to be generally agreed that Eliot's opinion of Arnold was low, and can readily turn to 'Arnold and Pater' or *The Use of Poetry and the Use of Criticism* to prove our point. It is plain enough that Eliot deplored what one commentary dismisses as Arnold's 'Cloud Cuckoo Land' (x 312): his notion that Poetry would in time become the mainstay of those values which Religion once sustained and is no longer powerful or pervasive enough to sustain. Granted the later poet's veneration for the Established Church a certain intolerance towards his predecessor on this score is understandable, but I am sure I am not the only reader to have felt a touch of jealousy in the intolerance, too, a faint sense of grievance that – in the matter of general outlook at least – Arnold had often rather irritatingly got there first.

The ungenerosity of this response should be balanced against the high regard for Arnold's writings it imputes, a regard which is amply corroborated in the *Criterion*'s commentaries and which makes Arnold's presence there much less surprising. Apart from the single outburst against his heretical views on Poetry and Religion just mentioned, the references to him are respectful to the point of open admiration (II 371, III 1, IX 4–5, IX 381), and indeed a work like *Culture and Anarchy* has to be seen as central to Eliot's whole purpose in what he himself was doing. Significantly, it is repeatedly quoted or alluded to – more frequently, I believe, than any other modern book. Eliot recalls

Arnold's picture of the Populace 'bawling, hustling and smashing' (v 286); he applies the criteria of Sweetness and Light to the *Sunday Express* just as Arnold might have done (VIII 3); he reproves his age for its incautious trust in 'machinery' (VI 290), recommends a variant of Arnold's Hellenism (III 342), and indeed at one point implicitly avows himself a member of that 'Party' which had been rallied in *Culture and Anarchy*, approvingly quoting the passage concerned:

> We have not won our political battles, we have not carried our main points, we have not stopped our adversaries' advance, we have not marched victoriously with the modern world; but we have told silently upon the mind of the country, we have prepared currents of feeling which sap our adversaries' position when it seems gained, we have kept up our own communications with the future. (III 162)

Arnold's influence extends beyond matters of content to matters of style, even to the style in which many of the commentaries are couched. Eliot's strictures on the prose of Churchill as 'constantly pitching the tone a little too high' (XIII 271) are very similar to Arnold's on the prose of Macaulay; he is at one with Arnold in disliking and avoiding the practice of 'writing down' to an audience (II 233); and anyone who remembers Arnold's fun with names, such as Lord Elcho or Mr Odger, and his constantly ironic surface, will recognise the derivativeness of Eliot's more sardonic paragraphs:

> Thus Mr Lansbury, hastily summoned from East London to visit the Roman Wall, has the warmest sympathy both with the National Preservation Trust and with Mr Wake whose aim is to reduce unemployment by quarrying in a capitalist way. Thus we are to treat various headstrong murmuring childish peoples with the greatest respect for their sovereign independence and liberty, and at the same time to do our best to protect our mill owners, mill workers and traders, as well as to prevent these equal peoples, equal to ourselves, from oppressing and murdering each other and sundry minor peoples and untouchables not yet equal to themselves and to us. . . . Thus we must give everybody the vote and at the same time provide against anybody having a mind of his own. . . . We must profess Free Trade but protect the Motor Car Industry. And this is what is complacently worshipped as the great British instinct for Compromise. (IX 589–90)

The commentaries' prose in this vein is habitually more turgid than Arnold's ever was, but the effort of emulation seems to be obvious.

There were other supports besides Arnold for Eliot to lean on when he began his editorship. Some were personal friends (Richard Aldington, Charles Whibley, and one might add his first wife, contributing under her pen-name of Fanny Marlow); others were academic eminences with whose interests his own were partly identified, such as F. H. Bradley and Sir James Frazer; others again were not people at all, but corporate enterprises which helped to supply him with a sense of community: the Egoist Press (II 373), the Ballet Russe (III 161), and the Phoenix Theatre (IV 418). A confident spokesman for the new modernity, a declared ally of Joyce and Yeats against such non-artists as Shaw and Wells, Eliot sometimes comes close to sounding the note of Crispin Crispianus, and even when he is quoting Max Scheler at length on the parlous state of Europe an underlying buoyancy somehow persists (IV 223). No one is likely to underestimate the special kind of encouragement his own contemporaries provided – or even the remote example of the *Edinburgh* or *Blackwood's* (V 187) – but it is worth emphasizing again that the influence of Arnold may have outweighed them all. If Eliot repeatedly quotes him, and often imitates his polemic style, he also professes precisely the sort of internationalism Arnold had professed before him, invoking 'the European Idea' and stressing the need 'to keep the intellectual blood of Europe circulating throughout the whole of Europe' (IX 182) by presenting to English readers 'the best of foreign thought and literary art' (VIII 577). His whole stance as an editor may fairly be called Arnoldian. In commentary after commentary we find him emphasizing the virtues of detachment, of independent thinking (IX 3, XIII 452), of 'solitary, rather than group thought' (XI 270), of 'That balance of mind which a few highly-civilized individuals, such as Arjuna, the hero of the *Bhagavad Gītā*, can maintain in action' (XVI 290), of 'the just impartiality' a Christian philosopher employs (XVIII 58). Mere interest in literature for literature's sake, like Edmund Gosse's, will never be enough without 'restless curiosity' and 'the demon of thought' (X 716), but such impulses are truly productive only in isolation (III 3), far from the mob excitement which honest freethinker and Christian alike are bound to avoid (XI 470). Pronouncements like these might stand as paraphrases of the spirit of *Culture and Anarchy*, the attitude of mind which could prefer the defeat of the Oxford Movement to all the popular success of 'Liberalism', and the inward pursuit of perfection to all the heady distractions of Nonconformity or Jacobinism.

Detachment is to be doubly valued in a time of ferment, and much of
Eliot's editorializing can be praised as a staunch endeavour to champion
a Tory (and often agrarian) position against the extremisms, Fascist and
Communist, of his time. Even as between Conservative and Labour
governments his impartiality is conspicuous. He quotes Dryden's
epigram about 'old consciences with new faces' to suggest how little
there is to choose between them (VIII 377), and analyses certain assumptions common to both to show how fallacious these often are (X 2). His
own position is quite distinct from modern Conservatism, being royalist
(XIII 629) and Tory, firmly grounded on that 'definite and uncompromising theory of Church and State' without which 'Toryism is merely
a fasces of expedients' (XI 69). In his rather special sense of the term it
is thoroughly reactionary: 'The only reactionaries today are those who
object to the dictatorship of finance and the dictatorship of a bureaucracy
under whatever political name it is assembled; and those who would
have some law and some ideal not purely of this world' (XV 667). The
distaste for bureaucracy here may not be very easy to reconcile with his
explicit preference in earlier commentaries for some form of Platonic
oligarchy rather than democracy (II 233–5, VIII 377–81), but the emphasis
on 'some law and some ideal not purely of this world' is characteristic,
and crucial. Time and again we find him taking up what looks like a
purely political problem or a problem in economics – the 'standard of
living', for example (X 4), or the reform of the House of Lords (XI 69) –
and measuring it against the scale of wisdom or benevolence recommended to him by his religious beliefs. 'Education in Political Economy
is vain . . . so long as it is offered as a pure science unfettered by moral
principles', he declares (X 309), and what is equally pernicious is to
suggest that economic problems have a special priority which entitles
them to be disposed of first. 'We are constantly being told that the
economic problem cannot wait. It is equally true that the moral and
spiritual problems cannot wait: they have already waited far too long'
(XII 647).

This cast of mind made it inevitable that, when his commentaries
became increasingly devoted to politics, as they did after volume X, Eliot
should have reserved most of his attention for an appraisal of Communism. Certain forms of right-wing extremism, like that of Charles
Maurras, were so congenial to him as to appear almost invulnerable;
and the less congenial forms of Italian Fascism and the Mosley programme he easily dismissed as un-English (VII 98) and as 'lacking . . .

:he evidence of profound moral conviction' (x 483; see also VIII 280–90). Left-wing extremism was a very different matter, and a sentence he quotes from A. J. Penty's *Communism and the Alternative* neatly summarizes his reason for finding it formidable: 'The strength of Communism finally rests on the fact that the Communist is a man of principle' (XIII 276). In an interesting passage he even brackets Tories and Communists together, discerning a fundamental distinction between their seriousness and the expediency of other political creeds:

> But our present danger is that our public men will be divided into trimmers and men of principle; that men of principle, men who refuse to listen to that siren song that the true spirit of Britain is 'the spirit of compromise', must become either extreme Tories or extreme Communists, with (no doubt) a respect for each other that they cannot feel for the trimmers, and perhaps in consequence a sense of moral relief at having something positive to fight. There is a very practical sense in which it is possible to 'love one's enemies'; and the Tory of to-morrow and the Communist of to-morrow will perhaps love each other better than they can love the politicians. (IX 590)

The gloomy irony of this prophecy is worth remembering, as we shall see; but for the moment it is enough to observe that its spirit of *odi atque amo* plainly appeared in Eliot's subsequent commentaries. Recognizing the hunger for a cause in the England of the time, and Communism's quasi-religious appeal to his younger contemporaries (XI 467), he forsook the tepid and mildly suspicious attitude he had adopted in the twenties – a period during which Russia apparently impressed him chiefly as a nation in dire need of Arnold's Culture (III 163) – and by the early thirties his discussions of Communism were growing lengthy and grave. Fabianism he saw as anachronistic (x 715) and lacking in religious fervour (XI 468). The danger of Communism, to which by this stage he was fully alive, was that it appealed to precisely those generous and philanthropic feelings he had himself tried to foster, and with all the conviction of a faith:

> Communism . . . has come as a godsend (so to speak) to those young people who would like to grow up and believe in something. Once they have committed themselves, they must find (if they are honest, and really growing) that they have let themselves in for all the troubles that afflict the person who believes in something. . . . They have joined that bitter fraternity which lives on a higher level

of doubt; no longer the doubting which is just play with ideas, on the level of a France or of a Gide, but that which is a daily battle. (XII 472)

Similar to Christianity in this respect, Communism was also similar in that it was generally intelligible: 'there is something in it which minds on every level can grasp' (XII 644).

It was indeed far too seductive a force to be met with the politics of a Laski or Lord Lymington: 'The Bolsheviks . . . believe in something which has what is equivalent for them to a supernatural sanction; and it is only with a genuine supernatural sanction that we can oppose it' (XI 71). Accordingly, through a whole series of later commentaries, he returns again and again, more and more fretfully, to the status which this pseudo-religion can claim. The results, I am afraid, cannot be called impressive. Eliot felt instinctively that much of the Communism in evidence during the thirties was more of a 'vogue' than a matter of deep conviction (XII 244), and he was prescient enough to foresee the possibility of 'a universal Russian imperialism, an imperialism more grandiose than anything heretofore achieved' (XVI 474). But when the chance was offered him for incisive refutation of Communism's claims he seemed to grow muddled and assertive, so that the final effect is closer to wistfulness than assurance. This impression arises partly from contradictions. In an early commentary even Henri Massis is pressed into the role of internationalist, along with Valéry and Spengler, so that Eliot's 'appeal to reason' may be contrasted with the 'emotional summons to international brotherhood' which, by implication, is attributed to Communism (VI 98); yet in a commentary of 1934 it is the rationality of Communism that is stressed:

> Communism is at least a respectable political theory, with its own standards of orthodoxy. . . . It appears to recognize a primacy of intellect, rather than of hysteria; and in times like ours we need ideas, not only our own, but antagonistic ideas against which our own may keep themselves sharp. . . . (XIII 273)

Again, when Eliot offers a persuasive distinction between the 'monistic' fallacy of Communism, purporting as it does to furnish an economic system and a religion in one, and the dualistic view of Christianity, with its separation of things temporal from things eternal (XIV 431–6), and seems half disposed to rest his whole case on this rather academic fulcrum, the argument is strained out of recognition as soon as we remind ourselves that he has offered to combat Communism with an identically 'monistic' creed, compounded out of Toryism and Christianity:

> The only hope is in a Toryism which, though not necessarily distinct for Parliamentary purposes, should refuse to identify itself philosophically with that 'Conservatism' which has been overrun first by deserters from Whiggism and later by business men. And for such a Toryism not only a doctrine of the relation of the temporal and spiritual in matters of Church and State is essential, but even a religious foundation for the whole of its political philosophy. Nothing less can engage enough respect to be a worthy adversary for Communism. (XI 71)

The spectacle is that of a writer so entangled in his own prejudices and predilections as to be intelligible only to those who share them. Even when he attempts incisiveness the result must strike an impartial reader as dubious, or at any rate disingenuously phrased: 'To surrender individual judgement to a Church is a hard thing; to surrender individual responsibility to a party is, for many men, a pleasant stimulant and sedative' (XIII 453). Was it the recognition of a lack of cogency, here and elsewhere, that kept him arguing so long?

So I come back to the point I touched on earlier, that the composition of these commentaries may gradually have affected his own attitude in ways that were unsuspected, and scarcely benign. Mr Graham Hough, asking questions with a frankness that was long overdue, has effectively demonstrated how incoherent were the aesthetic assumptions underlying the literary achievements of 'the men of 1914'.[1] That a similar incoherence underlay their political attitudes the case of Pound inclines one to credit, and the supposition is not discouraged by Eliot's high regard for Massis, Maurras, and *L'Action Française*. Indeed at this date it is surely possible to remark how strange Eliot's acceptance of Christianity itself often appeared. What rejoicing it entailed – which was subaudible – required the construction of something 'Upon which to rejoice', a sort of prior suspension of disbelief; and what faith it attained seems to have been valued chiefly for the mental relief it was able to supply: 'The man who is properly disillusioned is almost unconscious of the fact; and he knows that it is childish to let his mind dwell upon the things he no longer believes in; and that it is adult to believe in something and occupy his mind with that' (XII 470). As we have seen, too, conversion – to Christianity as well as to Communism – could be described as an induction only into 'that bitter fraternity which lives on a higher level of doubt'. Bitter? Said of *Christians?* There is a masochistic smugness about the adjective which bespeaks an insecurity in the writer's own innermost convictions. That such insecurity would in any case have led to dogmatic inflexibility seems probable; but the practice of writing out quarterly defences of his beliefs can only have helped to fix and arrest them. If the least impressive side of the later Eliot's work is its doctrinaire stiffness and complacency, as many would agree, it is a side which the *Criterion*'s commentaries may thus, imperceptibly, have done a good deal to engrain.

II

So much for the overt side of Eliot's editorship; what about the more general and less public side?

In the sombre 'Last Words' printed in its final issue, written out of 'a depression of spirits so different from any other experience of fifty years as to be a new emotion' (XVIII 274), Eliot himself divided the *Criterion*'s existence into two broad phases. The first phase, roughly pre-1930 (down to volume IX), seemed to him in retrospect a period of promise and achievement, and he notes with justifiable pride that the *Criterion* was then the first English periodical to print such European authors as 'Marcel Proust, Paul Valéry, Jacques Rivière, Jean Cocteau, Ramon Fernandez, Jacques Maritain, Charles Maurras, Henri Massis, Wilhelm Worringer, Max Scheler, E. R. Curtius' (XVIII 271) and perhaps Pirandello, thus introducing them to many readers for the first time. During the second phase after 1930, however, as he goes on to admit, the sense of enterprise which had animated the quarterly seriously declined. 'The "European Mind", which one had mistakenly thought might be renewed and fortified, disappeared from view'; the list of contributors became unwillingly more insular; and political and theological argument assumed a salience it had not had before. So far as it goes his analysis is both correct and enlightening, but perhaps it needs to be sharpened if we are to see the quarterly's lifespan in a proper perspective.

During the first phase, as the manifesto printed at the beginning of volume IV readily attests, the *Criterion*'s focus was a literary one. 'A literary review should maintain the application, in literature, of principles which have their consequences also in politics and in private conduct', Eliot wrote in his first volume (421), 'and it should maintain them without tolerating any confusion of the purposes of pure literature with the purposes of politics or ethics.' Not only was literature to be kept separate from religion, since to conflate them 'can only have the effect of degrading literature and annihilating religion' (II 373); in the pages of the *Criterion* at least it was also to be kept quite distinct from politics: 'With the benefits or disadvantages of the present administration of Italy, except in so far as they can be shown to advance or obstruct Italian literature and culture, we have nothing to do' (VI 221). Literary quality was everything, for 'one of the most important of our tasks is to keep the reader in contact with the best creative writing of our time – weighing the work of the oldest and of the youngest generations in the same scales' (VII iv 5). Chary of espousing any particular programme which might limit his scope, the editor was careful to define his over-all policy in the broadest Arnoldian terms, laying claim only to a 'common tendency' among his contributors (IV 3, V 2) – a tendency loosely associated with the label of Classicism (II 231, IV 5) – and as late as 1928 he was observing that what united so many diverse contributions was 'not a common adhesion to a set of principles, even of literary criticism, but a common interest in what we believe to be the most important matters of our time' (VII iv 4). At a stage when, in addition to many distinguished foreigners, the *Criterion* was printing such British authors as Lawrence, Joyce, Aldous Huxley, Yeats, E. M. Forster, Virginia Woolf, Wyndham Lewis, and Eliot himself there was little need for diffidence about this policy's vagueness, and indeed the optimism behind it may be gauged from Eliot's decidedly sanguine prescription for what a quarterly publication should aim to be:

. . . the bound volumes of a decade should represent the development of the keenest sensibility and the clearest thought of ten years. Even a single number should attempt to illustrate, within its limits, the time and the tendencies of the time. It should have a value over and above the aggregate value of the individual contributions. Its contents should exhibit heterogeneity which the intelligent reader can resolve into order. (IV 2)

Such perfection even the *Criterion* scarcely reaches, even in its best volumes: the passage is more of an adjuration to the band of brothers, and to the editor himself, than a hardheaded assessment of possibilities.

But at least during this phase the quarterly's position, if slightly less elevated, was perfectly secure. The creative prose it published was of the order of Lawrence's stories, while among the poems there were both *The Waste Land* and 'The Tower'. Among the essays there was a wide diversity, ranging from W. J. Lawrence on the *Hamlet* first quarto to Rivière on Freud, yet the difficult aim of a 'common tendency' was honourably maintained throughout their range: we are never very far from the 'classical, reactionary, and revolutionary' temper which Eliot found in the mind of Hulme and which, as he said, 'should be the twentieth-century mind, if the twentieth-century is to have a mind of its own' (II 231). If a potentiality exists for inner tension between the literary standard ('the best') and what might be called the intellectual standard ('classical' and 'reactionary'), its existence is still a mere hypothesis, since for roughly a decade the two things coincide. Lucky in their timing, those first nine or ten volumes remain models of their kind.

What about the second phase? Writing of the last months of the quarterly, and virtually ignoring the editor's involvement in politics, Herbert Howarth sees the *Criterion* crisply and consciously terminated, turned off like a tap: 'When the Czech crisis of 1938 proved that a European war could not be escaped and that, for who could know how long, European communications would be severed, he decided to discontinue the *Criterion*. He set matters in order to close down, and the last number appeared in New Year 1939.'[2] This is generous as well as brisk, but it seems to me wildly oversimplified. What confronts us during the second phase is a long and insidious decline, during which the relaxed and confident association of editor and contributors was progressively jeopardized. And Communism is the key.

Eliot was well aware of the necessity for any journal to grow and develop (V 1) and he had long foreseen that one field in which his magazine's interest was bound to enlarge was that of politics (V 283). 'It appears that [today] the existence and the concept of literature depends upon our answer to other problems', he remarks, ungrammatically, in an early book review (IV 751), and in commentaries printed at about the same time (IV 4, IV 420) he points out that involvement in political, social, philosophical and religious questions is inescapable.

The man of letters of to-day is interested in a great many subjects – not because he has many interests, but because he finds that the study of his own subject leads him irresistibly to the study of the

others; and he must study the others if only to disentangle his own,
to find out what he is really doing himself. (VI 386)

Such an interest, such an involvement, need not in happier times have
proved disruptive, but for someone of Eliot's generation – and convictions – the thirties must have been an unnerving period during
which to experience it. Communism, the very ideology which he
censured for its inability to encourage or even to understand the
activity of the artist (XI 471, XI 678), an ideology to which he was in
any case almost congenitally hostile, now emerged as the faith and hope
of a new generation of poets; and however much he might deplore their
convictions his literary judgement compelled him to recognize their
poems. If he was to continue his policy of keeping his readers 'in
contact with the best creative writing of our time' – and why should it
be changed ? – there was no real choice but to publish them. Auden and
Spender had to go in, along with Yeats and himself – 'weighing the
work of the oldest and of the youngest generations in the same scales' –
and after Auden's admission with 'Paid on Both Sides' in January 1930
and Spender's with 'Four Poems' in October of that year they soon
became regular contributors. Likeminded juniors came with them.

Any editor of stamina is prone to witness the eclipse of his own
generation, but this was a much more drastic development, transforming
the potential tension between the quarterly's literary and intellectual
standards into a reality and thrusting the editor into the predicament
of his Magus. His fellow-poets had become an alien people clutching
heathen gods; some older writers like John Middleton Murry had
defected to their side; a fierce new internationalism was everywhere
displacing the Arnoldian kind he had tried to promote. To many of
his younger contributors Spain presented a ringing challenge, but all
he could find in the conflict there was 'the perfect opportunity for
extremists of both extremes' (XVI 670). In its golden years the dynamism
of the *Criterion* had been centripetal; now it was centrifugal, and
alarmingly uncontrolled. For what 'common tendency' could there
possibly be between avowed Communists – or surrealists such as Hugh
Sykes Davies and Roger Roughton – and an editor dedicated to the
principles of Anglicanism, Classicism, and the Toryism of a bygone age ?

It is tempting, and would be genial, to interpret this simply as a
misfortune, an irony of the times, were it not for the fact that some
degree of editorial weakness or partisanship seems to have exacerbated
the result. Discussions of the other great quarterly of the thirties – in

conversation, if not in print – often fasten on the fact that *Scrutiny*'s interests were too coherent, too narrow, adducing this as a disabling defect; but as against the vacillations of the *Criterion* contemporary with it *Scrutiny*'s firmness strikes me as exemplary. Recently Mr Stephen Spender has presented *Scrutiny* as a sort of haven of malevolence, with fledgeling reviewers being instructed by the editors 'as to the lines on which they should attack other young writers.'[3] As a belated Scrutineer myself I may say that I had no experience of any such thing, but if it were true would it be so very far removed from some of the reviewing practices of the *Criterion*? Why, for example, should the editor have turned over *The Dog Beneath the Skin* to Auden's friend, John Garrett, for wildly eulogistic acclaim (XIV 687), while reserving the product of a rival editor, *Revaluation*, for assessment (XVI 350) by a predictably venomous Spender himself? In the *Criterion* even the Marxist maunderings of *The Magnetic Mountain* came to be cited with respect (XIV 703). There is something unclear, ambiguous, even disingenuous about the quarterly's closing years. The one recourse Eliot seems to have had against the false position in which he had allowed himself to be placed, and the Marxism he had somehow come to countenance, was a steady championing of Christianity, whether directly in commentaries or indirectly in contributions and reviews. Consider the prominence of some of those essays in the last five volumes: 'Philosophy Now' by the Rev. M. C. D'Arcy, S.J., 'Religion And The Totalitarian State' by Christopher Dawson, or P. S. Richards on 'The Religious Philosophy of P. E. More'. Consider the roster of reviewers who were also clerics: M. C. D'Arcy, Geoffrey Curtis, F. N. Davey, V. A. Demant, R. Newton Flew, Charles Harris, Frederic Hood, Cyril E. Hudson, and Charles Smyth. Parts of the *Criterion* resembled a supplement to the *Tablet* – while, incomprehensibly, other parts were crowded with Marxists and moderns. Years before Eliot had noted that 'The selection of books for review . . . is regularly one of the most difficult of editorial problems' (V 188), but by this date the necessity to balance Leftist enthusiasm with theology must have intensified it to the point of nightmare. Can we wonder at his plaintive insistence on detachment, on 'balance of mind'? Is it surprising that he should at the same time have entrenched himself deeper and deeper behind the defences of religious orthodoxy?

Take something like 'The Tower', or even F. T. Prince's 'Epistle To A Patron', and set beside it the verses the *Criterion* was publishing in 1938 (XVII 662), by one of the regular reviewers, Bro. George Every, S.S.M.:

> Charity is a hard saying.
> She does not dwell apart from faith in a person,
> The poor who are with us always,
> The bereaved, the émigrés,
> Hope that man is, through the pain in the womb of a woman,
> Born not alone for death, through death reborn.
> Each soul shall serve with his face in the common place
> On the hard, shabby, deal pews.

Or take the prolix, lacklustre commentaries in the same volume and compare them with their equivalents in the twenties. Collocations of this sort will bring home the quarterly's sickness with unusual force, but we do well to remember that it had been a wasting one, and active for some time. During the early years of his editorship Eliot had taken his duties very seriously, going out of his way to criticize contributions before publication so that they might be improved (V 2), but by 1932 he was writing of his daily routine as 'boring' (XI 274), as no better than a chore. When in that same year the editors of *Scrutiny* brought out their first issue it contained a Manifesto in which dissatisfaction with the *Criterion* was already explicit: 'But its high price, a certain tendency to substitute solemnity for seriousness, and, during the last two years, a narrowing of its interests, prevent it from influencing more than a small proportion of the reading public' (I 3 n.). The disparagement seems to have stimulated Eliot to write a very *Scrutiny*-like commentary for one issue (XIII 624–8) but, trapped as he soon became between two opposed camps of contributors, there was little he could do as an editor to overcome it. The times were out of joint, and the storm clouds of war steadily gathered. As he wrote in his vale-diction, 'It will perhaps need more severe affliction than anything we have yet experienced, before life can be renewed' (XVIII 274). Ever since the autumn of 1922 the magazine had been sustaining a remarkable quarterly (and at one stage monthly) standard, but as the thirties drew on the dissociation between its various contributors became intolerable, condemning it to extinction. It is ironic, from this distance, to reflect that the chief damage was inflicted by a thoughtless political enthusiasm which its exponents were later themselves to outgrow. On the other hand we should remind ourselves that the disenchantment and anxiety which brought Eliot's editorship to an end were at the same time engendering reflections that went much deeper, and which ultimately bore fruit in the courageously introspective sections of *Four Quartets*.

NOTES

1. See his 'Reflections on a Literary Revolution', in *Image and Experience* (1960), especially pp. 8–36.

2. *Notes on Some Figures behind T. S. Eliot* (1965) p. 263. For one whose interpretations seldom venture beyond applause Howarth can be strangely cavalier about facts. He makes a fanciful section about Eliot regarding Hofmannsthal as a 'fraternal figure' turn upon a dramatically laconic obituary notice:

> Eliot wrote a single sentence for the next issue of the *Criterion*, October 1929: 'Of your charity pray for the soul of Hugo von Hofmannsthal.' Nothing more. None of the material with which, writing obituary tributes, such as that to Virginia Woolf, he has sometimes both expressed his loyalty to the dead and attempted to avoid a judgement. The formal sentence bespeaks a community with the poet. . . . (pp. 292–3)

In actual fact the tribute concerned is twelve sentences long (IX 5–6).

3. See 'Remembering Eliot', in *Sewanee Review*, LXXIV (1966) 76–7.

Eliot and Matthew Arnold

IAN GREGOR

MATTHEW ARNOLD and T. S. Eliot suggest comparison not only because of the decisive influence they exerted on the literary taste of their age, but also their unusual self-awareness of the function they felt themselves called upon to perform, an awareness revealed in their poetry no less than their criticism. We find Arnold writing to his mother in 1863, '[I] hope to have a busy year. It is very animating to think that one at last has a chance of *getting at* the English public. Such a public as it is, and such a work as one wants to do with it.'[1] Eliot, reviewing Arnold's work, is prompted into describing the public role of the critic, 'From time to time, every hundred years or so, it is desirable that some critic shall appear to review the past of our literature, and set the poets and the poems in a new order. . . . Dryden, Johnson and Arnold have each performed the task as well as human frailty will allow' (*UPUC* pp. 108–9). That Eliot is also of this exclusive company it would be difficult for anyone aware of the modern literary scene to deny. Uniquely and economically, Arnold and Eliot sum up in their respective writings, as poets who were also critics, the fine point of the literary consciousness of their age, and to consider them in juxtaposition is to consider the different sensibilities of an age, as much as that of individuals.

Certainly, it was Eliot's sharp awareness of Arnold as the spokesman for an age that shaped his critical estimate of him. To distinguish himself from Arnold became for Eliot a way of characterising that revolution of taste which he was concerned to bring about, a revolution which, while it set 'the poets and the poems in a new order', also enabled him to create a climate of opinion favourable to his own poetic practice. When we see Arnold in this perspective we begin to understand something about why he haunted Eliot at every stage of his career, 'a familiar compound ghost' arousing him to admiration and dislike.

In Rugby and Boston, Arnold and Eliot found a way of life which remained with them always. Though both men became cultural cosmopolitans, they travelled as missionaries, exhibiting always an olympian zeal, a detached concern which exhibited itself in a prose both magisterial and urbane. From Rugby where no one 'ties their shoes without asserting a principle',[2] and from Boston – described by Eliot as 'refined beyond the point of civilisation' – both men set out, amply equipped with purpose and principle to fulfil the role of the man of letters in the modern world. The careers that follow have their striking similarities – the early work of esoteric and personal poetry leading to poetry of a more public character, the poetry leading to literary criticism and that in turn leading to social and religious criticism. But the most striking similarity is not in the details, but in the self-conscious standpoint from which they were seen. As professor of Poetry at Oxford, Arnold found a platform that enabled him 'to get at the English Public', and within that uncompromisingly academic context he began a career in criticism which started by examining the qualities of contemporary Homeric translation and ended by considering the spiritual anarchy that threatened a nation. As editor of the *Criterion*, Eliot had 'the aim of bringing together the best in new thinking and new writing in its time from all countries of Europe that had anything to contribute to the common good'. Its decease in 1939 was due to the fact that that aim had become no longer possible. But if Arnold and Eliot see that the boundaries of a literary interest cannot be drawn, that it is an index to the spirit of the age, they also see that such an interest must find its roots in a feeling for literature itself. For Arnold 'the great safeguard is never to let oneself become abstract',[3] and Eliot describes a characteristic Arnoldian procedure when he writes, 'you have only to examine the mass of newspaper leading articles, the mass of political exhortation, to appreciate the fact that good prose cannot be written without convictions' (*ICS* p. 20). It is their concern with language and tone that remind us that the public role of these critics was intimately related to their lives as poets. Before considering this further, it is worth looking at Eliot's formally declared reactions to Arnold.

These are expressed most substantially in 'The Return of Matthew

Arnold', part of a *Criterion* commentary written in 1925; the essay on 'Arnold and Pater', written in 1930, and published in *Selected Essays* (1932); a lecture on Arnold given at Harvard in 1933 and published the same year in *The Use of Poetry and the Use of Criticism;* some paragraphs in the first chapter of *Notes towards the Definition of Culture* (1948). From these pieces, together with scattered remarks to be found elsewhere, we can see that Eliot's criticism of Arnold, though it may change in tone with the years, returns continually to the same basic objections. Arnold is more of a propagandist for criticism than a critic, he shows himself insufficiently aware of the technique of poetry, the specific nature of art. Arnold is a vague and imprecise thinker, an easy prey to the temptation of confusing genres. In his early essay in the *Criterion* we find Eliot writing, '. . . Arnold was neither thorough enough, nor comprehensive enough, to make any fundamental alterations of literary values; he failed to ascend to first principles; his thought lacks the logical rigour of his master Newman; his taste is biased by convictions and prejudices which he did not take the trouble to dissect to their elements. The best of Arnold's criticism is an illustration of his ethical views . . .' (III 162). The limitation implied in the last phrase is something to which Eliot constantly returns and it takes its place beside Eliot's repeated charge that Arnold did not know enough or practice a strict enough discipline about the kind of criticism he was employing, literary, theological, philosophical, and as a consequence he blurred the frontiers and asked questions of one genre appropriate to the other. This was especially true, Eliot felt, of Arnold's thinking that poetry could take the place of religion, and it is in sentences like the following that Arnold attracts Eliot's sharpest fire. 'More and more mankind will discover that we have to turn to poetry to interpret life for us, to console us, to sustain us. Without poetry, our science will appear incomplete; and most of what now passes with us for religion and philosophy will be replaced by poetry.'[4] These territorial extensions of poetry proceeded in Eliot's view from the fact that, though Arnold admired the classical virtues, he was a romantic at heart, an attentive listener to the Inner Voice. Arnold never reflected with sufficient rigour on his own practice as a poet, and when he did it was always to convert art into ethics – 'what does the Scholar Gypsy *do* for you?' – or to write in oracular terms of Fading Power.

While admitting the justice of Eliot's analysis, it is interesting to note how Eliot's own later critical practice becomes less at variance with Arnold's. While he always insisted on the boundary between religion and poetry, he became less sure as time went by just where it lay, and his distinctions about the use of the word 'culture' entail as many confusions as Arnold's assimilations.* There is another essay in this volume devoted to a detailed examination of Eliot's concept of culture, and all I wish to do here is to make the general point that the kind of justice or injustice which Eliot does to Arnold's criticism seems to matter less as his own work falls into perspective. To bring the two names into conjunction seems less and less a matter of comparing their relative merits as social and literary critics, and increasingly a matter of being able to see the way in which their criticism is part of their whole creative achievement. Their poetic preoccupations help to bring their criticism into focus and it is to that I would like to turn.

II

The self-consciousness that Arnold exhibits as a critic is no less present in his poetry. 'My poems represent, on the whole,' he writes, 'the main movement of mind of the last quarter of a century and thus they will probably have their day as people become conscious to themselves of what that movement of mind is. . . .'[5] Making conscious the mind of the age, this is the poetic concern, complementing the critical concern, 'to propagate the best that is known and thought in the world, and thus to establish a current of fresh and true ideas'.[6] Complementing it in its self-awareness, and yet, of necessity, going much deeper, because the poet is himself part of the mind of the age and his particular mode of awareness something which lies beyond conscious control. We can see what this involves in the opening lines of 'The Buried Life':

> Light flows our war of mocking words, and yet,
> Behold, with tears mine eyes are wet!
> I feel a nameless sadness o'er me roll.
> Yes, yes, we know that we can jest,

* For instance, it is worth contrasting the varying emphases that Eliot is putting on 'culture' in the following sentences: 'a "culture" is conceived as the creation of the society as a whole' and 'in the past the repository of this culture has been the élite, the major part of which was drawn from the dominant class of the time'. ('The Class and the Élite', in *NDC* pp. 37, 42.)

'The creation' . . . 'the repository' – the words are significantly indicative of shifts in the meaning of the word 'culture' which Eliot, for all his elaborate tentativeness of approach, was never really able to reconcile.

> We know, we know that we can smile!
> But there's a something in this breast,
> To which thy light words bring no rest,
> And thy gay smiles no anodyne.
> Give me thy hand, and hush awhile,
> And turn those limpid eyes on mine,
> And let me read there, love! thy inmost soul.

What is immediately striking about the poem is the way Arnold finds, in a vividly recalled personal incident, an experience which modulates easily into the impersonal experience of 'the age'. The controlled mockery of the war of words conceals a deeper war within, and to listen to that we can only make a gesture, 'give me thy hand', and be silent. The poet would seem to wish to remove a barrier of language – we talk so as not to hear – and confront us with 'the eyes' which have not so much to be gazed upon as 'read'. The poem, in trying to tap the buried life, is trying to find a way of communicating the truth and in terms of 'the self' and 'the heart', the poet gives his pledges:

> . . . long we try in vain to speak and act
> Our hidden self, and what we say and do
> Is eloquent, is well – but 'tis not true.[7]

The rhetoric of the poem seems in a paradoxical way to wish to annihilate itself, to create a situation where 'eloquence' can only testify to its own falsity. The creation of the poem is itself a kind of prison which keeps the buried self inaccessible; it is another episode in 'the war of words'. Arnold sees in our self-consciousness a fatal division between our experience and the way we try to communicate it. Language distorts and we can only hope to find expression in a shared gesture, a glance of mutual understanding. When Arnold comes to praise Wordsworth it is because he seemed to bring directly into his verse the experience of his life:

> Wordsworth's poetry is great because of the extraordinary power with which Wordsworth feels the joy offered to us in nature . . . and because of the extraordinary power with which, in case after case, he shows us this joy, and renders it so as to make us share it.[8]

This direct interchangeability of subject and object, the disappearance of the poem, as it were, is illuminated when Arnold, seeking to define Wordsworth's unique and unmatchable quality, observes, 'Nature

herself seems . . . to take the pen out of his hand and to write for him
with her own bare, sheer, penetrating power'. When the poet is left
holding his own pen, we are offered eloquence for truth. The truth of
any poem can only be found because of the truth of the poet and so we
find Arnold defining style 'as the expression of the nobility of the poet's
character'.[9] Only in a hand worthy of receiving it can Nature place
her pen.

'There are many people who appreciate the expression of sincere
emotion in verse, and there is a smaller number of people who appreciate
technical excellence. But very few know when there is an expression
of *significant* emotion, emotion which has its life in the poem and not
in the history of the poet.'[10] Eliot's famous words, written in 1919, are
sufficient to remind us how sharply his early views were at variance
with Arnold's. We can see the nature of the difference in practice, if,
remembering the opening lines of 'The Buried Life', we consider the
following lyric:

> Eyes that last I saw in tears
> Through division
> Here in death's dream kingdom
> The golden vision reappears
> I see the eyes but not the tears
> This is my affliction
>
> This is my affliction
> Eyes I shall not see again
> Eyes of decision
> Eyes I shall not see unless
> At the door of death's other kingdom
> Where, as in this,
> The eyes outlast a little while
> A little while outlast the tears
> And hold us in derision.

Here the rhetoric of the poem is calculated to distance the personal
emotion behind it, so that although we feel the occasion to be highly
particularised and intensely felt it has been impersonalised into 'art'.
The absence of punctuation, the elaborate pattern of repetitions, the
all-enclosing finality of the closing line, make us see this poem in terms
of a sculpture in language, an object for our regard, spare, self-contained, self-sufficient. Where Arnold employs a strategy that seeks to
do away with the artifice of language in order to convey the truth,

Eliot's 'truth' only comes into existence when the poem has been completed. In 'The Buried Life', Arnold seeks 'to read' the eyes, in Eliot it is the eyes which hold us in derision; they look at us, not we at them. Behind Eliot's practice lies admiration, not for poets, whose pens have been guided by Nature, but for those who, like Jonson, 'created his own world',[11] and Shakespeare, who 'was occupied with the struggle – which alone constitutes life for a poet – to transmute his personal and private agonies into something rich and strange, something universal and impersonal'.[12] It is within this perspective that we can see why such words as 'technique' and 'practitioner' are so loaded in Eliot's conception of criticism. The poet 'must borrow every changing shape/ To find expression'.

In *Empedocles on Etna* Arnold attempts to find a changing shape in the dramatised conflict between Empedocles and Callicles, a conflict that could bear the sub-title 'The function of poetry at the present time'. In Empedocles, Arnold finds a dramatic embodiment for the conflict within the poet, of private concern and public duty. Callicles, a lyric scholar-gypsy, tries to reveal the powers of poetry, but to Empedocles they seem to promise only a world of solitude, where we are 'dead to every natural joy'. The world without is there, but the poet has no response; it remains a catalogue of unrelated nostalgic pleasures:

> A flute-note from the woods,
> Sunset over the sea;
> Seed-time and harvest,
> The reapers in the corn,
> The vinedresser in his vineyard,
> The village-girl at her wheel.[13]

Unable to resolve his conflict, in fear of becoming a wanderer through the world, 'nothing but a devouring flame of thought', Empedocles throws himself into the crater. It is Arnold's dramatic resignation from his life as a poet. He continued to write poetry, but it was in the margins of his other work – his conception of the role of the poet in his age he found himself unable to fulfil. He seemed able to offer only a 'zest to our melancholy and a grace to our dreams', and only in the painful self-awareness of these limitations could he construct the material of a poetic, which he thought could communicate 'the main movement of mind of the last quarter of a century'. Arnold carried to a new extreme the romantic paradox of wresting poetry out of elegies lamenting an inability to write. It was a dying song and Arnold came more and more to find in criticism the appropriate and congenial dialogue with his age.

The world that Eliot finds in *The Waste Land* is no less fragmented and inchoate than Arnold found in 'Empedocles', but Eliot's dry thoughts in a dry season' take a characteristically different form from Arnold's. The fragments which so oppress Arnold become for Eliot not simply what the poem is 'about' but its organising principle. It is not necessary to contend for any unity of argument to suggest that the poem has a unity of mood, and however easily we can dispense with Eliot's elucidatory note on Tiresias, it points us to an inclusive point of view. Within that point of view, we find the poet able to accept 'the fragments' for what they are, 'to be shored against his ruins', and he is able to do this primarily because his attitude to time is different from Arnold's. Where Arnold continually contrasts the tedium of the present with 'the days when wits were fresh and clear', Eliot refuses to see the the past in this way. The present is neither more nor less tedious than the past. Together they form a continuum, Elizabeth and Essex lead on to the Thames daughters. And so in the background of *The Waste Land* there is not a precise mythological tale like Empedocles, but a generalised myth suggesting that the human drama, forever changing, will be forever the same in different ages and different places.

Arnold's view of time is another facet of the way in which he is involved within his poetry, whereas Eliot's views of the impersonality of the poet is no less related to seeing all time as 'eternally present'. Nevertheless, there is some point in thinking that *The Waste Land* might have constituted a poetic terminus for Eliot, had it not been for the fact that in the 1920s he began to find in Christianity a way of looking at time which fitted in with his own and yet offered him a personal and poetic liberation, which renewed his inspiration.[14] The poem as a self-contained whole, impersonal, disparate, this position remains, but now the severity of exclusion is seen not in terms of a self-justifying art, but as declaring the frontiers of art, the necessary declaration of humility. 'The stony rubbish' of *The Waste Land*, 'the charr'd, blacken'd, melancholy waste' of Empedocles, Eliot's later poetry will reveal as 'emptiness, absence, separation from God'. And with that recognition we have the beginning of wisdom. It is the same world that Eliot sees in his early and later poetry; it is the viewpoint which has changed. In the early poems 'The worlds revolve like ancient women/Gathering fuel in vacant lots', becomes in the later poems 'conditions/That seem unpropitious. But perhaps neither gain nor loss./For us, there is only the trying. The rest is not our business.' What was seen with despair is seen again with hope. It is precisely this sense of the limitations of poetry that takes Eliot, as his career develops, into writing a public poetry that would have been understood by Arnold. It is an interesting paradox that Arnold, who saw in poetry the inclusive view of life, and Eliot, who never forgot 'that when we consider poetry it is as poetry we must consider it and not as another thing', should in the end discover in their poetry a similar truth, though the way of attaining it remains as different as ever.

I would like to conclude this paper by illustrating this with reference to two poems where Arnold and Eliot consider old age. Arnold's poem reads:

> What is it to grow old?
> Is it to lose the glory of the form,
> The lustre of the eye?
> Is it for beauty to forgo her wreath?
> – Yes, but not this alone.
>
> Is it to feel our strength –
> Not our bloom only, but our strength – decay?
> Is it to feel each limb
> Grow stiffer, every function less exact,
> Each nerve more loosely strung?
>
> Yes, this, and more; but not
> Ah, 'tis not what in youth we dream'd 'twould be!
> 'Tis not to have our life
> Mellow'd and soften'd as with sunset-glow,
> A golden day's decline.
>
> 'Tis not to see the world
> As from a height, with rapt prophetic eyes,
> And heart profoundly stirr'd;
> And weep, and feel the fulness of the past,
> The years that are no more.
>
> It is to spend long days
> And not once feel that we were ever young;
> It is to add, immured
> In the hot prison of the present, month
> To month with weary pain.

It is to suffer this,
And feel but half, and feebly, what we feel.
Deep in our hidden heart
Festers the dull remembrance of a change,
But no emotion – none.

It is – last stage of all –
When we are frozen up within, and quite
The phantom of ourselves,
To hear the world applaud the hollow ghost
Which blamed the living man.

At the heart of the poem is the inability to respond, the absence of joy that is Arnold's central concern. The past is irretrievably cut off from the present, 'the years that are no more' have only an archaic, nostalgic ring for the man who is 'immured/In the hot prison of the present'. The personal emotion, the immediate interchange with life – these proofs for Arnold of poetic authenticity – have been removed by time, leaving only ironically 'the hollow ghost', the Poetic Figure, to hear the public praise. It constitutes the last rites for the buried life.

In 'Little Gidding', Eliot reflects on growing old:

Let me disclose the gifts reserved for age
    To set a crown upon your lifetime's effort.
    First, the cold friction of expiring sense
Without enchantment, offering no promise
    But bitter tastelessness of shadow fruit
    As body and soul begin to fall asunder.
Second, the conscious impotence of rage
    At human folly, and the laceration
    Of laughter at what ceases to amuse.
And last, the rending pain of re-enactment
    Of all that you have done, and been; the shame
    Of motives late revealed, and the awareness
Of things ill done and done to others' harm
    Which once you took for exercise of virtue.

Our response is ambivalent in that, although we are aware that the passage is dramatised, the language exhibits such precision, such personal authority, that we feel we might be reading the epitaph for everyman. This counterpoint of feeling between the highly personal and the wholly public is characteristic of the *Quartets* as a whole. Where Arnold confronts his experience directly, Eliot seeks to communicate not an epistemology, but rather the *experience* of an epistemology. Arnold, like Wordsworth, tries to show us and render the joy which he feels should inhere in experience, fails and is driven to silence; Eliot, concerned with the transmutation of experience, is left 'trying to get the better of words'. In *Four Quartets* Eliot at last manages to make the private experience wholly public in such a way that criticism, which must be personal, seems oddly disoriented. The problem is that the poem is about its own creation, but not as something as an event in the life of the poet like *The Prelude*, but as a creation which sees itself defining, in a unique way, its own limitations, endorsing the reality of a divine experience, about which, by definition, it can say nothing.

At the end of the Harvard lectures, *Poetry and Drama* (1950), Eliot defines art in terms that would surely have won Arnold's approval:

> For it is ultimately the function of art, in imposing a credible order upon ordinary reality, and thereby eliciting some perception of an order *in* reality, to bring us to a condition of serenity, stillness and reconciliation; and then leave us, as Virgil left Dante, to proceed toward a region where that guide can avail us no further. (p. 35)

How closely Arnold would concur with this formulation is suggested by his own definition of art:

> The grand power of poetry is its interpretative power; by which I mean, not a power of drawing in black and white an explanation of the mystery of the universe, but the power of so dealing with things as to awaken in us a wonderfully full, new, and intimate sense of them. . . . When this sense is awakened in us, as to objects without us, we feel ourselves to be in contact with the essential nature of these objects, to be no longer bewildered and oppressed by them, but to have their secret, and to be in harmony with them; and this feeling calms and satisfies us as no other can.[15]

For both men poetry becomes both the perception and the creation of an order, with a final distinction that, whereas for Arnold it always remains an interpretation of reality, the poet speaking to others, for Eliot it is a revelation, the poet speaking primarily to himself.

NOTES

1. *The Letters of Matthew Arnold*, 1848–88, ed. G. W. E. Russell, 2 vols (1895) I 201.

2. Fitzjames Stephens' description in his review of *Tom Brown's Schooldays*, in the *Edinburgh Review*, CVII (Jan 1858) 186.

3. 'The Function of Criticism at the Present Time', in *Essays in Criticism* First Series (1865).

4. 'The Study of Poetry', in *Essays in Criticism*, Second Series (1888).

5. *Letters*, II 9.

6. 'The Function of Criticism at the Present Time'.

7. 'The Buried Life', lines 64–6.

8. 'Wordsworth', in *Essays in Criticism*, Second Series (1888).

9. *The Letters of Matthew Arnold to Arthur Hugh Clough*, ed. H. F. Lowry (1932) p. 101.

10. 'Tradition and the Individual Talent', in *SE* p. 22.

11. 'Ben Jonson', in *SE* p. 156.

12. 'Shakespeare and the Stoicism of Seneca', in *SE* p. 137.

13. 'Empedocles on Etna', lines 252–7.

14. For enabling me to see this I am indebted to a persuasively argued essay on Eliot by J. Hillis Miller in *Poets of Reality* (1966) pp. 131–89.

15. 'Maurice de Guérin', in *Essays in Criticism*, First Series (1865).

Eliot and a Common Culture

TERRY EAGLETON

I

IN 1939, in *The Idea of a Christian Society*, Eliot pointed out that what he meant by a political philosophy was 'not merely even the conscious formulation of the ideal aims of a people, but the substratum of collective temperament, ways of behaviour and unconscious values which provides the material for the formulation. What we are seeking is not a pro-gramme for a party, but a way of life for a people . . .' (p. 18). It is worth beginning an essay on Eliot's idea of culture with this emphasis, not only because it is central to the work in which it occurs but because it reveals the continuity of that work with Eliot's later cultural thinking. It is this thinking, embodied most obviously in the later *Notes towards the Definition of Culture* (1948), which I want to examine here; I want also to relate it to the contemporary debate on culture by comparing Eliot's thought with that of a later writer on culture, Raymond Williams.

The Idea of a Christian Society is not explicitly concerned with 'culture': it is part of a wider contemporary discussion, one involving Dawson and Maritain, Demant and Maurras, the pages of the *Criterion* and the *Colosseum*, the Sheed & Ward *Essays in Order* series and a good deal more literature, about the future directions of what was felt to be a disintegrating society. Eliot's position, briefly, is that liberalism is finished: it offers only a negative conception of society, and as such must yield to positive order and belief. That order will for him be Christian, but not necessarily one governed by a consciously Christian group or composed of a consciously Christian people. The first of these requirements he thinks unnecessary because what is crucial is the 'frame' of the society, its distinctive moral atmosphere, and 'What the rulers believed, would be less important than the beliefs to which they

would be obliged to conform.' (p. 28) The second requirement he
thinks impossible: a consciously Christian society could not exist
because he believes the majority of people to be incapable of any
significant degree of conscious belief:

> For the great mass of humanity whose attention is occupied mostly
> by their direct relation to the soil, or the sea, or the machine, and to
> a small number of persons, pleasures and duties, two conditions are
> required. The first is that, as their capacity for *thinking* about the
> objects of faith is small, their Christianity may be almost wholly
> realised in behaviour: both in their customary and periodic religious
> observances, and in a traditional code of behaviour towards their
> neighbours. The second is that, while they should have some per-
> ception of how far their lives fall short of Christian ideals, their
> religious and social life should form for them a natural whole, so
> that the difficulty of behaving as Christians should not impose an
> intolerable strain. (pp. 28-9)

Eliot takes it as fundamental that most people, whom he sees as
living already a kind of 'organic' life – note the emphasis on 'soil' and
'sea', before what one would have thought was the more typical
'machine' – can live spiritual values only obliquely, embodied in
unconscious habits of behaviour and the texture of a way of life. Unity
of belief and behaviour will be the general condition of a good society,
but one inferior in quality to that tension between the two which
characterises the aware Christian, struggling with his sense of inadequacy
to ideals which finally transcend any possible common life. Dislocation
of consciousness and behaviour, that is, can be a mark of human
superiority: the two are unified only in the savage or the saint. Again,
in the later *Notes* Eliot remarks that 'The reflection that . . . even the
most conscious and developed of us live also at the level on which
belief and behaviour cannot be distinguished, is one that may, once we
allow our imagination to play upon it, be very disconcerting. . . . To
reflect that from one point of view religion is culture, and from another
point of view culture is religion, can be very disturbing' (*NDC* p. 32).
Eliot's attempt, in the *Notes*, to find a way of expressing the connection
of religion and culture which suggests neither the separateness implied
in 'relation' nor the fusion of 'identification' is a consequence of his
concern to embody belief in behaviour while avoiding the corollary
that behaviour may exhaust belief. His cultural thinking, then, begins
with two related difficulties, both peculiar to his conservative and

religious viewpoint: he does not believe that more than a small minority can ever be cultured in one strong traditional sense of the term – capable of subtle and complex response – and he does not believe that any particular way of life can be more than an inadequate embodiment of his deepest values.

What Eliot means by a Christian society, therefore, is one whose common and unconscious rhythms will 'incarnate' Christian value. 'For the great majority of the people – and I am not here thinking of social classes, but of intellectual strata – religion must be primarily a matter of behaviour and habit, must be integrated with its social life, with its business and pleasures . . . for behaviour is as potent to affect belief, as belief to effect behaviour' (*ICS* p. 30). The Christian society 'would be a society in which the natural end of man – virtue and well-being in community – is acknowledged for all, and the supernatural end – beatitude – for those who have eyes to see it' (p. 34). Insight into this supernatural end will be the characteristic of the *conscious* Christian majority, and more particularly of that section of the Church which Eliot calls the 'Community of Christians' (p. 35), a version of Coleridge's clerisy, whose role, as the spiritual *élite*, would be actively to nourish the values which the rest of society lived unconsciously. It is only from these men that 'one would expect a consciously Christian life on its highest social level' (p. 28); the rest of society, unable to bear too much reality, would live its Christianity through behaviour and conformity – its faith would be 'communal before being individual'.

This distinction between levels of consciousness, and the confident placing of these levels in direct relation to levels of spirituality, is crucial to Eliot's thought. It is dramatised in the tension between Thomas and the Women of Canterbury in *Murder in the Cathedral*; it is there, too, in his idea of levels within a theatre audience capable of receiving meanings at different depths. This is clearly a profoundly conservative estimation of human capacities, but the form of the expression interestingly obscures its political content. Eliot, as we have seen above, has already placed the whole discussion outside the bounds of politics: political philosophy is less important than a people's whole way of life, and when that way of life is then authoritatively described in terms of a ritual of unconscious conformism, the fact that this itself is a political attitude can easily be missed. The cultural argument is detached from a particular definition of politics – politics as 'philosophy', as conscious and rational discussion – only to be embodied in a form which confusingly is both a highly political version of man and yet one presented as beyond politics. (We shall see later how Eliot uses a similar method in *Notes*.)

By appealing to the quality of unconsciousness in a common life, Eliot can press for a return to a Christian society in the context of a disbelief in the ability of most people to believe very much at all. The continuity of this position with the attitudes of *Notes* becomes clear once it is seen that the communal instinctive life which Eliot described in the first essay is now a major part of what is meant by 'culture'. There is one, important difference, however: the reservation in the former work that what was at stake was not social but intellectual levels has almost entirely dropped out. A distinction between conscious and unconscious degrees of life is still the decisive factor in the structure of a society, but the correlation of these degrees with traditional social classes is now much more direct. Eliot is arguing for a common culture, a way of life shared organically by a whole people; but the culture will be shared at different levels, and the levels are determined by grades of consciousness. 'According to my view of culture, the whole of the population *should* 'take an active part in cultural activities' – not all in the same activities or on the same level' (*NDC* p. 38). The society will be stratified into social classes largely corresponding to these levels, and the strength of the whole culture will depend on the extent to which each class fulfils its particular function. The function of the ruling class – the traditional English upper class, interacting with an intellectual *élite* – will be 'to bring about a further development of the culture in organic complexity: culture at a more conscious level, but still the same culture' (p. 37). The liberal theory of society, of equality of opportunity and meritocratic *élites*, is rejected as an atomistic conception which destroys common belief and the continuity essential for genuine culture;[1] the traditional ruling class, by preserving and transmitting its culture from generation to generation within stable forms and manners, will act as the tip of developed spiritual and artistic consciousness in the society, and as such will be sustaining, not merely itself, but the whole culture.

But the culture as a whole can only be lived unconsciously, through established form and habit: this, Eliot sees, is part of the nature of culture, once it is defined as 'not merely the sum of several activities, but a *way of life*' 'the *whole way of life* of a people, from birth to the grave, from morning to night and even in sleep . . .' (pp. 41, 31). A culture, on these terms, can never be consciously grasped as an entity: it 'can never be wholly conscious – there is always more to it than we are conscious of; and it cannot be planned because it is always the unconscious background of all our planning. . . . Culture cannot altogether be brought to consciousness; and the culture of which we are wholly conscious is never the whole of culture' (pp. 94, 107). In his introduction, Eliot quotes a passage which includes under the culture of an industry the geography of its raw materials, its markets, inventions, scientific background, but adds significantly that 'an industry, if it is to engage the interest of more than the conscious mind of the worker, should also have a way of life somewhat peculiar to its initiates, with its own forms of festivity and observances' (p. 16 n). Later in the essay, in discriminating between kinds of good manners, he makes the distinction in terms of 'more and less conscious "good manners" ' (p. 42 n); at another point he remarks that the upper levels of society will not possess *more* culture than the lower levels, but will represent 'a more conscious culture and a greater specialisation of culture' (p. 48). It is interesting to see that the distinction between conscious and unconscious life is being presented in terms of the two meanings of 'culture': culture as the whole body of artistic and intellectual work is the reserve of the conscious *élite* and the acme of a society's awareness; culture defined anthropologically as a particular way of life is a network of unconscious habits.

II

It is useful to compare Eliot's model of a common culture to one which, despite many points of contact, ultimately opposes it. In the conclusion to his *Culture and Society 1780–1950* (1958), Raymond Williams places a similar emphasis on the unconsciousness of a lived culture, but links it to a different structure of values:

A culture, while it is being lived, is always in part unknown, in part unrealized. The making of a community is always an exploration, for consciousness cannot precede creation, and there is no formula for unknown experience. A good community, a living culture, will, because of this, not only make room for but actively encourage all and any who can contribute to the advance in consciousness which is the common need. . . . We need to consider every attachment, every value, with our whole attention; for we do not know the future, we can never be certain of what may enrich it. (p. 334)

For Williams a culture's unconsciousness, its lack of availability as a whole to anyone living within it, is a consequence of its openness to every offered value; the culture can never be brought fully to consciousness because it is never fully finished. The making of a culture is a continual exchange and extension of meanings, a network of shared activities and definitions never self-conscious as a whole, but growing towards the 'advance in consciousness', and thus in full humanity, of a total society. The making of a *common* culture is the collaborative making of meanings; a culture is common, for Williams, not only when it is commonly shared but when it is commonly made, through the fullest active participation of all its members. For Eliot a culture is common when commonly shared, at different levels of participation and response; the conscious making and nourishing remains the reserve of a few. But for Williams common sharing is not a sufficient criterion: the full meaning of a common culture is not that the ready-made creations of others should be taken over and lived passively by a people, but that a way of life should be continually remade and redefined in that people's common action and consciousness. It is for this reason that Williams's idea of culture explicitly demands, and is inseparable from, political change: it requires and implies an ethic of common responsibility and 'the full democratic process'.

The essential point of difference between the two versions of a common culture is that, in Williams's version, the conscious and unconscious life which, for Eliot, are characteristic of different social classes become aspects of a single creative process. Williams's common culture is at once more and less conscious than Eliot's: more conscious, because it engages the active participation of all its members; less conscious, because what will then be created according to this rule can be neither prescribed in advance nor fully known in the making. Williams makes this point explicitly, in relation to the meaning of the word 'culture':

> We have to plan what can be planned, according to our common decision. But the emphasis of the idea of culture is right when it reminds us that a culture, essentially, is unplannable. We have to ensure the means of life, and the means of community. But what will then, by these means, be lived, we cannot know or say. The idea of culture rests on a metaphor: the tending of natural growth. And indeed it is on growth, as metaphor and as fact, that the ultimate emphasis must be placed. (p. 335)

The idea of culture as the active tending of spontaneous growth holds the elements of conscious and unconscious life in fusion; a truly common culture is one which, precisely because it engages the fullest conscious collaboration of all its members, can never be wholly self-transparent. Eliot's idea of culture, in contrast, forces a wedge between these two aspects. For him, consciousness and unconsciousness are qualities of different social groups within the culture: the minority fosters conscious values and transmits them through rhythm and texture to the majority. It follows that for Eliot the culture *can* be to some extent prescribed: he can say now what the values are, as indeed he does in *The Idea of a Christian Society*. Eliot has already a very clear idea of what form of common life he wants to see; moreover, it will be a form of life based on a structure of values which ultimately transcends culture and as such cannot be radically modified by the activity it generates. Both Williams and Eliot point to the values of an existing social class as a symbol of the future society; the difference is that whereas Williams imagines these values as undergoing a radical reworking when extended to new groups, rejecting any simple panacea of 'proletarian' culture, Eliot does not anticipate any such re-creation. It is precisely because Eliot's idea of culture involves unconsciousness in the majority that he can consciously prescribe the values: since the people are excluded from active remaking, the essentials of the culture can be said to exist already. Eliot does not need to wait and see what will emerge spontaneously from a common collaboration, since in his scheme there will be no such collaboration.

It is true that at points Eliot suggests a more reciprocal relation between the more and less conscious levels within his society. He insists in the *Notes* that 'this higher level of culture must be thought of both as valuable in itself, and as an enriching of the lower levels: thus the movement of culture would proceed in a kind of cycle, each class nourishing the others' (p. 37). In practice, however, his thinking seems centred on the distilling of the known values of a Christian upper class to different cultural levels, and the idea that the distilling will involve change in the values themselves is never concretely entertained. There can certainly be no question of any direct offering of the values of conscious culture to lower levels in the society, for this will be to destroy standards: 'to aim to make everyone share in the appreciation of the fruits of the more conscious part of culture is to adulterate and cheapen what you give' (p. 106-7). And so any real measure of political democracy is rejected: 'A democracy in which everybody had an equal responsibility in everything would be oppressive for the conscientious and licentious for the rest' (p. 48). Popular education is equally mistaken: 'our headlong rush to educate everybody' is simply preparing the ground 'upon which the barbarian nomads of the future will encamp in their mechanised caravans' (p. 108). (It is only occasionally, in phrases like the last, that the full force of the deeply emotional snobbery behind the intellectual argument can be felt.)

What is striking about Eliot's idea of a common culture is its static quality, and it is this which Williams criticises in his chapter on Eliot in *Culture and Society*. Both Eliot and Williams are concerned to contrast a *common* with a *uniform* culture; both stress the unevenness and variety of any lived common experience. But for Eliot the unevenness springs ironically from a quite rigid structure of levels: all will not experience alike because all will not participate alike. Williams, while agreeing that full participation by one individual in the whole culture will be impossible, locates the essential variety of development in the culture's content, rather than simply in its form: a culture will reveal the unevenness of any process of growth which engages the activity of a great number of men, but it is the variety of what is created, rather than of levels of conscious creation, which is seen as primary. Williams's point is that the metaphor of levels is too crude: this will not be the way an actual society will be experienced in the consciousness of those variously engaged in creating it. What we can expect is 'not a simple equality (in the sense of identity) of culture; but rather a very complex system of specialised developments – the whole of which will form the whole culture, but which will not be available or conscious, as a whole, to any individual or group living within it' (p. 238). Williams's criticism of Eliot is that, in his idea of levels of consciousness as 'a fixed percentage of a given whole' (p. 237), he seems always to have in mind 'a society which is at once more stable and more simple than any to which his discussion is likely to be relevant' (p. 236). The judgement seems particularly just on a thinker who can at one point gravely announce that 'on the whole, it would appear to be for the best that the great majority of human beings should go on living in the place in which they were born' (p. 52). When the human beings begin to move, Eliot's structures begin to crumble.

There are places in the *Notes*, especially in the discussion of regional cultures, where Eliot seems to be moving towards a sense of culture as complex collaboration, but this dynamic image is constantly thrown out of focus by the superimposition of a concept of levels incompatible with it. When Eliot remarks that 'a national culture, if it is to flourish, should be a constellation of cultures, the constituents of which, benefiting each other, benefit the whole' (p. 58), he is very close to Williams's idea of a series of related complex developments; the suspicion that the idea of such a constellation of 'organic' regional cultures is part of a general over-simplifying of industrial society is perhaps less important than this fact. But the image of a number of regional cultures in creative tension with each other is then extended to the image of social classes in the same tension at precisely the point where the argument had seemed to move beyond this 'vertical' seeing into a more complex understanding. The disjunction can be traced within single sentences: 'As a society develops towards functional complexity and differentiation, we may expect the emergence of several cultural levels. . . .' (p. 25). Here, the break from 'functional complexity and differentiation', terms fully compatible with democratic equality, to 'several cultural levels', is puzzling, despite the air of logic. The same break comes in an earlier description of cultural activity: '. . . it is only by an overlapping and sharing of interests, by participation and mutual appreciation, that the cohesion necessary for culture can obtain. A religion requires not only a body of priests who know what they are doing, but a body of worshippers who know what is being done' (p. 24). The image seems to contradict the reality it offers to illustrate: the relation of an active priestly caste to a passively worshipping congregation seems an appropriate enough description of the kind of society outlined in *The Idea of a Christian Society* and in much of the *Notes*, but hardly of 'participation and mutual appreciation', least of all in the kind of liturgy Eliot would favour.

The confusion of simple and complex ideas of society connects with a further confusion in Eliot's use of the term 'culture'. Eliot uses both the traditional definitions of culture – roughly, the arts on one hand and a way of life on the other – but without always making it clear which definition he is drawing on at a particular point. What he means by culture, he says, is 'first of all what the anthropologists mean: the way of life of a particular people living together in one place' (p. 120); but at other times culture as a value-term seems uppermost in his mind – 'Culture may even be described simply as that which makes life worth living' (p. 27) – and, hovering between these two versions, is a sense of culture as the whole complex of a society's manners, arts, religion and philosophy which can be pressed into the service of either definition. The culture of a society is at one point 'that which makes it a society' (p. 37); at another point we are told that it is possible to anticipate a period 'of which it is possible to say that it will have *no* culture' (p. 19). Raymond Williams has pointed out that, when Eliot comes to spell out in detail what he means by culture as a whole way of life, he gives a selection of topics – Derby Day, Henley Regatta, Cowes, boiled cabbage, Elgar – which amounts ironically to the *alternative* definition of culture as manners and arts: in Williams's phrase, 'sport, food, a little art' (p. 234).

The point is not that the term should not be used in this double sense – Eliot's deliberate double use of it, when he speaks of 'the hereditary transmission of culture within a culture' is quite legitimate – but that one definition may be made subconsciously to do service for the other. For the question of whether one is thinking of culture chiefly in terms of a body of artistic and intellectual work, or of a way of life in its artistic, political, social and economic totality, is vital to the question of whether Eliot's 'organic' conception of class can stand. If culture is thought of in the first sense, it is possible to argue that the governing social class, by fostering this artistic work, has in the long run benefited the whole society as much as itself, provided one takes account, too, of the snobbery and exclusiveness which have seemed at times inseparable from this role.* But if culture is to include the whole way of life of a class – its values, ideologies, institutions – then it can plausibly be argued that the 'culture' of the English ruling class has operated at the *expense* of a full and satisfying life for the 'lower orders'. We have to ask in what sense it can be said that the possessive individualism of the ruling agrarian class in the late eighteenth century benefited those peasants dispossessed by enclosures – in what sense this was, in Eliot's phrase, 'an enriching of the lower levels'. We can ask similar questions about the economic practice and philosophy of the industrial middle class over recent history, or at the simplest level how the access of one social group today to, say, private medical care or private education is an 'enriching' of those who rely on the National

---

* Although it is difficult to see how, short of pressing the 'organic' idea to the point of mystical influence (which this social tradition has in fact done at points), even this can be argued on Eliot's terms, if any *actual* extension of high art to the people is denied.

Health Service and state schools. It is because Eliot always seems to have in mind the other meaning of culture – culture as arts – while discussing the relations between classes that these questions are not raised, and his interchangeable use of 'class' and 'group' is symptomatic of this weakness. The complex, institutional reality of 'class' is seen in essentially personal terms: a face-to-face group of cultivated men, a network of related families and private houses.

Another way in which this shift in the meaning of 'culture' confuses the argument is that a particular image of artistic creation and transmission becomes the archetype of all cultural activity. This is clear in *The Idea of a Christian Society:*

> When we speak of culture, I suppose that we have in mind the existence of two classes of people: the producers and the consumers of culture – the existence of men who can create new thought and new art (with middlemen who can teach the consumers to like it) and the existence of a cultivated society to enjoy and patronise it. (p. 77)

This hardly serves as an illuminating model of artistic creation and response – the passivity of 'enjoy' and 'consume', the leisurely relaxation of 'patronise', the casual reliance on a cynically commercial image, are far from the sense of active recreation which real criticism involves – and it serves even less, for the same reasons, as the model of a whole way of life. The image of the active artist and the passive consumer fits well with the idea of the conscious tip and unconscious masses, but its failure as an adequate image of critical response is also its failure as a description of the activity involved in the common creation of a culture. If a culture is an active interchange of meanings, the artistic process can be offered as an image of this only if it is understood as reciprocal, as involving criticism: Dr Leavis made the point in his 1962 Richmond Lecture, when he described criticism as the type of 'collaborative human creativity'. Eliot first of all narrows 'culture' to the artistic process, and then gives a version of this process which both shares in and underlines the inadequacy of his sense of culture in its wider definition.

There is a related confusion in Eliot's uncertainty as to whether culture should be located primarily 'in the pattern of the society as a whole' as he argues at one point, or in that series of smaller, 'organic' groups which the idea of a 'constellation' suggests. He describes culture in the *Notes* as that which makes a society what it is, but at a later point in the text insists more narrowly on the family as the primary channel of cultural transmission. True culture will be preserved by a network of these select families; a strong national educational provision is rejected as a soulless ordering of organic growth. The tension, here again, is between the two definitions of culture: culture as arts and manners – feasibly, though surely not wholly, transmitted by the family – or culture in the sense of a society's whole institutional life, which indeed goes beyond the family to 'the pattern of the society as a whole'. It is because Eliot is reluctant to think in complex, institutional terms – because, in a sense, his offered institutions are *personal*: the tight group of families, the private exchange of literary men between nations in preference to cultural organisations – that the confusion arises. Eliot rarely faces the actual consequences of defining culture as a whole way of life, in an industrial society; when at one point he describes the whole complex of educative influences on children – 'not only of family and environment, but of work and play, of newsprint and spectacles and entertainment and sport' (p. 106) – the effect, given the carefully distancing archaism 'spectacles', is suddenly of that quite different tradition of cultural criticism, locating a quality of life in particular institutions, which Dr Leavis, Raymond Williams and Richard Hoggart have in their different ways emphasised, and the implicit criticism of Eliot's own abstract method is severe.

This reluctance to situate the cultural argument within discussion of specific structures relates to that need to place it outside politics which we have noted already. It is characteristic of the ambivalence of the *Notes* that Eliot can recognise on one page that 'the political, the economic and the cultural problems cannot be isolated from each other' (p. 53), and advise Europe on another page to 'preserve our common culture uncontaminated by political influences' (p. 123). The distinction which runs throughout the *Notes* is a form of that dualism of belief and behaviour which we saw in *The Idea of a Christian Society*: the lack of any dialectical relation there between cultural values and the socio-political forms which embody them parallels the mechanistic notion in the same text that a society's culture 'provides the material' for its political formulations, as though concepts followed, rather than structured, experience. By placing culture above politics, in the timeless values of a small personal group, or below politics, in the unconscious rhythms of an instinctive way of life, Eliot evades a number of crucial questions. On one front, politics is attacked as a set of formulations falsely abstracted from a whole texture of life; on another, it is criticised as part of the shallow, unreflective quality of that life, from the standpoint of a finely conscious *élite*. The result is a peculiar kind of mystification: by setting his ideas of conscious and unconscious life at extreme poles outside that normative range of human activity, incorporating both kinds of life in interaction, which Williams takes as his concern, Eliot can attack the assumptions of that concern from either pole, retreating from one to the other in a continually confusing way.

The mystification is there most notably in the whole of the introduction to the *Notes*, and it is worth examining this in some detail because it says much about Eliot's method of argument, especially of the moral significance of *tone*. The tone of the introduction is one of authoritative caution: the reader is warned that the term 'culture' has been misused, and that the extreme of the author's ambition is to rescue it from contexts where it does not belong. The caution is that of an urge towards clarity, after a long and muddled debate; the book's epigraph, significantly, is that part of the *Oxford English Dictionary*'s definition of 'definition' which speaks of 'the setting of bounds; limitation'. We are told in the first paragraph that the author's intention is not 'to outline a social or political philosophy' but 'to help define a word, the word *culture*', and part of this attempt will consist in disentangling culture from politics and education. Authority as much as caution is needed for such a complex operation, as the book's title suggests: these are 'notes', but towards 'the definition'. When the caution expresses itself further in the assertion that no attempt should ever be made directly to improve a culture, but that we should look always to 'minute particulars', the authoritativeness seems to be taking over from the modest clarifying – this is, after all, a large kind of political statement in its implications – but the limiting concern set by the precise tone partly conceals the movement of emphasis. The urge to precise definition in fact turns out to be deceptive, in a similar way to the deceptiveness of balancing 'collective temperament' against 'political philosophy'. Under cover of the clarifying tone, Eliot is able to rescue culture from other people's political structures in what appears to be a limiting operation but is in fact an expansion of the term to a point where it can *include* his own politics while appearing non-political. It will become clear later, of course, that Eliot's version of culture is thoroughly political, mobilising his deepest instinctive beliefs about man in society, but since the political emphases are all made in terms of organic growth, personal value, traditional rhythm, Eliot can talk about politics while seeming only to be talking about culture. When others try to drag politics into the argument, he can censure this from an apparently unbiased and unpolitical standpoint, unpolitical only because he has widened the description of culture to include his own politics and at the same time made this appear a salutary narrowing, detaching culture from the distracting political concerns of others. Those, therefore, who attack his idea of culture on political grounds can be told simply that they have not understood the meaning of culture; they cannot be seen as attacking the political structure of Eliot's cultural theory because he will not admit the existence of this as an element in the debate:

> The writer himself is not without political convictions and prejudices; but the imposition of them is no part of his present intention. What I try to say is this: here are what I believe to be essential conditions for the growth and for the survival of culture. If they conflict with any passionate faith of the reader – if, for instance, he finds it shocking that culture and equalitarianism should conflict, if it seems monstrous to him that anyone should have 'advantages of birth' – I do not ask him to change his faith, I merely ask him to stop paying lip-service to culture. (p. 16)

The precision – it is culture, not politics, which is in question – and the authoritativeness (now grown almost to insolence), are aspects of the same approach. The objector is not asked to change his faith, since political faith is not in question. When an opponent brings the charge against Eliot that his theory of culture is undemocratic, the argument is about politics; when Eliot himself asserts that culture involves inequality, it is about culture. On these terms, there is no more need to answer an opponent's political objections than there is to defend one's own political position: for the purposes of this argument, the former are irrelevant and the latter non-existent.

III

The separation of culture from politics has been a persistent feature of cultural argument in this century, yet it is one which is difficult to understand once both terms have been fully described, as languages concerned with the whole structure and quality of life in a society. The suppression of this relation between culture and politics has been pointed to by Raymond Williams as a major flaw in Eliot's thinking: it leads him contradictorily to demand a community of belief and value within the context of a commitment to political and economic structures deeply atomistic in their effect. The attempt to go beyond the single definition of culture as the arts to the idea of a whole way of life has been an attempt to relate the quality of a society's highest values to the quality of its common institutional life. The connection can be made in various ways: it can be made superficially, at the level of a society's 'tone' and 'style', without relation to the forms of its politics, industry, communications; this happens in some of Eliot's work, as it does in some of Arnold's. Again, the relation can be firmly made but in a chiefly negative way: high art and common life were connected in some past society, but their present relationship is one of a mutually defining hostility. Culture (art) is related to culture (society) by its effort to keep clear of its inevitably impoverishing influence; this will demand the existence of an aware and defensive *élite*, concerned to protect a living tradition from the infection of 'mass' society. This is a position which has involved a good deal of indiscriminate judgement of that society; in some cases it has ended ironically with a crude, dehumanising caricature of contemporary culture, one blind to its points of growth and deeply conservative in its final effect. The efforts of those working to change the society in its fundamental structures, strongly aware of dehumanisation but aware also of the possibilities for a general human- isation of the common life, have been too easily dismissed from this standpoint. In its own way it can become as static and prescriptive as Eliot's own model: industrial democratic society is seen, inevitably and continuingly, as 'mass' society, shallow and faceless.

Eliot is concerned to reject this position:

> It is commonly assumed that there is culture, but that it is the property of a small section of society; and from this assumption it is usual to proceed to one of two conclusions: either that culture can only be the concern of a small minority, and that therefore there is no place for it in the society of the future; or that in the society of the future the culture which has been the possession of the few must be put at the disposal of everybody. (*NDC* pp. 32–3)

It is part of the strength of Eliot's conception of culture that he refuses to confine it wholly to an *élite*; culture is ideally a whole way of life, lived commonly and variously by a whole people. I have criticised the

way in which, in establishing this position, Eliot summarily relegates
the majority of mankind to the level of unconscious and instinctive life;
he would agree with the 'minority' argument that fully *conscious* culture
cannot be widely shared. Nevertheless, he is concerned that 'high'
culture should be lived in some oblique way by a people as a whole,
and it is this which ties his argument most closely to the third, more
positive connection of art and society, the radical case for a common
culture represented by Raymond Williams.

For Williams, belief in the possibility of a common culture is a belief
in the capacity of 'high' culture, when shared and re-created by a whole
community, to be enriched rather than adulterated; it is also a belief
that this wide artistic sharing can make sense only within the admission
of the people as a whole to full participation in the making of 'culture'
as a way of life, in its social, political and economic forms. Eliot, of
course, sees such an operation as disastrous, as the emotive force of his
phrase '[to] put [art] at the disposal of everybody' reveals. But the
difference lies partly in whether society is conceived of as static or
moving, as a finished structure or an ongoing human creation. Williams's
belief in the possibility of a genuinely common culture is based on his
recognition that the growth of literacy, industrialism and political
democracy in Britain has been growth towards total control by a whole
society over its own life, a reaching for common responsibility through
the struggles of a long revolution still far from finished. It is a process
which has been faced at many points by the conservative response which
Eliot represents: the urge to erect barriers, to draw the line before one's
own feet and place culture, literacy, democracy on *this*, not *that* side,
has been a recurrent reaction, and Burke's contempt for the 'swinish
multitude' has taken many subsequent forms. Each time, however, the
revolution for wider participation and responsibility has continued;
each grudgingly lowered barrier, each new form of incorporation, has
been the cue for a further participation, until the whole process can
only be denied or halted by replacing the images of growth with those
of stasis. The conservative version of a stable and stratified society,
with given degrees and relations of culture, and the 'liberal minority'
version, with its faith in the few just men sustaining a personal tradition
within an impersonal and unchanging 'mass' society, both end by doing
this. Eliot's cultural work has been one major example of the conservative
reaction, and as such is a challenge which must be met if a common
culture in its fullest sense is to exist.

NOTES

1. T. B. Bottomore has criticised Eliot's implication that our present meritocracy involves a 'circulation of personnel' among its *élites* which is destructive of continuity; he notes that 'there is not at the present time any substantial circulation of individuals between the élites and the rest of the population' (*Élites and Society*, New Thinker's Library (1964) p. 118).

2. cf. F. R. Leavis and M. Yudkin, *Two Cultures? The Significance of C. P. Snow* (1962) p. 10.

Notes on Contributors

F. W. BATESON, Fellow in English, Corpus Christi College, Oxford, is editor of the *Cambridge Bibliography of English Literature* and *Essays in Criticism*, and author of several works of criticism including *Wordsworth: a reinterpretation* and *A Guide to English Literature*.

HAROLD F. BROOKS, Reader in English, Birkbeck College, London, is one of the general editors of the Arden Shakespeare and author of many articles on renaissance and seventeenth-century literature.

ADRIAN CUNNINGHAM, Lecturer, Department of Religious Studies, University of Lancaster, is an editor of *Slant*, and at present writing a book on the sociology of religion.

DONALD DAVIE, Professor of English, Stanford University, California, has published several volumes of poetry and works of literary criticism, including *Ezra Pound: poet as sculptor*, and has recently edited a collection of essays, *Russian Literature and Modern English Fiction*.

TERRY EAGLETON, Fellow in English, Wadham College, Oxford, has published *Shakespeare and Society*, and is co-editor of a collection of essays, *From Culture to Revolution*.

IAN GREGOR, Professor of Modern English Literature, University of Kent, is co-author of *The Moral and the Story* and *William Golding: a critical study*, and editor of a critical edition of Arnold's *Culture and Anarchy* shortly to be published.

IAN HAMILTON, poetry and fiction editor of the *Times Literary Supplement*, and editor of the *Review*, has also edited *The Poetry of War, 1939–1945, Alun Lewis: selected poetry and prose* and *The Modern Poet: essays from the Review*. *The Visit*, a collection of poems, is due to be published shortly.

MARTIN JARRETT-KERR, C.R., Associate Lecturer, Department of Theology, University of Leeds, has written a number of works of criticism. Two publications shortly to appear are a critical study of William Faulkner and *Christians and the Third World*.

GABRIEL PEARSON, Lecturer in English, University of Essex, is co-editor of *Dickens and the Twentieth Century* and author of critical essays on Berryman, Lowell, Bellow, Malamud and Arnold.

JOHN PETER is Professor of English, University of Victoria, British Columbia.

FRANCIS SCARFE is Director of the British Institute in Paris and Professor of French in the University of London. His recent publications include the Penguin *Baudelaire*, *La Vie et l'Œuvre de T. S. Eliot* and *The Life and Work of André Chenier*.

RICHARD WOLLHEIM is Professor of Philosophy and Mind, University College, London. His recent publications include *F. H. Bradley* and *Art and Its Objects: an introduction to aesthetics*.

KATHARINE WORTH, Lecturer in English, Royal Holloway College, London, is editor of the Modern Drama section of the *Cambridge Bibliography of English Literature*, volume 6. Essays on John Osborne, N. F. Simpson and John Arden were published in a symposium, *Experimental Drama*.

Index